DECISIVE

ALSO BY CHIP HEATH AND DAN HEATH

Switch
Made to Stick

DECISIVE

How to
Make Better
Choices
in Life
and Work

CHIP HEATH AND DAN HEATH

RANDOM HOUSE CANADA

PUBLISHED BY RANDOM HOUSE CANADA

Copyright © 2013 Chip Heath and Dan Heath

www.randomhouse.ca

Library and Archives Canada Cataloguing in Publication

Heath, Chip
Decisive : how to make better choices in life and work / Chip Heath and Dan Heath.

Issued also in electronic format.

ISBN 978-0-307-36113-4

1. Decision making. I. Heath, Dan, 1973– II. Title.

BF448.H42 2013   153.8'3   C2012-905597-2

Jacket design by Justin Gammon

Printed and bound in the United States of America

1 3 5 7 9 8 6 4 2

To our wives,
Susan and Amanda,
the best decisions
we ever made

CONTENTS

PREPARE TO BE WRONG

DECISIVE

Introduction

Shannon, the head of a small consulting firm, is agonizing about whether to fire Clive, her IT director. Over the past year, Clive has consistently failed to do more than the minimum required of him. He's not without his talents—he's intelligent and has a knack for improvising cheap solutions to technical problems—but he rarely takes any initiative. Worse, his attitude is poor. In meetings, he is often critical of other people's ideas, sometimes caustically so.

Unfortunately, losing Clive would cause problems in the short-term. He understands how to maintain the company's database of clients better than anyone else.

What would you advise her to do? Should she fire him or not?

IF YOU REFLECT ON the past few seconds of your mental activity, what's astonishing is how quickly your opinions started to form. Most of us, reflecting on the Clive situation, feel like we already know enough to start offering advice. Maybe you'd advise Shannon to fire Clive, or maybe you'd encourage her to give him another chance. But chances are you didn't feel flummoxed.

"A remarkable aspect of your mental life is that you are rarely stumped," said Daniel Kahneman, a psychologist who won the Nobel Prize in economics for his research on the way that people's decisions depart from the strict rationality assumed by economists. In his fascinating book, *Thinking, Fast and Slow*, he describes the ease with which we draw conclusions: "The normal state of your mind is that you have intuitive feelings and opinions about almost everything that comes your way. You like or dislike people long before you know much about them; you trust or distrust strangers without knowing why; you feel that an enterprise is bound to succeed without analyzing it."

Kahneman says that we are quick to jump to conclusions because we give too much weight to the information that's right in front of us, while failing to consider the information that's just offstage. He called this tendency "what you see is all there is." In keeping with Kahneman's visual metaphor, we'll refer to this tendency as a "spotlight" effect. (Think of the way a spotlight in a theater directs our attention; what's inside the spotlight is crisply illuminated.)

The Clive situation above is an example of the spotlight effect. When we're offered information about Clive—he does only the bare minimum, he doesn't take initiative, he has a poor attitude, and his boss might fire him—we find it very easy to take that readily available set of information and start drawing conclusions from it.

But of course a spotlight only lights a spot. Everything outside it is obscured. So, in Clive's situation, we don't immediately think to ask a lot of obvious questions. For instance, rather than fire Clive, why not change his role to match up better with his strengths? (After all, he's good at improvising cheap solutions.) Or maybe Clive could be matched with a mentor who'd help him set more ambitious goals and deliver less scathing criticism.

Furthermore, what if we dug deeper and discovered that Clive's colleagues adore his crusty, straight-talking ways? (Maybe he's the IT version of Dr. House.) And what makes us think that Shannon's take on Clive is impeccably accurate? What if she is a terrible manager? When we begin shifting the spotlight from side to side, the situation starts to look very different. We couldn't possibly hope to make a good decision about Clive without doing this spotlight shifting. Yet developing an opinion was easy without doing it.

And that, in essence, is the core difficulty of decision making: What's in the spotlight will rarely be everything we need to make a good decision, but we won't always remember to shift the light. Sometimes, in fact, we'll forget there's a spotlight at all, dwelling so long in the tiny circle of light that we forget there's a broader landscape beyond it.

IF YOU STUDY THE kinds of decisions people make and the outcomes of those decisions, you'll find that humanity does not have a particularly impressive track record.

Career choices, for instance, are often abandoned or regretted. An American Bar Association survey found that 44% of lawyers would recommend that a young person not pursue a career in law. A study of 20,000 executive searches found that 40% of senior-level hires "are pushed out, fail or quit within 18 months." More than half of teachers quit their jobs within four years. In fact, one study in Philadelphia schools found that a teacher was almost two times more likely to drop out than a student.

Business decisions are frequently flawed. One study of corporate mergers and acquisitions—some of the highest-stakes decisions executives make—showed that 83% failed to create any value for shareholders. When another research team asked 2,207 executives to evaluate decisions in their organizations, 60% of the executives reported that bad decisions were about as frequent as good ones.

On the personal front we're not much better. People don't save enough for retirement, and when they do save, they consistently erode their own stock portfolios by buying high and selling low. Young people start relationships with people who are bad for them. Middle-aged people let work interfere with their family lives. The elderly wonder why they didn't take more time to smell the roses when they were younger.

Why do we have such a hard time making good choices? In recent years, many fascinating books and articles have addressed this question, exploring the problems with our decision making. The biases. The irrationality. When it comes to making decisions, it's clear that our brains are flawed instruments. But less attention has been paid to another compelling question: Given that we're wired to act foolishly sometimes, how can we do better?*

Sometimes we are given the advice to trust our guts when we make important decisions. Unfortunately, our guts are full of questionable advice. Consider the Ultimate Red Velvet Cheesecake at the Cheesecake Factory, a truly delicious dessert—and one that clocks in at 1,540 calories, which is the equivalent of three McDonald's double cheeseburgers plus a pack of Skittles. This is something that you are supposed to eat after you are finished with your real meal.

The Ultimate Red Velvet Cheesecake is exactly the kind of thing that our guts get excited about. Yet no one would mistake this guidance for wisdom. Certainly no one has ever thoughtfully plotted out a meal plan and concluded, *I gotta add more cheesecake.*

Nor are our guts any better on big decisions. On October 10, 1975, Liz Taylor and Richard Burton celebrated the happy occasion of their wedding. Taylor was on her sixth marriage, Burton on his third. Samuel

---

*See page 255 for a more thorough list of our recommended decision books, but to understand the problems we face in making decisions, essential reading would include Daniel Kahneman's book, *Thinking, Fast and Slow*, mentioned above, and Dan Ariely's *Predictably Irrational*. One of the handful of books that provides advice on making decisions better is *Nudge* by Richard Thaler and Cass Sunstein, which was written for "choice architects" in business and government who construct decision systems such as retirement plans or organ-donation policies. It has been used to improve government policies in the United States, Great Britain, and other countries.

Johnson once described a second marriage as the "triumph of hope over experience." But given Taylor and Burton's track record their union represented something grander: the triumph of hope over a mountain of empirical evidence. (The marriage lasted 10 months.)

Often our guts can't make up their minds at all: an estimated 61,535 tattoos were reversed in the United States in 2009. A British study of more than 3,000 people found that 88% of New Year's resolutions are broken, including 68% of resolutions merely to "enjoy life more." Quarterback Brett Favre retired, then unretired, then retired. At press time he is ~~playing~~ retired.

If we can't trust our guts, then what can we trust? Many businesspeople put their faith in careful analysis. To test this faith, two researchers, Dan Lovallo, a professor at the University of Sydney, and Olivier Sibony, a director of McKinsey & Company, investigated 1,048 business decisions over five years, tracking both the ways the decisions were made and the subsequent outcomes in terms of revenues, profits, and market share. The decisions were important ones, such as whether or not to launch a new product or service, change the structure of the organization, enter a new country, or acquire another firm.

The researchers found that in making most of the decisions, the teams had conducted rigorous analysis. They'd compiled thorough financial models and assessed how investors might react to their plans.

Beyond the analysis, Lovallo and Sibony also asked the teams about their decision *process*—the softer, less analytical side of the decisions. Had the team explicitly discussed what was still uncertain about the decision? Did they include perspectives that contradicted the senior executive's point of view? Did they elicit participation from a range of people who had different views of the decision?

When the researchers compared whether process or analysis was more important in producing good decisions—those that increased revenues, profits, and market share—they found that "process mattered more than analysis—by a factor of six." Often a good process led to better analysis—for instance, by ferreting out faulty logic. But the reverse was not true: "Superb analysis is useless unless the decision process gives it a fair hearing."

To illustrate the weakness of the decision-making process in most organizations, Sibony drew an analogy to the legal system:

> Imagine walking into a courtroom where the trial consists of a prosecutor presenting PowerPoint slides. In 20 pretty compelling charts, he demonstrates why the defendant is guilty. The judge then challenges some of the facts of the presentation, but the prosecutor has a good answer to every objection. So the judge decides, and the accused man is sentenced. That wouldn't be due process, right? So if you would find this process shocking in a courtroom, why is it acceptable when you make an investment decision?
>
> Now of course, this is an oversimplification, but this process is essentially the one most companies follow to make a decision. They have a team arguing only one side of the case. The team has a choice of what points it wants to make and what way it wants to make them. And it falls to the final decision maker to be both the challenger and the ultimate judge. Building a good decision-making process is largely ensuring that these flaws don't happen.

Dan Lovallo says that when he talks about process with corporate leaders, they are skeptical. "They tend not to believe that the soft stuff matters more than the hard stuff," he said. "They don't spend very much time on it. Everybody thinks they know how to do this stuff." But the ones who do pay attention reap the rewards: A better decision process substantially improves the results of the decisions, as well as the financial returns associated with them.

The discipline exhibited by good corporate decision makers— exploring alternative points of view, recognizing uncertainty, searching for evidence that contradicts their beliefs—can help us in our families and friendships as well. A solid process isn't just good for business; it's good for our lives.

Why a process? Because understanding our shortcomings is not enough to fix them. Does knowing you're nearsighted help you see better? Or does knowing that you have a bad temper squelch it? Similarly, it's hard to correct a bias in our mental processes just by being aware of it.

Most of us rarely use a "process" for thinking through important decisions, like whether to fire Clive, or whether to relocate for a new job, or how to handle our frail, elderly parents. The only decision-making process in wide circulation is the pros-and-cons list. The advantage of this approach is that it's deliberative. Rather than jump to conclusions about Clive, for example, we'd hunt for both positive and negative factors—pushing the spotlight around—until we felt ready to make a decision.

What you may not know is that the pros-and-cons list has a proud historical pedigree. In 1772, Benjamin Franklin was asked for advice by a colleague who'd been offered an unusual job opportunity. Franklin replied in a letter that, given his lack of knowledge of the situation, he couldn't offer advice on whether or not to take the job. But he did suggest a process the colleague could use to make his own decision. Franklin said that his approach was "to divide half a sheet of paper by a line into two columns, writing over the one Pro and over the other Con." During the next three or four days, Franklin said, he'd add factors to the two columns as they occurred to him. Then, he said:

> When I have thus got them all together in one view, I endeavour
> to estimate their respective weights; and where I find two, one
> on each side, that seem equal, I strike them both out: If I find a
> reason Pro equal to some two reasons Con, I strike out the three.
> If I judge some two reasons Con equal to some three reasons Pro,
> I strike out the five; and thus proceeding I find at length where
> the balance lies; and if after a day or two of farther consideration
> nothing new that is of importance occurs on either side, I come to
> a determination accordingly. [Capitalization modernized.]

Franklin called this technique "moral algebra." Over 200 years after he wrote this letter, his approach is still, broadly speaking, the approach people use when they make decisions (that is, when they're not trusting their guts). We may not follow Franklin's advice about crossing off pros and cons of similar weight, but we embrace the gist of the process. When we're presented with a choice, we compare the pros and cons of our options, and then we pick the one that seems the most favorable.

The pros-and-cons approach is familiar. It is commonsensical. And it is also profoundly flawed.

Research in psychology over the last 40 years has identified a set of biases in our thinking that doom the pros-and-cons model of decision making. If we aspire to make better choices, then we must learn how these biases work and how to fight them (with something more potent than a list of pros and cons).

Prepare to encounter the four most pernicious villains of decision making—and a process that we can use to counteract their influence.

1

The Four Villains of Decision Making

1.

Steve Cole, the VP of research and development at HopeLab, a nonprofit that fights to improve kids' health using technology, said, "Any time in life you're tempted to think, 'Should I do this OR that?' instead, ask yourself, 'Is there a way I can do this AND that?' It's surprisingly frequent that it's feasible to do both things."

For one major project, Cole and his team at HopeLab wanted to find a design partner, a firm that could help them design a portable device capable of measuring the amount of exercise that kids were getting. There were at least seven or eight design firms in the Bay Area that were capable of doing the work. In a typical contracting situation, HopeLab would have solicited a proposal from each firm and then given the winner a giant contract.

But instead of choosing a winner, Cole ran a "horse race." He shrank down the scope of the work so that it covered only the first step of the project, and then he hired five different firms to work on the first step independently. (To be clear, he wasn't quintupling his budget—as a non-profit, HopeLab didn't have unlimited resources. Cole knew that what he'd learn from the first round would make the later rounds more efficient.)

With his horse race, Cole ensured that he'd have multiple design alternatives for the device. He could either pick his favorite or combine the best features of several. Then, in round two of the design, he could weed out any vendors who were unresponsive or ineffective.

Cole is fighting the first villain of decision making, narrow framing, which is the tendency to define our choices too narrowly, to see them in binary terms. We ask, "Should I break up with my partner or not?" instead of "What are the ways I could make this relationship better?" We ask ourselves, "Should I buy a new car or not?" instead of "What's the best way I could spend some money to make my family better off?"

In the introduction, when we asked the question "Should Shannon fire Clive or not?" we were stuck in a narrow frame. We spotlighted one alternative at the expense of all the others.

Cole, with his horse race, is breaking out of that trap. It wasn't an obvious move; he had to fight for the concept internally. "At first, my colleagues thought I was insane. At the beginning, it costs some money and takes some time. But now everybody here does it. You get to meet lots of people. You get to know lots of different kinds of things about the industry. You get convergence on some issues, so you know they are right, and you also learn to appreciate what makes the firms different and special. None of this can you do if you're just talking to one person. And when all of those five firms know that there are four other shops involved, they bring their best game."

Notice the contrast with the pros-and-cons approach. Cole could have tallied up the advantages and disadvantages of working with each vendor and then used that analysis to make a decision. But that would have reflected narrow framing. Implicitly, he would have been assuming that there was one vendor that was uniquely capable of crafting the perfect solution, and that he could identify that vendor on the basis of a proposal.

2.

There's a more subtle factor involved too—Cole, in meeting with the teams, would have inevitably developed a favorite, a team he clicked with. And though intellectually he might have realized that the people he likes personally aren't necessarily the ones who are going to build the best products, he would have been tempted to jigger the pros-and-cons list in their favor. Cole might not even have been aware he was doing it, but because pros and cons are generated in our heads, it is very, very easy for us to bias the factors. We think we are conducting a sober comparison but, in reality, our brains are following orders from our guts.

Our normal habit in life is to develop a quick belief about a situation and then seek out information that bolsters our belief. And that problematic habit, called the "confirmation bias," is the second villain of decision making.

Here's a typical result from one of the many studies on the topic: Smokers in the 1960s, back when the medical research on the harms of smoking was less clear, were more likely to express interest in reading an article headlined "Smoking Does Not Lead to Lung Cancer" than one with the headline "Smoking Leads to Lung Cancer." (To see how this could lead to bad decisions, imagine your boss staring at two research studies headlined "Data That Supports What You Think" and "Data That Contradicts What You Think." Guess which one gets cited at the staff meeting?)

Researchers have found this result again and again. When people have the opportunity to collect information from the world, they are more likely to select information that supports their preexisting attitudes, beliefs, and actions. Political partisans seek out media outlets that support their side but will rarely challenge their beliefs by seeking out the other side's perspective. Consumers who covet new cars or computers will look for reasons to justify the purchase but won't be as diligent about finding reasons to postpone it.

The tricky thing about the confirmation bias is that it can look very scientific. After all, we're collecting data. Dan Lovallo, the professor and decision-making researcher cited in the introduction, said, "Confirmation bias is probably the single biggest problem in business, because even the most sophisticated people get it wrong. People go out and they're collecting the data, and they don't realize they're cooking the books."

At work and in life, we often pretend that we want truth when we're really seeking reassurance: "Do these jeans make me look fat?" "What did you think of my poem?" These questions do not crave honest answers.

Or pity the poor contestants who try out to sing on reality TV shows, despite having no discernible ability to carry a tune. When they get harsh feedback from the judges, they look shocked. Crushed. And you realize: This is the first time in their lives they've received honest feedback. Eager for reassurance, they'd locked their spotlights on the praise and support they received from friends and family. Given that affirmation, it's not hard to see why they'd think they had a chance to become the next American Idol. It was a reasonable conclusion drawn from a wildly distorted pool of data.

And this is what's slightly terrifying about the confirmation bias: When we want something to be true, we will spotlight the things that support it, and then, when we draw conclusions from those spotlighted scenes, we'll congratulate ourselves on a reasoned decision. Oops.

3.

In his memoir, *Only the Paranoid Survive*, Andy Grove recalled a tough dilemma he faced in 1985 as the president of Intel: whether to kill the company's line of memory chips. Intel's business had been built on memory. For a time, in fact, the company was the world's only source of memory, but by the end of the 1970s, a dozen or so competitors had emerged.

Meanwhile, a small team at Intel had developed another product, the microprocessor, and in 1981 the team got a big break when IBM chose Intel's microprocessor to be the brain of its new personal computer. Intel's team scrambled to build the manufacturing capacity it would need to produce the chips.

At that point, Intel became a company with two products: memory and microprocessors. Memory was still the dominant source of the company's revenue, but in the early 1980s, the company's competitive position in the memory business came under threat from Japanese companies. "People who came back from visits to Japan told scary stories," said Grove. It was reported that one Japanese company was designing multiple generations of memory all at once—the 16K people were on one floor, the 64K people were a floor above, and the 256K team was above them.

Intel's customers began to rave about the quality of the Japanese memories. "In fact, the quality levels attributed to Japanese memories were beyond what we thought possible," said Grove. "Our first reaction was denial. This had to be wrong. As people often do in this kind of situation, we vigorously attacked the data. Only when we confirmed for ourselves that the claims were roughly right did we start to go to work on the quality of our product. We were clearly behind."

Between 1978 and 1988, the market share held by Japanese companies doubled from 30% to 60%. A debate raged inside Intel about how to respond to the Japanese competition. One camp of leaders wanted to leapfrog the Japanese in manufacturing. They proposed building a giant new factory to make memory chips. Another camp wanted to bet on an avant-garde technology that they thought the Japanese couldn't match. A third camp wanted to double down on the company's strategy of serving specialty markets.

As the debate continued with no resolution, the company began losing more and more money. The microprocessor business was growing rapidly, but Intel's failures in memory were becoming a drag on profits. Grove summarized the year 1984 by saying, "It was a grim and frustrating year. During that time, we worked hard without a clear notion of how things were ever going to get better. We had lost our bearings."

In the middle of 1985, after more months of fruitless debate, Grove was discussing the memory quandary in his office with Intel's chairman and CEO, Gordon Moore. They were both fatigued by the internal deliberations. Then Grove had an inspiration:

> I looked out the window at the Ferris Wheel of the Great America amusement park revolving in the distance, then I turned back to Gordon and I asked, "If we got kicked out and the board brought in a new CEO, what do you think he would do?" Gordon answered without hesitation, "He would get us out of memories."
>
> I stared at him, numb, then said, "Why shouldn't you and I walk out the door, come back in, and do it ourselves?"

This was the moment of clarity. From the perspective of an outsider, someone not encumbered by the historical legacy and the political infighting, shutting down the memory business was the obvious thing to do. The switch in perspectives—"What would our successors do?"—helped Moore and Grove see the big picture clearly.

Of course, abandoning memory was not easy. Many of Grove's colleagues were furiously opposed to the idea. Some held that memory was the seedbed of Intel's technology expertise and that without it, other areas of research were likely to wither. Others insisted that Intel's sales force could not get customers' attention without selling a full range of products—memories as well as microprocessors.

After much "gnashing of teeth," Grove insisted that the sales force tell their customers that Intel would no longer be carrying memory products. The customers' reaction was, essentially, a big yawn. One said, "It sure took you a long time."

Since that decision in 1985, Intel has dominated the microprocessor market. If, on the day of Grove's insight, you had invested $1,000 in Intel, by 2012 your investment would have been worth $47,000 (compared with $7,600 for the S&P 500, a composite of other big companies). It seems safe to say that he made the right decision.

GROVE'S STORY REVEALS A flaw in the way many experts think about decisions. If you review the research literature on decisions, you'll find that many decision-making models are basically glorified spreadsheets. If you are shopping for an apartment, for instance, you might be advised to list the eight apartments you found, rank them on a number of key factors (cost, location, size, etc.), assign a weighting that reflects the importance of each factor (cost is more important than size, for instance), and then do the math to find the answer (um, move back in with Mom and Dad).

There's one critical ingredient missing from this kind of analysis: emotion. Grove's decision wasn't difficult because he lacked options or information; it was difficult because he felt conflicted. The short-term pressures and political wrangling clouded his mind and obscured the long-term need to exit the memory business.

This brings us to the third villain of decision making: short-term emotion. When we've got a difficult decision to make, our feelings churn. We replay the same arguments in our head. We agonize about our circumstances. We change our minds from day to day. If our decision was represented on a spreadsheet, none of the numbers would be changing—there's no new information being added—but it doesn't feel that way in our heads. We have kicked up so much dust that we can't see the way forward. In those moments, what we need most is perspective.

Ben Franklin was aware of the effects of temporary emotion. His moral algebra wisely suggests that people add to their pros-and-cons list over several days, giving them a chance to add factors as they grow more or less excited about a particular idea. Still, though, to compare options rigorously is not the same as seeing the bigger picture. No doubt Andy Grove had been compiling his pros-and-cons list about whether to exit the memory business for many years. But the analysis left him paralyzed, and it took a quick dose of detachment—seeing things from the perspective of his successor—to break the paralysis.

4.

The odds of a meltdown are one in 10,000 years.

　　—Vitali Sklyarov, minister of power and electrification in the Ukraine, two months before the Chernobyl accident

Who the hell wants to hear actors talk?

　　—Harry Warner, Warner Bros. Studios, 1927

What use could this company make of an electrical toy?

　　—William Orton, president of the Western Union Telegraph Company, in 1876, rejecting an opportunity to purchase Alexander Graham Bell's patent on the telephone

Our search for the final villain of decision making takes us back to January 1, 1962, when a young four-man rock-and-roll group named the Beatles was invited to audition in London for one of the two major British record labels, Decca Records. "We were all excited," recalled John Lennon. "It was Decca." During an hourlong audition, they played fifteen different songs, mostly covers. The Beatles and their manager, Brian

Epstein, were hopeful they'd get a contract, and they waited anxiously for a response.

Eventually they received the verdict: Decca had decided to pass. In a letter to Epstein, Dick Rowe, a prominent talent scout at Decca Records, wrote, "We don't like your boys' sound. Groups are out; four-piece groups with guitars, particularly, are finished."

As Dick Rowe would soon learn, the fourth villain of decision making is overconfidence. People think they know more than they do about how the future will unfold.

Recall that Andy Grove's colleagues had dire predictions of what would happen if Intel stopped making memory chips. *We will lose the seedbed of our R&D. Our sales force can't succeed without a full line of products.* History proves that they were wrong: Intel's R&D and sales stayed strong. But what's interesting is that, at the time they made these proclamations, they didn't feel uncertain. They weren't hedging their remarks by saying, "It's possible that . . ." or "I just worry that this could happen someday. . . ." They knew they were right. They just knew it.

A study showed that when doctors reckoned themselves "completely certain" about a diagnosis, they were wrong 40% of the time. When a group of students made estimates that they believed had only a 1% chance of being wrong, they were actually wrong 27% of the time.

We have too much confidence in our own predictions. When we make guesses about the future, we shine our spotlights on information that's close at hand, and then we draw conclusions from that information. Imagine the head of a travel agency in 1992: *My travel agency is the market leader in Phoenix, and we have the best customer relationships. This area is growing so rapidly, we could easily double in size over the next ten years. Let's get ahead of the curve and build those additional branches.*

The problem is that we don't know what we don't know. *Whoops, the Internet. So much for my travel agency.*

The future has an uncanny ability to surprise. We can't shine a spotlight on areas when we don't know they exist.

. . .

LET'S SUM UP WHERE we are. If you think about a normal decision process, it usually proceeds in four steps:

- You encounter a choice.
- You analyze your options.
- You make a choice.
- Then you live with it.

And what we've seen is that there is a villain that afflicts each of these stages:

- You encounter a choice. **But narrow framing makes you miss options.**
- You analyze your options. **But the confirmation bias leads you to gather self-serving information.**
- You make a choice. **But short-term emotion will often tempt you to make the wrong one.**
- Then you live with it. **But you'll often be overconfident about how the future will unfold.**

So, at this point, we know what we're up against. We know the four top villains of decision making. We also know that the classic pros-and-cons approach is not well suited to fighting these villains; in fact, it doesn't meaningfully counteract any of them.

Now we can turn our attention to a more optimistic question: What's a process that *will* help us overcome these villains and make better choices?

5.

In the fall of 1772, a man named Joseph Priestley was struggling with a career decision, and the way he handled the decision points us toward a solution.

Priestley, a brilliant man with an astonishing variety of talents, did not lack for career options. He was employed as a minister for a Dissenting church in Leeds, England. ("Dissenting" meant that it was not affiliated with the Church of England, the state-sanctioned religion.) But he was a man with many hobbies, all of which seemed to take on historical significance. As an advocate for religious tolerance, he helped to found the Unitarian Church in England. As a philosopher, he wrote works on metaphysics that were cited as important influences by John Stuart Mill and Jeremy Bentham.

An accomplished scientist, Priestley is credited with the discovery of 10 gases, including ammonia and carbon monoxide. He is best known for discovering the most important gas of them all: oxygen.*

A political rabble-rouser, Priestley spoke out in favor of the French Revolution, which aroused the suspicion of the government and his fellow citizens. Later, as tempers flared, a mob burned down his home and church, forcing him to flee, first to London and eventually to the United States, where he spent the rest of his life.

Priestley was a theologian, a chemist, an educator, a political theorist, a husband, and a father. He published more than 150 works, ranging from a history of electricity to a seminal work on English grammar. He even invented soda water, so every time you enjoy your Diet Coke, you can thank Priestley.

In short, Priestley's career was a bit like an eighteenth-century version of *Forrest Gump*, if Gump were a genius. He intersected with countless

---

*Priestley had focused the sun's rays on a sample of mercuric oxide inside a sealed container and was surprised to find that mice survived well in the resulting gas. Later he tested it on himself and proclaimed that it was "five or six times better than common air" for breathing.

movements of historical and scientific significance. But in the fall of 1772, he had a much more prosaic problem on his hands: money.

Priestley, like any father, worried about the financial security of his growing family. His salary as a minister—100 pounds a year—was not sufficient to build substantial savings for his children, who eventually numbered eight. So he started looking for other options, and some colleagues connected him with the Earl of Shelburne, a science buff and a supporter of Dissenting religious groups in England's House of Lords. Shelburne was recently widowed and looking for intellectual companionship and help in training his children.

Lord Shelburne offered Priestley a job as a tutor and an adviser. For a salary of 250 pounds a year, Priestley would supervise the education of Lord Shelburne's children and counsel him on political and governmental matters. Priestley was impressed by the offer—particularly the money, of course—but was also cautious about what he'd be signing on for. Seeking advice, he wrote to several colleagues he respected, including a wise and resourceful man he'd met while writing the history of electricity: Benjamin Franklin.

FRANKLIN REPLIED WITH THE moral-algebra letter cited in our introduction, suggesting that Priestley use the process of pros and cons to guide his decision.

Thanks to the record provided by Priestley's letters to friends, it's possible to imagine how Priestley would have used the moral-algebra process. The pros: good money; better security for his family.

The cons were more plentiful. The job might require a move to London, which bothered Priestley, who described himself as "so happy at home" that he hated to contemplate being apart from his family. He worried, too, about the relationship with Shelburne. Would it feel like master and servant? And even if it started off fine, what would happen if Shelburne grew tired of him? Finally, Priestley worried that the commitments would distract him from more important work. Would he end up spending his days teaching multiplication to kids instead of blazing new intellectual paths in religion and science?

From the perspective of the pros-and-cons list, accepting the offer looks like a pretty bad decision. There's basically one big pro—money—stacked up against an array of serious cons. Fortunately, though, Priestley largely ignored Franklin's advice and found ways to circumvent the four villains of decision making.

First, he rejected the narrow frame: *Should I take this offer or not?* Instead, he started pushing for new and better options. He considered alternative ways to bring in more income, such as speaking tours to lecture on his scientific work. In the spirit of "AND not OR" he negotiated for a better deal with Shelburne, at a time when people rarely questioned the nobility. Priestley ensured that a tutor, rather than he, would handle the education of Shelburne's kids, and he arranged to spend most of his time in the country with his family, making trips to London only when Shelburne really needed him.

Second, he dodged the confirmation bias. Early in the process, Priestley received a strong letter from a friend who argued vehemently against Shelburne's offer, insisting that it would humiliate Priestley and leave him dependent on a nobleman's charity. Priestley took the objection quite seriously, and at one point he reported that he was leaning against the offer. But rather than stewing over his internal pros-and-cons list, he went out and collected more data. Specifically, he sought the advice of people who *knew* Shelburne, and the consensus was clear: "Those who are acquainted with Lord Shelburne encourage me to accept his proposal; but most of those who know the world in general, but not Lord Shelburne in particular, dissuade me from it." In other words, the people who knew the lord best were the most positive about the offer. Based on these converging assessments, Priestley began to consider the offer more seriously.

Third, Priestley got some distance from his short-term emotions. He sought advice from friends as well as more neutral colleagues such as Franklin. He didn't allow himself to be distracted by visceral feelings: the quick flush of being offered a 150% raise or the social shame of being thought "dependent" by a friend. He made his decision based on the two factors he cared most about in the long term: his family's welfare and his scholarly independence.

Finally, he avoided overconfidence. He expected the relationship to fare well, but he knew that he might be wrong. He worried, in particular, about leaving his family exposed financially if Shelburne had a sudden change of heart about the arrangement. So he negotiated a sort of insurance policy: Shelburne agreed to pay him 150 pounds a year for life, even if their relationship was terminated.

In the end, Priestley accepted the offer, and he worked for Lord Shelburne for about seven years. It would be one of the most prolific periods of his career, the period of his most important philosophical work and his discovery of oxygen.

Shelburne and Priestley eventually parted ways. The reasons aren't clear, but Priestley said they separated "amicably," and Shelburne honored his agreement to provide 150 pounds a year to the newly independent Priestley.

6.

We believe Priestley made a good decision to work with Shelburne, though it's impossible to say for certain. After all, it's possible that spending time with Shelburne distracted him just enough to stop him from making yet another world-historical contribution (cinnamon rolls? the Electric Slide?). But what we do know is that there's a lot to admire about the *process* he used to make the decision, because he demonstrates that it's possible to overcome the four villains of decision making.

Of course, he's not the only one to triumph: Steve Cole at HopeLab beat narrow framing by thinking "AND not OR." Andy Grove overcame short-term emotions by asking, "What would my successor do?"

We can't *deactivate* our biases, but these people show us that we can *counteract* them with the right discipline. The nature of each villain suggests a strategy for defeating it:

1. You encounter a choice. *But narrow framing makes you miss options. So . . .*

   → **Widen Your Options.** How can you expand your set of choices? We'll study the habits of people who are expert at uncovering new options, including a college-selection adviser, some executives whose businesses survived (and even thrived) during global recessions, and a boutique firm that has named some of the world's top brands, including BlackBerry and Pentium.

2. You analyze your options. *But the confirmation bias leads you to gather self-serving info. So . . .*

   → **Reality-Test Your Assumptions.** How can you get outside your head and collect information that you can trust? We'll learn how to ask craftier questions, how to turn a contentious meeting into a productive one in 30 seconds, and what kind of expert advice should make you suspicious.

3. You make a choice. *But short-term emotion will often tempt you to make the wrong one. So . . .*

   → **Attain Distance Before Deciding.** How can you overcome short-term emotion and conflicted feelings to make the best choice? We'll discover how to triumph over manipulative car salesmen, why losing $50 is more painful than gaining $50 is pleasurable, and what simple question often makes agonizing decisions perfectly easy.

4. Then you live with it. *But you'll often be overconfident about how the future will unfold. So . . .*

   → **Prepare to Be Wrong.** How can we plan for an uncertain future so that we give our decisions the best chance to succeed? We'll show you how one woman scored a raise by mentally simulating the negotiation in advance, how you can rein in your spouse's crazy business idea, and why it can be smart to warn new employees about how lousy their jobs will be.

Our goal in this book is to teach this four-step process for making better choices. Note the mnemonic WRAP, which captures the four verbs. We like the notion of a process that "wraps" around your usual way of making decisions, helping to protect you from some of the biases we've identified.

The four steps in the WRAP model are sequential; in general, you can follow them in order—but not rigidly so. Sometimes you'll double back based on something you've learned. For example, in the course of gathering information to Reality-Test Your Assumptions, you might discover a new option you hadn't considered before. Other times, you won't need all of the steps. A long-awaited promotion probably won't require much distance before you accept and pop the champagne.

At its core, the WRAP model urges you to switch from "auto spotlight" to manual spotlight. Rather than make choices based on what naturally comes to your attention—visceral emotions, self-serving information, overconfident predictions, and so on—you deliberately illuminate more strategic spots. You sweep your light over a broader landscape and point it into hidden corners.

NOW YOU'VE REACHED THE part of the book where we are supposed to assure you that, if you follow these four steps religiously, your life will be a picture of human contentment. You will lack for nothing, and your peers will herald your wisdom. Alas. If our own experience is any guide, then you are still going to make a healthy share of bad decisions.

Here is our goal: We want to make you a bit better at making good decisions, and we want to help you make your good decisions a bit more decisively (with appropriate confidence, as opposed to overconfidence). We also want to make you a better adviser to your colleagues and loved ones who are making decisions, because it's usually easier to see other people's biases than your own.

This book will address decisions that take longer than five minutes to make: Whether to buy a new car, take a new job, or break up with your boyfriend. How to handle a difficult colleague. How to allocate budgetary resources between departments. Whether to start your own business.

If a decision takes only seconds—if, for instance, you are an NFL quarterback choosing which open receiver to hit with a pass—then this book will not help you. Much has been written in recent years about intuitive decisions, which can be surprisingly quick and accurate. But— and this is a critical "but"—intuition is only accurate in domains where it has been carefully trained. To train intuition requires a predictable environment where you get lots of repetition and quick feedback on your choices. (For a longer discussion of this issue, see the endnotes section.)

If you're a chess grand master, you should trust your gut. (You've had thousands of hours of study and practice with prompt feedback on your moves.) If you're a manager making a hiring decision, you shouldn't. (You've probably hired only a small number of people over the years, and the feedback from those hires is delayed and often confounded by other factors.)

Our hope is that you'll embrace the process we outline in *Decisive* and practice it until it becomes second nature. As an analogy, think of the humble grocery list. If you're forgetful (as we are), it's hard to imagine shopping without a list. Over time, the routine sharpens; you get better at recording, right away, the random items that occur to you, and when you shop, you begin to trust that everything you need to buy will be on the list. The grocery list is a correction for the deficiency of forgetfulness. And it's a much better solution than focusing really hard on not being forgetful.

Because we wanted the WRAP process to be useful and memorable, we have done our best to keep it simple. That was a challenge, because the decision-making literature is voluminous and complex. As a result, we've had to omit some very interesting work to let the most useful research shine through. (If you're hungry for more, see the end of the book for reading recommendations.)

Occasionally some aspect of the WRAP process will lead to a

home-run insight, as in the cases of Steve Cole's "horse race" and Andy Grove's question "What would our successors do?" More commonly, it will yield small but consistent improvements in the way you make decisions—and that's critical too. Think of a baseball player's batting average: If a player gets a hit in one out of every four at-bats (a .250 average) over the course of a season, he is mediocre. If he hits in one out of three (.333), he's an All-Star. And if he hits .333 over his career, he'll be a Hall-of-Famer. Yet the gap in performance is small: only one extra hit in every twelve at-bats.

To get that kind of consistent improvement requires technique and practice. It requires a process. The value of the WRAP process is that it reliably focuses our attention on things we otherwise might have missed: options we might have overlooked, information we might have resisted, and preparations we might have neglected.

A more subtle way the WRAP process can help us is by ensuring that we're *aware* of the need to make a decision. And that leads us to David Lee Roth.

ROTH WAS THE LEAD singer for Van Halen from the mid-1970s to the mid-1980s, an era when the band cranked out one smash hit after another: "Runnin' with the Devil," "Dance the Night Away," "Jump," "Hot for Teacher," and more. Van Halen toured tirelessly, with over a hundred concerts in 1984 alone, and behind the band's head-banging appeal was some serious operational expertise. It was one of the first rock bands to bring major stage productions to smaller markets. As Roth recalled in his autobiography, "We'd pull up with nine eighteen-wheeler trucks, full of gear, where the standard was three trucks, max."

The band's production design was astonishingly complex. The contract specifying the setup was, according to Roth, "like a version of the Chinese Yellow Pages" because it was so technical and complex it was like reading a foreign language. A typical article in the contract might say, "There will be fifteen amperage voltage sockets at twenty-foot spaces, evenly, providing nineteen amperes. . . ."

While Van Halen had its own road crew, much of the prep work had to be done in advance, before the eighteen-wheelers arrived. Van Halen and its crew lived in fear that the venues' stagehands would screw up something and leave the band exposed to injury. (This was the same era when Michael Jackson's head was set on fire by some misfiring stage pyrotechnics as he filmed a Pepsi commercial.) But, given the band's frantic touring schedule, there wasn't time to do a top-to-bottom quality check at each venue. How could the band know when they were at risk?

During this same period of touring, rumors circulated wildly about Van Halen's backstage antics. The band members were notorious partiers, and while there's nothing particularly noteworthy about a rock band that likes to party, Van Halen seemed committed to a level of decadence that was almost artistic. Roth wrote in his autobiography, "Well, we've heard about throwing a television out a window. How about getting enough extension cords . . . so that the television can remain plugged in all the way down to the ground floor?"

Sometimes, though, the band's actions seemed less like playful mayhem and more like egomania. The most egregious rumor about the band was that its contract rider demanded a bowl of M&Ms backstage—with all the brown ones removed. There were tales of Roth walking backstage, spotting a single brown M&M, and freaking out, trashing the dressing room.

This rumor was true. The brown-free bowl of M&Ms became the perfect, appalling symbol of rock-star diva behavior. Here was a band making absurd demands simply because it could.

Get ready to reverse your perception.

The band's "M&M clause" was written into its contract to serve a very specific purpose. It was called Article 126, and it read as follows: "There will be no brown M&M's in the backstage area, upon pain of forfeiture of the show, with full compensation." The article was buried in the middle of countless technical specifications.

When Roth would arrive at a new venue, he'd immediately walk backstage and glance at the M&M bowl. If he saw a brown M&M, he'd demand a line check of the entire production. "Guaranteed you're going to arrive at a technical error," he said. "They didn't read the contract. . . . Sometimes it would threaten to just destroy the whole show."

In other words, David Lee Roth was no diva; he was an operations master. He needed a way to assess quickly whether the stagehands at each venue were paying attention—whether they'd read every word of the contract and taken it seriously. He needed a way, in other words, to snap out of "mental autopilot" and realize that a decision had to be made. In Van Halen's world, a brown M&M was a tripwire.

COULDN'T WE ALL USE a few tripwires in our lives? We'd have a "trigger weight" that signaled the need to exercise more, or a trigger date on the calendar that reminded us to ask whether we're investing enough in our relationships. Sometimes the hardest part of making a good decision is knowing there's one to be made.

In life, we spend most of our days on autopilot, going through our usual routines. We may make only a handful of conscious, considered choices every day. But while these decisions don't occupy much of our time, they have a disproportionate influence on our lives. The psychologist Roy Baumeister draws an analogy to driving—in our cars, we may spend 95% of our time going straight, but it's the turns that determine where we end up.

This is a book about those turns. In the chapters to come, we'll show you how a four-part process can boost your chances of getting where you want to go.

INTRODUCTION AND CHAPTER ONE IN ONE PAGE
The Four Villains of Decision Making

1. Danny Kahneman: "A remarkable aspect of your mental life is that you are rarely stumped."

   - *Should Shannon fire Clive? We form opinions effortlessly.*

2. What's in our spotlight = the most accessible information + our interpretation of that information. But that will rarely be all that we need to make a good decision.

3. Our decision "track record" isn't great. Trusting our guts or conducting rigorous analysis won't fix it. But a good process will.

   - *Study: "Process mattered more than analysis—by a factor of six."*

4. We can defeat the four villains of decision making by learning to shift our spotlights.

5. Villain 1: Narrow framing (unduly limiting the options we consider)

   - *HopeLab had five firms work simultaneously on stage 1; "Can I do this AND that?"*

6. Villain 2: The confirmation bias (seeking out information that bolsters our beliefs)

   - *The tone-deaf American Idol contestant . . .*
   - *Lovallo: "Confirmation bias is probably the single biggest problem in business."*

7. Villain 3: Short-term emotion (being swayed by emotions that will fade)

   - *Intel's Andy Grove got distance by asking, "What would our successors do?"*

8. Villain 4: Overconfidence (having too much faith in our predictions)

   - *"Four-piece groups with guitars, particularly, are finished."*

9. The pros-and-cons process won't correct these problems. But the WRAP process will.

   - *Joseph Priestley conquered all four villains.*

10. To make better decisions, use the WRAP process:

    Widen Your Options.
    Reality-Test Your Assumptions.
    Attain Distance Before Deciding.
    Prepare to Be Wrong.

Widen Your Options

Reality-Test Your Assumptions

Attain Distance Before Deciding

Prepare to Be Wrong

2

Avoid a Narrow Frame

1.

In July 2012, a user named claireabelle posted a dilemma on the "Q&A Community" of the Web site Ask.com:

> **claireabelle:** Break up or not? I don't know what to do. Every time I go to my boyfriend's house or hang out with his family, I feel like I'm constantly being judged. His sister, who is the same age as me, is very mood-swingy towards me. His older brother hates me and calls me a b*tch. His mom is rude to me and makes insulting jokes at me. What do I do? I like him, but I'm tired of being judged and feeling weird when I'm with them.*

Within a day, she had almost a dozen responses, including these:

> **Shalie333:** As long as he is not treating you this way, then I wouldn't break up with him. Just try not hanging out with his family as much!

---

*Note that we have corrected the punctuation and capitalization in these entries (though not the grammar). This diminishes authenticity but greatly enhances one's sanity in reading it.

eimis74523: Don't talk nonsense, if he loves her he should stand up for her. If my family would do this to my gf, I would tell them to [bleep] themselves up. You should tell him that you're going to leave him because of his family and then see how he reacts—then you'll see if he loves you.

yolo1212: Do whatever feels right.

14Sweetie: Breaking up isn't the answer if he treats you good. Make other plans to hang out other places and explain to him why. If he can't handle this and work with how you feel, then he doesn't deserve you.

lovealwayz: This is the truth, leave him if he doesn't say anything to his family about it, because if he doesn't then he don't care. :(

Kuckleburg: . . . RUN . . . RUN FAST. This family is creepy.

The "break up" dilemma is a classic of the teenage decision-making genre, along with others like what to wear, whom to hang out with, what car to buy, and how long to wait before wrecking it. Note that claire-abelle above has framed her decision narrowly when she asks, "Should I break up or not?" Some of the commenters accept this narrow frame— "RUN . . . RUN FAST"—whereas others try to widen the set of options she is considering, as with the advice to "make other plans to hang out other places and explain to him why."

A researcher named Baruch Fischhoff, a professor at Carnegie Mellon University, wanted to understand more about the teenage decision-making process, so he and his colleagues interviewed 105 teenage girls in Pittsburgh, Pennsylvania, and Eugene, Oregon. They asked the girls to describe in detail recent decisions in seven different domains: school, parents, clothes, peers, health, money, and free time.

In the interviews, the teens reported some peculiar decisions. Most of us think of a "decision" as a situation where we must choose among two or more options: Should we eat at Chipotle or Subway? Which color shirt should we buy: the navy, the black, or the white one? But teenagers' decisions rarely had this structure. When Fischhoff began to categorize the teens' decisions, he found that the most common type was one that lacked any choice at all. It was what he called a "statement of resolve." An example would be "I'm going to stop blaming others."

In the second-most-common type of decision, teens assessed a single option, such as "I'm deciding whether or not I should smoke cigarettes with my friend" or, as in the case of claireabelle, "I'm deciding whether or not to break up with my boyfriend." (We'll refer to decisions like these as "whether or not" decisions.) This isn't a decision among multiple alternatives, as with picking between Chipotle and Subway—it's simply an up-or-down vote on a single alternative.

These two categories—statements of resolve and "whether or not" decisions—composed about 65% of teenagers' decisions. In other words, if a teenager is making a "decision," chances are there's no real choice being made at all!

(As an aside, when we first came across Fischhoff's study, we were shocked by the lack of consideration teens gave to their options. But when we shared the results of the study with our sister, who has raised two teenagers, she was unimpressed. "What do you expect?" she said. "Kids get to their teen years, the hormones kick in, and they spend a few years operating without a frontal lobe.")

Teenagers are blind to their choices. They get stuck thinking about questions like "Should I go to the party or not?" The party is in their mental spotlight, assessed in isolation, while other options go unexplored. A more enlightened teen might let the spotlight roam: "Should I go to the party all night, or go to the movies with a few friends, or attend the basketball game and then drop by the party for a few minutes?"

In short, teens are prone to narrow framing, the first of our villains of decision making. They see only a small sliver of the spectrum of options available to them. And, as it turns out, when it comes to making decisions, organizations are a lot like teenagers.

2.

In 1983, William Smithburg, the CEO of Quaker, made a bold decision to acquire the parent company of Gatorade for $220 million. According to a summary of reports from the time, "Smithburg made the Gatorade purchase impulsively, basing the acquisition on his taste buds; he tried the product and liked it." And his taste buds proved savvy: Thanks to Quaker's aggressive marketing, Gatorade grew ferociously. The $220 million purchase grew in estimated value to $3 billion.

About a decade later, in 1994, Smithburg proposed buying another beverage brand, Snapple, for a stunning $1.8 billion. It was a price that some analysts squawked might be a billion dollars too high, but, because of Gatorade's massive success, the Quaker board of directors didn't protest.

To Smithburg, the Snapple acquisition must have seemed like a replay of Gatorade. Here was another chance to make a bold bet; as researcher Paul Nutt wrote, Smithburg had received "accolades" for the Gatorade deal and "wanted another flashy acquisition." Snapple was another niche brand with the potential to cross over to the mass market.

The high cost of the acquisition, Smithburg knew, would leave Quaker deep in debt, but to him this was actually a bonus. He was worried about a hostile takeover of Quaker, and he believed the debt would deter potential raiders. So with the board's support, Smithburg moved quickly, and the deal was completed in 1994.

It was a fiasco.

The Snapple acquisition has become known as one of the worst decisions in business history. Quaker discovered that Snapple was almost nothing like Gatorade. The brand's teas and juices demanded very different approaches to manufacturing and distribution. And Quaker managed to make a mess of Snapple's brand image, abandoning the quirky, authentic voice that had helped Snapple succeed. (These trouble spots could have been surfaced before the acquisition, if Quaker's execs had bothered to investigate.)

When Snapple's sales didn't take off the way Gatorade's had, Quaker executives had an emergency on their hands. The debt burden threatened to bring down the company. Three years later, Snapple was hurriedly sold off to Triarc Corporation for $300 million, one sixth the original price. Humiliated, Smithburg stepped down as CEO.

He later reflected, "There was so much excitement about bringing in a new brand, a brand with legs. We should have had a couple of people arguing the 'no' side of the evaluation."

That's a pretty staggering confession. Under Smithburg's leadership, Quaker was contemplating the largest acquisition in its history, with deal terms that had been mocked widely by industry analysts, and yet, unbelievably, there was *no one within Quaker arguing against the acquisition!*

Quaker wasn't even making a "whether or not" choice; it was making a "yes or yes" choice.

QUAKER'S DECISION WAS PRETTY egregious, but the company is hardly alone in making an ill-advised acquisition. A KPMG study of 700 mergers and acquisitions (mentioned previously in the introduction) found that 83% of them did not boost shareholder value. This suggests a good rule of thumb for business leaders: If you've spent weeks or months analyzing a potential target, and what you've learned has convinced you to make an offer, don't. Five times out of six you'll be right!

Of course, we shouldn't expect acquisitions, with their attendant forces of ego and emotion and competition, to be typical of organizational decision making. The average manager, making a normal decision outside the world of deal making, should easily dodge the teenage trap. Right?

For the answer we turn to Paul Nutt, who may know more than anyone alive about how managers make decisions. In 2010, Nutt retired from the business-school faculty of Ohio State University, having spent his 30-year career collecting decisions the way some people collect stamps. He analyzed decisions made by businesses: *McDonald's consider-*

ing a new design for its stores. And nonprofits: *a 250-bed rural hospital deciding whether to add a detox unit.* And government agencies: *Florida's Medicaid program contemplating how to revamp its fraud-management system.*

In each situation, Nutt gathered data in a prescribed way. First he interviewed the primary decision maker, often a CEO or COO. Then he cross-checked their reports with two other "informants," usually senior managers who had watched the decision process unfold. Finally he evaluated whether the decisions had succeeded. Not trusting the judgment of the primary decision makers, who'd be biased in their own favor, he asked the informants to assess the quality of the decision. Did the decision produce an option that was successfully adopted? Was the success sustained over time?

A 1993 study by Nutt, which analyzed 168 decisions in this laborious way, came to a stunning conclusion: Of the teams he studied, only 29% considered more than one alternative.* By way of comparison, 30% of the teens in the Fischhoff study considered more than one alternative.

According to Paul Nutt's research, then, most organizations seem to be using the same decision process as a hormone-crazed teenager.

Organizations, like teenagers, are blind to their choices. And the consequences are serious: Nutt found that "whether or not" decisions failed 52% of the time over the long term, versus only 32% of the decisions with two or more alternatives.

Why do "whether or not" decisions fail more often? Nutt argues that when a manager pursues a single option, she spends most of her time asking: "How can I make this work? How can I get my colleagues behind me?" Meanwhile, other vital questions get neglected: "Is there a better way? What else could we do?"

Finding answers to those questions—"Is there a better way? What else could we do?"—is the goal of this part of the WRAP framework,

---

*Note that we are counting a "whether or not" decision as one alternative. It's one alternative that will be either accepted or rejected.

"Widen Your Options." Can we learn to escape a narrow frame and discover better options for ourselves?

The first step toward that goal is to learn to distrust "whether or not" decisions. In fact, we hope when you see or hear that phrase, a little alarm bell will go off in your head, reminding you to consider whether you're stuck in a narrow frame.

If you're willing to invest some effort in a broader search, you'll usually find that your options are more plentiful than you initially think.

3.

Heidi Price was so frustrated by one of her family's decisions that she ended up founding a business to help other families avoid the same frustration. In 2003, she was trying to help her daughter, a high school senior, pick the right college. It was a struggle finding information they could trust. All the college brochures looked alike—down to the obligatory photo of a polyracial group of students reading under a tree. (Surely those photos should be modernized to show a polyracial group of students using their smartphones to crib from Wikipedia?)

After months of consideration, her daughter eventually decided to enroll in an honors program at the University of Kansas, but the difficulty of the search nagged at Price. They'd been inundated with information, but it had been tough to tease out what was important. Curious, Price started to dig into the research on undergraduate education: What factors really made a difference for students? She started sharing her discoveries with friends, and soon they were asking for her advice: *Which college do you think is right for my kid?*

Convinced there was a need for a better college-selection process, Price and a partner cofounded College Match, a small firm in Kansas City that helps match students with the college that's right for them. One of Price's early clients was actually her nephew, Caufield Schnug, who had grown up in Texas, though he was far from the stereotypical

Texas teenager. He didn't play sports. He wasn't a football fan. He was liberal, bright, and quirky—while in high school, he got interested in guitars, played in a band, won a writing contest, and helped his dad with a screenplay.

Often bored by school, his grades were mediocre. He was unlikely to be admitted to the best-ranked state schools, the University of Texas and Texas A&M. When his dad took him to see his other options in the state, he had to be cajoled to get out of the car.

At one university, his visit coincided with a fraternity party where drunk students were spraying one another with hoses. "One part of me thought it was fun and another part thought it was barbaric," said Schnug. The *Animal House* vision of college held no allure for him. "I wanted to find out what was wrong with me—if I was good at anything. I felt like I was smart. I felt like I had interests, but what were they? I didn't want to drink a six-pack. That wasn't my mission."

Price had several suggestions for Schnug, but one stood out in her mind: Hendrix College, a small liberal-arts school in Conway, Arkansas, known for its artsy, liberal culture. Schnug had never heard of Hendrix, but he agreed to visit. The change in atmosphere appealed to him—he would leave the big, hip city of Austin and move to an uncool, rural Arkansas town. "I can be 'monkish' here," he remembers thinking. "I felt like I could focus on my studies."

Schnug blossomed at Hendrix. It was the right environment for him. "My first year at Hendrix, I read three or four books every week. I watched one or two or three foreign films every single day. I took philosophy courses. I turned into an academic person," he said.

Schnug thrived academically, double-majoring in film studies and English, and he studied abroad for two semesters, including a fall term at Oxford University. While traveling in Barcelona, he made a documentary about Gaudí's architecture.

It was a far cry from Old Milwaukee kegs and fraternity hose-downs.

Eventually he decided that he wanted to get a PhD in film studies. (Getting a PhD was an aspiration his family would never have anticipated before Hendrix.) After gaining acceptance to several programs, he chose Harvard. He was one of only three students admitted to the school's Film & Visual Studies program in 2012.

HEIDI PRICE HELPS STUDENTS and parents to take off their blinders, to see that their universe of schools is not the 20 schools that sit atop the rankings but rather the 2,719 schools that offer four-year degrees in the United States, most of which admit the majority of their applicants. The top-ranked schools are unquestionably fine institutions, but the rankings may signify less than meets the eye. Parents are often surprised to learn that the vaunted *U.S. News & World Report* rankings rely on statistics such as faculty compensation and the percentage of alumni who make donations, which have little to do with the experience of students. (Nothing in the rankings directly measures whether students are enjoying their college experience or whether they are learning anything.)

Parents are often shocked, too, to hear that, once you control for aptitude, a person's lifetime earnings don't vary based on what college they attended. In other words, if you're smart enough to get into Yale, it doesn't really matter (from an income perspective) whether you go there or instead choose your much cheaper state university.

The question a college-bound senior should be asking, according to Price, is not "What's the highest-ranking college I can convince to take me?" Rather, it should be "What do I want out of life, and what are the best options to get me there?" Those two questions are in no way synonymous, and once families start thinking about the latter one, they often find that they have many more good options than they ever thought possible.

Spiritual advisers are often called on to do a similar kind of "reframing." Father J. Brian Bransfield, associate general secretary of the United States Conference of Catholic Bishops, said that the parishioners who seek out his advice have a tendency, as do Price's clients, to unduly narrow their options. Individuals will often approach him with a dilemma:

Should I marry this person? Should I take the job I've been offered in another city? Should I become a priest?

His parishioners will often fret, "I just don't know what God wants me to do," and look at Bransfield expectantly, hoping he can act as a spokesperson. "There's a myth that there's only one thing that God wants you to do," he said. "We spend so much time trying to figure out that one thing and become so fearful of making a mistake." Bransfield challenges them to broaden their perspective:

> Actually, there are 18 things that God would be very happy if you chose. You're not cornered into becoming a priest or not. You're not cornered into marrying this woman or not. There are 6 billion people in the world. You're telling me that God looked at you and said, "There is only 1 thing you can do in your life, I know it and you have to guess it or else"? Could it be that you are putting *your* constraints on God?

Bransfield's parishioners would often react with surprise to this message: "Really?" They're relieved to hear that they're not cornered. They've just been wearing blinders.

Why is it so hard for all of us to see the bigger picture? To understand what lulls us into adopting a narrow frame, we will dig into a seemingly easy decision—a customer choosing a stereo to buy—and reveal the complexity that lies underneath it.

4.

In the early 1990s, Shane Frederick, then a graduate student, was shopping for a stereo in Vancouver, and he found himself "frozen in indecision" between a $1,000 Pioneer and a $700 Sony. He ended up spending almost an hour agonizing over the decision until finally a salesman approached him and asked a question: "Well, think of it this way—would

you rather have the Pioneer or the Sony and $300 worth of albums?"
That question broke Frederick's mental logjam; he decided to buy the
Sony. The extra features of the Pioneer were cool, he figured, but not
nearly as cool as a bunch of new music.

That day in the electronics store landed Frederick a new stereo, but it
would also, later in his career, spark a line of research. At the time he was
stereo shopping, he was getting a master's in environmental studies, but
later he switched to a PhD program in decision sciences. Recalling his
stereo experience, the first experiment he conducted as a doctoral student
explored the way consumers think about opportunity costs.

"Opportunity cost" is a term from economics that refers to what we
give up when we make a decision. For instance, if you and your spouse
spend $40 on a Mexican dinner one Friday night and then go to the mov-
ies ($20), your opportunity cost might be a $60 sushi dinner plus some
television at home. The sushi-and-TV combo is the *next-best thing* you
could have done with the same amount of time and money. Or if you
love both shopping and hiking, then the opportunity cost of a Saturday
afternoon at the mall might be the forgone opportunity to hike through
a nearby park. Sometimes you'll be offered an option with a very high
opportunity cost—for instance, if we invited you to our "neighborhood
sing-along" on the same night as the Super Bowl. Assuming you are sane,
you will turn down our invitation, because its opportunity cost is too high.

The stereo salesman's question was a classic prod to think about opportunity cost: For Frederick to buy the $1,000 Pioneer stereo meant
that he was sacrificing the chance to buy a $700 Sony stereo plus $300
worth of music. It intrigued Frederick that it simply hadn't occurred to
him to think that way. Some economists take it for granted that consumers make these opportunity-cost calculations. One journal article
summarized the typical assumption: "Decision makers confronted with
a showcase of beluga caviar consider how much hamburger they could
buy with the same money. . . . People intuitively take opportunity cost
into account."

But Frederick knew that, before the salesperson intervened, he hadn't done that analysis. Suspecting that other consumers were likely to fall into the same trap, he and his colleagues designed a study to test whether consumers spontaneously considered opportunity costs.

One of the questions in their study was this:

Imagine that you have been saving some extra money on the side to make some purchases, and on your most recent visit to the video store you come across a special sale on a new video. This video is one with your favorite actor or actress, and your favorite type of movie (such as a comedy, drama, thriller, etc.). This particular video that you are considering is one you have been thinking about buying for a long time. It is available for a special sale price of $14.99.

What would you do in this situation? Please circle one of the options below.

(A) Buy this entertaining video.

(B) Not buy this entertaining video.

Given this choice, 75% bought the video and only 25% passed. Probably you'd have made the same decision—after all, it's your favorite actor (Leonardo DiCaprio!) in your favorite type of film (sinking-ship movies!) and you've been considering it for a while.

Later the researchers asked a different group of people the same question, but with a minor modification (printed here in bold):

(A) Buy this entertaining video.

(B) Not buy this entertaining video. **Keep the $14.99 for other purchases.**

Surely the part in bold should not have to be stated. It's obvious and even a little insulting. Do we really need to remind people that they can use their money to buy things other than videos?

Nonetheless, when shown that simple, stupid reminder, 45% of the people decided *not* to buy the video. The reminder almost doubled the chance that people would pass on the purchase! Which makes us wonder whether Quaker would have benefited from a slight tweak to its choices:

(A)   Buy Snapple.

(B)   Don't buy Snapple. **Keep the $1.8 _billion_ for other purchases.**

This study presents very good news for all of us. It suggests that being exposed to even a weak hint of another alternative—*you could buy something else with this money if you want*—is sufficient to improve our purchasing decisions.*

We can understand if you're a little suspicious that our decisions can be improved so easily. It's rarely so simple to "repair" one of our cognitive biases. It's like learning that you can cure the avian flu by clapping your hands.

But here's the catch: You won't clap your hands if you don't realize you have the avian flu. Or to escape that metaphor: You won't think up additional alternatives if you aren't aware you're neglecting them. Often you simply won't recognize you're stuck in a narrow frame.

Think about Frederick's predicament. What's in his spotlight? The two stereos. He stares at them, mentally comparing their aesthetics and features and prices. It's a hard comparison; how much is it worth to have a wider frequency range? Or a slightly cooler speaker design? As he dwells on what's inside the spotlight, his brain obligingly ignores what's outside, like the music he could buy if he picked the cheaper stereo. In a sense, he was the victim of his own ability to focus.

Focusing is great for analyzing alternatives but terrible for spotting them. Think about the visual analogy—when we focus we sacrifice pe-

---

*Note that we aren't claiming it is a bad idea to buy the video. Buying it is probably the right decision for some people and the wrong one for others, depending on their bank account and their movie lust. But the one thing we can say for sure is that it would be a bad decision to buy it *without first considering what else the money could have bought.*

ripheral vision. And there's no natural corrective for this; life won't interrupt our focus to draw our attention to all of our options.

Frederick's stereo salesperson was surprisingly good-hearted to break his focus and prompt him to think about opportunity cost. A more mercenary salesperson, who wanted to maximize her commission, would never have gone there. She'd have kept Frederick's spotlight trained on the expensive stereo: "You know, Shane, it's ultimately a matter of quality. Do you think it's worth paying a little more to hear your favorite bands more clearly?" (You will never encounter a car salesman who says, "Hey, why not buy the entry-level model and use the savings to take your family on vacation?")

Our lack of attention to opportunity costs is so common, in fact, that it can be shocking when someone acknowledges them. Frederick and his coauthors highlight a speech from Republican president (and former general) Dwight D. Eisenhower in 1953, a few months after he took office in his first term: "The cost of one modern heavy bomber is this: a modern brick school in more than 30 cities. It is two electric power plants each serving a town of 60,000 people. It is two fine, fully equipped hospitals. It is some 50 miles of concrete highway. We pay for a single fighter with a half million bushels of wheat. We pay for a single destroyer with new homes that could have housed more than 8,000 people."

How much better would our decisions be if more people shared Eisenhower's willingness to consider opportunity costs? What if we started every decision by asking some simple questions: What are we giving up by making this choice? What else could we do with the same time and money?

5.

Another technique you can use to break out of a narrow frame is to run the Vanishing Options Test. The conceit here is that Aladdin's genie has an eccentric older brother who, instead of granting three wishes to a person, arbitrarily takes options away. Below, we give you a generic form of the Vanishing Options Test, which you can adapt to your situation:

> You *cannot* choose any of the current options you're considering. What else could you do?

To see how the Vanishing Options Test can help you evade a narrow frame, consider a conversation we had with Margaret Sanders, the director of career services for a graduate school of government. (Names in this case study are disguised to prevent embarrassment.) Sanders was struggling with a tough decision: Should she tolerate a marginally performing employee or, as she put it, "begin the ridiculously long and tedious process for documentation of poor performance that can eventually lead to termination"?

The employee in question was her administrative assistant, Anna, who had two primary responsibilities. First, she handled administrative tasks, such as tracking expenses and managing the group's database, and second, she served as the "front door"—the face of the office, the first point of contact for students seeking jobs or for recruiters seeking students. While Anna was good with the first set of tasks, she struggled with the social aspect of her job. She was much more introverted than Sanders had realized during their interview. "I think it hurts for her to talk to people," said Sanders. Unfortunately, the social side of the job was critical, and Anna's shyness made the center less effective.

But firing Anna was not an easy answer. The university had strict protocols for handling terminations. It would be many months, Sanders knew, before Anna would be gone—if she was gone at all—and in the meantime, it would be incredibly awkward to work with her in an intimate office of five people.

Dan Heath had the chance to speak with Sanders as she was agonizing about whether or not to fire Anna. And—to interrupt the story for a moment—we hope your "narrow frame" alarm bells went off as you read that phrase, "whether or not to fire Anna." That phrase "whether or not" is, as we've seen, a classic warning signal that you haven't explored all your options.

So, in keeping with that idea, Dan tried pushing Sanders with the Vanishing Options Test:

DAN: Imagine that I told you you're stuck with Anna indefinitely *and* you can't rely on her to be the "front door." She cannot be the face of the office anymore. What would you do?

SANDERS: Hmmm . . . We could move her out of the front door and try to staff the front door differently. Maybe the professional staff could take an hour each, and we could get some work-study students in to fill in the rest of the time.

DAN: Is that a viable option? Could you afford to hire work-study students?

SANDERS: They are super cheap. We only pay about 25% of their hourly rate, which comes out to about $2.50 per hour.

Notice how easy it was for Sanders to break out of her narrow frame with a bit of prodding. It took less than a minute for her to generate another reasonable option—to hire work-study students to serve as the "front door," with Anna shifting to full-time administrative duties. It was an option that would fix the problem and cost only $20 per day! (Not to mention the benefit from the extra time Anna could spend on database or accounting work.)

The breakthrough that Margaret Sanders experienced is not unusual. When people imagine that they *cannot* have an option, they are forced to move their mental spotlight elsewhere—really move it—often for the first time in a long while. (In contrast, when people are asked to "generate another option," they often halfheartedly shift the spotlight a couple of inches, suggesting a minor variant of an existing alternative.)

The old saying "Necessity is the mother of invention" seems to apply here. Until we are forced to dig up a new option, we're likely to stay fixated on the ones we already have. So our eccentric genie, who seems at first glance to be cruel—he's taking away our options!—may actually be kindhearted. Removing options can in fact do people a favor, because it makes them notice that they're stuck on one small patch of a wide landscape. (Of course, we should be clear that people respond much more cheerfully when you metaphorically, rather than literally, remove their options.)

IN THE CALL WITH Margaret Sanders, Dan was trying to act as a decision adviser, just as Heidi Price acted as a decision adviser for high school seniors and Father Bransfield did for parishioners. This is the same role that we're urging you to play with your colleagues and loved ones.

When you hear the telltale signs of a narrow frame—people wondering "whether or not" they should make a certain decision or rehashing arguments endlessly about the same limited set of choices—push them to Widen Their Options.

Prod them for their opportunity cost; what else could they do with the same time and money? Or try the Vanishing Options Test: Ask them what they'd do if their current alternatives disappeared.

Being stuck in a narrow frame is hard to recognize—but only when you're the one inside it. From the outside, as an adviser, you will be able to see clearly when your coworkers or your children are unduly limiting their choices. A wider view can sometimes make a big difference.

CHAPTER TWO IN ONE PAGE
Avoid a Narrow Frame

1. Teenagers get trapped in a narrow frame. They are blind to their choices.

    - *"Should I go to the party or not?"*

2. Unfortunately, most organizations tend to make decisions like teenagers.

    - *Quaker lost $1.5 billion in three years on the Snapple acquisition.*
    - *Nutt research: Only 29% of organizations considered more than one alternative (versus 30% of teens).*

3. Often our options are far more plentiful than we think.

    - *College-selection counselor Price helps students explore their full range of options.*

4. Why do we get stuck in a narrow frame? Focusing on our current options means that other things are out of our spotlight.

    - *Frederick got stuck choosing between two stereos—he failed to consider his other options.*

5. How do we escape a narrow frame? Think about opportunity cost.

    - *Keep the $14.99 for other purchases.*
    - *Eisenhower: One bomber = a modern brick school in more than 30 cities.*

6. Or try the Vanishing Options Test: What if your current options disappeared?

    - *Margaret Sanders realized she had a better option than firing Anna, the introverted receptionist.*
    - *When our options "disappear," we're forced to move our spotlights.*

7. It's easier to spot a narrow frame from the outside—watch for it as a decision adviser. "Whether or not" decisions should set off warning bells.

3

Multitrack

1.

In Sausalito, California, there is a small firm called Lexicon that has coined the names for 15 billion-dollar brands, including BlackBerry, Dasani, Febreze, OnStar, Pentium, Scion, and Swiffer. These names don't emerge from brainstorming sessions that yield sudden lightning-bolt insights—nobody gets struck by lightning 15 times. Rather, Lexicon's magic is its creative process, which helps the team avoid getting stuck in a narrow frame.

Consider the firm's 2006 work for Colgate, which was preparing to launch a disposable mini-toothbrush. The center of the brush held a dab of special toothpaste, which was designed to make rinsing unnecessary. So you could carry the toothbrush with you, use it in a cab or an airplane lavatory, and then toss it out.

When Lexicon founder and CEO David Placek first saw the toothbrush, he said, what stood out was its small size. So, if you were on the Lexicon team, with your mental spotlight pointed at the tiny toothbrush, you'd be tempted to start tossing out names that highlight its small size: Petite Brush, Mini-Brush, Brushlet, etc. Notice that, in brainstorming that way, you would have already locked yourself into a tight frame with two assumptions: (1) The name should connote smallness; and (2) "Brush" should be part of the name.

That early lock-in is something that the Lexicon team has learned to fight. Clients will often come to them with a narrow conception of what a good name is. Some at Intel, for instance, had wanted to call the Pentium "ProChip." Some at P&G had wanted to call the Swiffer "EZMop." Lexicon has learned that the best names emerge from what we'll call "multitracking"—considering several options simultaneously.

To get familiar with the new toothbrush, Placek's team at Lexicon began to use it in their daily lives, and what struck them was how odd it was, at first, not to spit out the toothpaste that it produced. (We *always* spit out the toothpaste.) Fortunately, unlike normal brushes, the new brush didn't create a big mass of minty lather. The mouthfeel was lighter and more pleasant, more like a breath strip. It was this lack of foaminess that was the brush's most distinctive trait. So it dawned on the team that the name of the brush should not signal smallness; it should signal lightness, cleanliness, softness.

Armed with that insight, Placek began to multitrack. He asked his network of linguists—70 of them in 50 countries—to brainstorm about metaphors, sounds, and word parts that connoted lightness. By working independently, they vastly increased the pool of considered names.

Meanwhile, he asked another two colleagues within Lexicon to help. But he kept these two in the dark about the client and the product. Instead, he gave this team—referred to as the "excursion team"—a fictional mission. He told them that the cosmetics brand Olay was interested in introducing a new line of oral-care products, and their job would be to help Olay brainstorm about product ideas.

Placek chose Olay because he believed that beauty was an implicit selling point for the new brush. "Good oral care means white teeth, and white teeth are better looking," Placek said. After a period of exploration, the excursion team pitched some intriguing product ideas, including the "Olay Sparkling Rinse," a mouthwash that would make your teeth gleam.

In the end, it was the insight about lightness, rather than beauty, that prevailed. The team of linguists produced a long list of possible words and phrases, and one word on the list jumped out at Placek's team: "wisp." It was the perfect association for the new brushing experience. It's not something heavy and foamy; it's barely there. It's a wisp. Thus was born the Colgate Wisp.

Notice what's missing from the Lexicon process: the part when everyone sits around a conference table, staring at the toothbrush and brainstorming names together. ("Hey, how about ToofBrutch—the URL is available!")

Lexicon refuses to single-track the process. In fact, in most of its naming projects, Lexicon forms three teams of two, with each group pursuing a different angle. Usually there is an excursion team, blind to the client and the product, that spends its time chasing analogies from related domains. In naming Levi's Curve ID jeans, which were engineered differently for different body types, the excursion team dug into references on surveying and architecture.

Lexicon's multitracking often leads to "wasted" work. In the Wisp case, the excursion team found themselves at a dead end with the Olay assignment. But it's precisely this willingness to work in parallel, and to endure inefficiency, that often leads to a break in the case. That's what happened with one of Lexicon's most famous projects: the BlackBerry, made by Research in Motion (RIM).

When RIM engaged Lexicon, Placek and his team knew that they were fighting negative associations with PDAs: They buzz, they vibrate, they irritate us and stress us out. He challenged the excursion team—again unfamiliar with the actual client—to catalog things in the world that bring us joy, that slow us down, that relax us. The goal was to discover names that might offset the negative PDA associations.

The list grew quickly: camping, riding a bicycle, having a martini on Friday night, taking a bubble bath, fly-fishing, cooking, having a martini on Thursday night, and on and on. Later someone added "picking straw-berries" to the list. Someone else plucked out the word "strawberry." But one of Lexicon's linguists said, "No. 'Strawberry' sounds slow." (Think of the similar vowels in "drawl," "dawdle," and "stall.")

Soon it was crossed out and replaced with the word "blackberry" un-derneath. *Someone else noticed that the keys on the PDA look like the seeds on a blackberry.* Epiphany!

Actually, no. The RIM clients were not positive at first because of the frame they'd started with. They'd been leaning toward more descriptive names such as "EasyMail." Placek said, "Most clients feel that they're going to know the perfect name as soon as they see it, but it doesn't hap-pen that way."

Eventually, the case for the name "BlackBerry" prevailed, and the rest is history.

The client's initial reluctance is instructive, though. Sometimes we'll know the right option when we see it, and sometimes we won't. But in this chapter we'll see that the simple act of surfacing another option—even if we ultimately decide against it—helps us to make better choices.

We've already encountered the dangers of narrow framing and the value of expanding our options, but we're about to see something new: the unexpected power of considering our options *simultaneously*.

A STUDY OF GRAPHIC designers demonstrates the value of multi-tracking. The designers, tasked with making a banner ad for a Web maga-zine, were randomly assigned to use one of two creative processes. Half of them were instructed to design one ad at a time, receiving feedback after each new design. Each designer started with a single ad and revised it five times based on rounds of feedback, yielding a total of six ads. The other half of the designers were instructed to use a "simultaneous" process, so that each one started with three ads and received feedback on all three. Then, in successive rounds, the set was whittled down with further feed-back to two ads and then one final ad.

All of the designers ultimately created the same number of ads (six) and received the same quantity of feedback (five ad critiques). The only difference was the process: simultaneous versus one at a time.

As it turned out, process mattered a great deal: The simultaneous designers' ads were judged superior by the magazine's editors and by independent ad execs, and they earned higher click-through rates on a real-world test of the banners on the Web site. Why?

The study's authors, trying to explain the better performance of the simultaneous designers, said, "Since [simultaneous] participants received feedback on multiple ideas simultaneously, they were more likely to read and analyze critique statements side-by-side. Direct comparison perhaps helped them better understand key design principles and led to more principled choices for subsequent prototypes."

In other words, the simultaneous designers, by multitracking, were learning something useful about the shape of the problem. They were able to triangulate among the features of their three initial ads—combining their good elements and omitting the bad.

You may recall this is the same logic used by Steve Cole—the "think AND not OR" guy from the first chapter—in explaining why it's helpful to hire multiple vendors for the same project. He said, "You get convergence on some issues, so you know they are right, and you also learn to appreciate what makes people different and special. None of this can you do if you're just talking to one person."

Multitracking has another advantage too, one that is more unexpected. It *feels* better. After the banner-ad study concluded, both sets of designers were interviewed. Asked to rate the usefulness of the feedback they received during the design process, over 80% of the simultaneous designers said the feedback was helpful. Only 35% of the one-at-a-time designers agreed, and in fact, over half of them believed the feedback they'd received was critical of them. (None of the simultaneous designers felt criticized.) The simultaneous designers also reported that, as a result of the experience, they felt more confident in their design abilities. The one-at-a-time designers didn't agree.

Why was the experiment so frustrating for the one-at-a-time designers? The study's authors speculated that people who work on a single track begin to take their work too personally, viewing criticism as a "rebuke of their only option." Or as one of the authors, Scott Klemmer, said, "If I have only one design, then my ego is perfectly conflated with my design. But if I have multiple designs, I can separate the two."

This is a critical point: Multitracking keeps egos in check. If your boss has three pet projects in play, chances are she'll be open to unvarnished feedback about them, but if there's only one pet project, it will be harder for her to hear the truth. Her ego will be perfectly conflated with the project.

So, given the clear benefits of multitracking, what explains the failure of most organizations to embrace it? Many executives are worried that exploring multiple options will take too long. It's a reasonable fear, but the researcher Kathleen Eisenhardt has found that the opposite is true. In a study of top leadership teams in Silicon Valley, an environment that tends to place a premium on speed, she found that executives who weigh more options actually make faster decisions.

It's a counterintuitive finding, but Eisenhardt offers three explanations. First, comparing alternatives helps executives to understand the "landscape": what's possible and what's not, what variables are involved. That understanding provides the confidence needed to make a quick decision.

Second, considering multiple alternatives seems to undercut politics. With more options, people get less invested in any one of them, freeing them up to change positions as they learn. As with the banner-ad study, multitracking seems to help keep egos under control.

Third, when leaders weigh multiple options, they've given themselves a built-in fallback plan. As an example, one company studied by Eisenhardt was pursuing negotiations with several partners simultaneously. When the negotiations with the first-choice partner failed, the president simply cut a deal with the second-choice partner. If, instead, the firm had pursued only one option initially, those negotiations might well have dragged on as the president fought to salvage the deal. (And he would have been tempted to concede too much to make it work.)

WITH SOME DECISIONS, FINDING more options is easy—you can just expand your search. You can interview three job candidates rather than one, or if you're shopping for a house, you can visit ten rather than five. After all, you can't move into the dream home you never saw.

There's no "right number" of houses to see or job candidates to interview. One rule of thumb is to keep searching for options until you fall in love at least twice. If you've only identified one good candidate for a job, for instance, you'll have the strong urge to talk yourself into hiring her, which is a recipe for the confirmation bias. You'll start to make excuses for the flaws you see: *She asked us not to call her old boss for a reference, but that's probably okay, because the boss sounded like a real jerk . . .*

The same search-expanding logic also applies to choosing a car or a college or a job, though there are certainly commonsense limits—i.e., you probably don't need to fall in love with two hair dryers before picking one, and God help you if you apply this advice to marriage.

So far in this chapter, we've emphasized the benefits of multitracking your options. We've implied that more is better. However, if you've ever walked into an ice cream store and found yourself stymied by the array of choices, you know there may be a limit to the amount of "more" we can take. This leads us to an important concern about multitracking. Psychologists such as Barry Schwartz have written about the dangers of "choice overload," our tendency to freeze in the face of too many options. Is multitracking likely to plunge people into choice overload?

There is research suggesting that extreme multitracking is detrimental. A classic study by Columbia's Sheena Iyengar and Mark Lepper monitored the behavior of consumers in a grocery store. One day, the store set up a sampling table with 6 different kinds of jam, and customers loved it; another day, the store set up a table with 24 different kinds of jam, and it was even more popular than the first. The surprise came at the cash register: Customers who'd chosen among 6 jams were 10 times more likely to actually buy a jar of jam than customers who'd chosen among 24! It was fun to sample 24 flavors, it seems, but painful to pick among them. The choice was paralyzing.

Most decisions, though, don't involve choice sets that force us to choose among 24 options. Remember what we saw in the last chapter: When most people and organizations make decisions, they are more likely to be choosing among, er, one kind of jam. (I'm deciding *whether or not* to buy this strawberry jam.)

We want to suggest that adding even one jar of jam to the table— that is, adding one more alternative to your decision—will substantially improve your decisions, and it stops well short of triggering decision paralysis. (Note for motivated readers: The endnotes contain a wonkish discussion that has more detail about why we don't think multitracking is likely to produce decision paralysis.)

For evidence that adding another alternative can lead to superior decisions, consider a study of every major decision made at a medium-sized private German technology firm. The researchers, professors at the University of Kiel in Germany, had discovered that the firm kept extremely detailed notes of its meetings, including deliberations on decisions. (The notes were sent to the firm's major investor to keep him abreast of what was happening.)

Over one particular 18-month period, the archives revealed that the executive board had debated and resolved 83 major decisions. Decisions never involved more than three alternatives, and 95% were either a "whether or not" decision (40%) or a two-alternative choice (55%). (Thus these decision makers were noticeably savvier about escaping narrow framing than the typical firm in Nutt's study on page 37.)

The university researchers discovered the archive many years after the decisions had been made, so it was possible, with the help of the executive board, to assess the quality of the decisions in light of their subsequent success or failure. In an intense rating procedure that involved hours of discussion and debate, the board categorized each of its 83 decisions as having proved to be very good, satisfactory, or poor.

When the researchers analyzed the data, the evidence was striking: When the executive board considered more than one alternative, they made six times as many "very good" decisions. (Specifically, 40% of the multi-option decisions were rated "very good," compared with only 6% of the "whether or not" decisions.) That is not a small effect.

That's why we believe decision paralysis is not a big factor in most circumstances—you don't need a plethora of choices to improve your decisions. You just need one extra choice, or two. Forget 24 different kinds of jam; we'll happily settle for two or three.

2.

Not all choices are created equal. If the simultaneous designers in the banner-ad study had created ads that differed only in the size of the font—*Do you like the 11-point or the 12-point version better?*—that's not really multitracking. It's more like multitweaking. To get the benefits of multitracking, we need to produce options that are meaningfully distinct.

We must be careful, too, to avoid sham options, which exist only to make the "real" option look better. More than a few real estate agents, for instance, have admitted to taking their clients to lousy properties first to make the subsequent visits more appealing.

This sham-option technique is used frequently in politics, where bosses demand choices but aren't always careful to assess the quality of the options. For insight on this subject, we turn to a formidable practitioner of the art of manipulation, former secretary of state Henry Kissinger.

In his memoir *White House Years*, he discusses a classic bureaucratic trick that was played on President Richard Nixon, who was considering what policy to adopt on a particular issue in Europe. The State Department presented a memo to Nixon with three "options." Kissinger noted that two options were obvious losers, leaving only one plausible choice:

> Here was the standard bureaucratic device of leaving the decision-maker with only one real option, which for easy identification is placed in the middle. The classic case, I joked, would be to confront the policymaker with the choices of nuclear war, present policy, or surrender.

Nixon may have thought he had options, but they were illusory. He was stuck in a narrow frame the whole time.

If the president can fall for it, so can you. Managers need to push for *legitimate* alternatives, not sham options. To diagnose whether your colleagues have created real or sham options, poll them for their preferences. If there's disagreement, that's a great sign that you have real options. An easy consensus may be a red flag.

Granted, it can sometimes be difficult to produce distinct options. The spotlight effect is partly to blame. If we're thinking about installing wood floors in our house, for example, it will be natural to consider different types of wood flooring. If we're really thinking out of the box, we might consider doing another home-improvement project instead. But truly distinct options—*Use more rugs? Stain the existing floor and go to Hawaii on the savings? Forget the floors and buy a car?*—are less likely to emerge, because they require greater swings of the spotlight.

Generating distinct options is even more difficult when our minds settle into certain well-worn grooves. Two of those grooves are common states of mind, studied widely by researchers, that play a role in almost every decision we make. One is triggered when we think about avoiding bad things, and one is triggered when we think about pursuing good things. When we're in one state, we tend to ignore the other.

To illustrate one of these states of mind, imagine a morning that goes as follows. Your teenage son talks to you about his duties as the president of a service-minded student club. You're proud of him, but you also hope he understands the commitments he's made. In your driveway, you bump into your next-door neighbor, who mentions that a home down the street recently sold, after six months, for far less than its asking price. On the way to work, you listen to a radio program about the potential dangers of a newly emerging technology.

Then, an hour after you arrive at the office, your boss pulls you aside and tells you about a new position that has opened up. It involves leading a small team in creating and launching a new product. It's a pretty risky product concept, but your boss thinks there's solid potential. He wonders if you'd be interested—it would involve a lateral move, with fewer direct reports than you currently have but potentially more glory if everything goes well.

What's your gut reaction to the offer? You might feel a little cautious. It doesn't really sound like a promotion, and you have a responsibility to get your team through its current project. And what happens if the new product is a flop? Will you have sabotaged your career prospects? You will definitely want to consider the position carefully. Better safe than sorry.

Now imagine a different morning. Your son tells you about his aspirations for a club he joined at school; you feel parental pride that he's pursuing big goals. Your neighbor tells you about how much he loves his herb garden, which gets you thinking about some landscaping ideas for your own backyard. On the way to work, you listen to a radio program about the opportunities opened up by a newly emerging technology. An hour after you arrive at work—the same as before—your boss tells you about a new position . . .

Now what's your gut reaction to the position? This time, you might feel a bit more open and enthusiastic. You're being trusted to lead a new product with great potential! Nothing ventured, nothing gained.

How you react to the position, in short, depends a great deal on your mindset at the time it's offered. Psychologists have identified two contrasting mindsets that affect our motivation and our receptiveness to new opportunities: a "prevention focus," which orients us toward avoiding negative outcomes, and a "promotion focus," which orients us toward pursuing positive outcomes.

In the first scenario above, you arrive at work with a prevention focus, which means that you are in a vigilant mood. You want to ensure that your son lives up to his duties. You're worried about your home losing its value. You really hope policy makers will stave off the dangers of the new technology. So when you think about the new position, your spotlight tends to highlight what could go wrong, what you could lose. Whereas in the second scenario you have a promotion focus, meaning that you are eager rather than vigilant—you're open to new ideas and new experiences.

Both are useful, and we shift between them as we consider different decisions in our lives. They don't coexist easily, though. It's hard to embrace both at once.

Yet the wisest decisions may combine the caution of the prevention mindset with the enthusiasm of the promotion mindset. Consider a study of the way 4,700 public companies navigated three global recessions (1980 to 1982, 1990 to 1991, and 2000 to 2002). Three Harvard researchers—Ranjay Gulati, Nitin Nohria, and Franz Wohlgezogen—pored over the companies' financial statements, analyzing the way they'd responded to the tough market conditions. The top-level findings were sobering: 17% of the companies didn't survive the relevant recession, and another 40% of them, three years after the recession ended, hadn't returned to their prerecession levels of sales and profits.

The researchers sorted the companies into categories based on how they reacted to the recession, and two of the categories were inspired by the promotion and prevention mindsets. Prevention-focused companies made primarily defensive moves—they tightened their belts and tried to reduce risks. Promotion-focused companies went on the offensive, continuing to make strategic bets and investments.

Both categories of companies tended to suffer because of their disproportionate focus on one set of tools. The researchers report that prevention-focused companies, with their focus on cost cutting, tended to adopt a "siege mentality." Inside these companies, they write, "pessimism permeates the organization. Centralization, strict controls, and the constant threat of more cuts build a feeling of disempowerment. The focus becomes survival—both personal and organizational."

The promotion-focused companies, on the other hand, tended to be naive and slow to react. The researchers said these companies developed "a culture of optimism that leads them to deny the gravity of a crisis for a long time."

The most successful companies acted more like multitrackers, combining the best elements of promotion and prevention. During the 2000 recession, for instance, Staples closed some underperforming stores and contained its operating costs, but it also hired 10% more workers, using them to roll out some new high-end services. Meanwhile, Staples' archrival, Office Depot, took a prevention-focused approach, cutting 6% of its workforce and failing to make comparable investments in new businesses. The difference in approach showed up on the companies' bottom lines: In the three years after the recession, Staples was about 30% more profitable than Office Depot.

The best multitrackers, such as Staples, cut costs by becoming more efficient rather than by laying off employees, and they kept investing in R&D and new business opportunities. They were cautious and eager at once, and their ambidextrousness boosted their chance of thriving. The researchers measured success by looking for companies that rebounded strongly after the recession, beating their rivals by 10% or more on *both* sales growth *and* profit growth. Multitrackers were 42% more likely to be strong rebounders than companies that were solely promotion focused, and they were 76% more likely to be strong rebounders than companies that were solely prevention focused. Thinking "AND not OR" turns out to be good corporate strategy.

BLENDING THE TWO MINDSETS, in short, is a recipe for a wiser decision. That's why we've got to be alert for any situation where one mindset prevails. In a budget-cutting environment, the prevention mindset will dominate: *How can we do the minimum amount of harm given that we have to make these cuts? How can we protect ourselves from calamity?* As a decision adviser in this situation, you can help your colleagues by nudging them toward the promotion focus: "We all know we need to cut 5%. But what if, instead, we could cut 8%, so that we could free up some money to invest in our most exciting opportunities? What's our best chance to make a great leap forward?"

In contrast, consider an aspiring screenwriter who has just moved to LA, imagining infinite opportunity—exciting new stories, fascinating new friends, lucrative new deals, and great industry parties. A compassionate friend might invoke the prevention mindset: *What can you do to make sure you don't get pinched economically while you're waiting for some of these wonderful opportunities to pan out?*

This blending of mindsets is as vital for our personal decisions as it is for organizational decisions, but we don't always manage to do it on our own. Consider the case of Doreen and Frank, as recounted in a book by University of Michigan psychologist Susan Nolen-Hoeksema. Doreen, a caseworker for the Los Angeles County welfare department, was deeply committed to her work. But it wasn't easy for her emotionally. She felt angry about her apathetic clients who didn't seem motivated to help themselves, and it broke her heart when needy clients were kicked off the welfare rolls.

The emotional roller coaster left Doreen increasingly stressed out, and the stress was interfering with her family relationships. Nolen-Hoeksema wrote, "On several evenings, Doreen has either exploded at one of her kids for something minor, like not turning off the television when she called him for dinner, or has secluded herself in the den all evening, trying not to blow up at the million things she found annoying around the house."

At the end of her rope, Doreen visited a mentor at her church, who encouraged her to be proactive about managing her stress. Later she wrote out a list of possible solutions:

1.   Quit my job.
2.   Go to half-time.
3.   Get my kids to be less irritating.
4.   Ask Frank to control the kids more.
5.   Find a less stressful job.
6.   Find some way to release the stress before I get home.

Notice that Doreen did a great job of generating multiple options. It will always be tempting, in situations like hers, to slip into a narrow frame, reducing the situation to a single choice, such as whether or not to quit (or whether or not to put muzzles on your children).

Unfortunately, though, many of her options were infeasible. Because her family needed the income she earned, the first two choices were out. Nor were options 3 and 4 possible: Her children were unlikely to transform suddenly into mute, compliant beings, and shifting more of the parental burden onto Frank (who was already pulling his weight) did not feel right. The fundamental problem, she realized, was not with her kids or her husband but with her overheated response to life's normal irritations.

That led her to focus on option 5, finding a less stressful job. Finding a job that was less emotionally taxing would provide instant stress relief. However, it also felt like a betrayal of one of her core religious beliefs, the imperative to serve the less fortunate.

Feeling stuck, she talked with her husband, Frank, about the last option—releasing stress before coming home. He threw out a few ideas: Why not listen to soothing music on the way home? (Doreen typically tuned in to a news show; hearing about the world's various problems and corruptions tended to further inflame her mood.) Frank also suggested that she leave work early and work out at the YMCA before heading home.

These are simple ideas, and many of us might have come up with similar ones. What we want to highlight is the everyday wisdom in Doreen's instinct to talk over her options with Frank (and her church mentor), as well as in Frank's subtle shift in focus. While Doreen was dwelling on ways to prevent or minimize stress (quitting her job, cutting back parental responsibilities), Frank pushed her to think about ways she could *increase her happiness* (by working out or listening to good music). He added the promotion mindset to her prevention mindset.

Encouraging our loved ones and colleagues to blend the two mindsets can help them escape from an emotional cul-de-sac.

WHEN LIFE OFFERS US a "this or that" choice, we should have the gall to ask whether the right answer might be "both."

In the last chapter, we saw the value of evading a narrow frame by seeking out more options. This chapter added a new wrinkle: It's worth cultivating multiple options at the same time. As we saw at the German technology firm, decisions with a couple of alternatives turned out dramatically better than decisions with one.

In our experience, some managers will try to excuse single-tracking by arguing, "Even though we're only considering one option right now, it's not really a 'whether or not' decision, because we've considered many other options over the last few years." Unfortunately, as we saw with the banner-ad study, exploring ideas sequentially—even though it yields multiple options over time—is not as powerful as exploring them simultaneously. Multitracking improves our understanding of the situations we're facing. It lets us cobble together the best features of our options. It helps us keep our egos in check.

Developing multiple alternatives will sometimes be difficult because our minds don't always think, "This *and* that." Often, for example, we'll get stuck in a mindset of prevention OR promotion. If we can do both, seeking out options that minimize harm AND maximize opportunity, we are more likely to uncover our full spectrum of choices.

There's an issue we have dodged so far, though. In this chapter, options have been plentiful. Lexicon considered dozens of names, the banner-ad designers created six ads, and Doreen produced six possible solutions (not counting suggestions from Frank). But what if you're in a situation where it's not so easy to generate new options? What if you're stuck at a seeming dead end?

That's the issue we'll explore next: Where can you go looking for new alternatives?

CHAPTER THREE IN ONE PAGE
Multitrack

1. Multitracking = considering more than one option simultaneously.

   - *The naming firm Lexicon widens its options by assigning a task to multiple small teams, including an "excursion team" that considers a related task from a very different domain.*

2. When you consider multiple options simultaneously, you learn the "shape" of the problem.

   - *When designers created ads simultaneously, they scored higher on creativity and effectiveness.*

3. Multitracking also keeps egos in check—and can actually be faster!

   - *When you develop only one option, your ego is tied up in it.*
   - *Eisenhardt's research on Silicon Valley firms: Multitracking minimized politics and provided a built-in fallback plan.*

4. While decision paralysis may be a concern for people who consider many options, we're pushing for only one or two extra. And the payoff can be huge.

   - *We're not advocating 24 kinds of jam. When the German firm considered two or more alternatives, it made* six times *as many "very good" decisions.*

5. Beware "sham options."

   - *Kissinger: "Nuclear war, present policy, or surrender."*
   - *One diagnostic: If people on your team disagree about the options, you have real options.*

6. Toggle between the prevention and promotion mindsets.

   - *Prevention focus = avoiding negative outcomes. Promotion focus = pursuing positive outcomes.*
   - *Companies who used both mindsets performed much better after a recession.*
   - *Doreen's husband, Frank, prompted her to think about boosting happiness, not just limiting stress.*

7. Push for "this AND that" rather than "this OR that."

4

Find Someone Who's Solved Your Problem

1.

The massive scale of Walmart—its $444 billion revenue in 2012 amounts to $64 for every person on earth—inspires a complicated mixture of emotions: awe, fear, admiration, and loathing. It's easy to forget, though, that Walmart began as a pipsqueak, a small business in Bentonville, Arkansas. Though the founder of Walmart, Sam Walton, became a global Goliath, he started as a small businessman.

In 1954, years before Walmart, Walton was running a variety store in Bentonville. Walton constantly scoured other stores for good ideas. So when he got wind that some Ben Franklin variety stores in Minnesota had created a new approach to the checkout line, he resolved to see it firsthand. He hopped on a bus and made the 600-mile journey to Pipestone, Minnesota.

When he finally arrived—imagine taking a 12-hour bus ride to do a bit of industry benchmarking—he was impressed by what he discovered. In the stores, all customers were funneled through a central checkout line at the front of the store. This was a departure from the industry norm of departmental checkout. In most stores, including Walton's own, customers shopping for kitchen supplies would pay at the kitchen counter, and if they also needed soap, they'd pay separately at the toiletries counter.

The centralized model had several key advantages, Walton realized. It required fewer checkout clerks, which reduced payroll. It reduced the handling of cash, which minimized errors and theft. It ensured that customers would only have to pay one time.

Convinced Franklin's process was superior, Walton quickly implemented the idea in his stores, and Walmart continues to use the same model today, as do most other big-box retailers.

Throughout Walton's career, he kept his eyes out for good ideas. He once said that "most everything I've done I've copied from someone else." In the early days of discount store chains, he crisscrossed the country in search of insights, visiting discounters ranging from Spartan and Mammoth Mart in the Northeast to FedMart in California. Through conversations with one of FedMart's leaders, Walton clarified his thinking on distribution, which would eventually become a defining strength of Walmart. And he admired the merchandise mix and displays in Kmart, founded in Garden City, Michigan, by S. S. Kresge. "I'll bet I've been in more Kmarts than anybody," Walton said.

Again and again in his career, Walton found clever solutions by asking himself, "Who else is struggling with a similar problem, and what can I learn from them?"

TO BREAK OUT OF a narrow frame, we need options, and one of the most basic ways to generate new options is to *find someone else who's solved your problem.* If you're not sure how to cope with a relative who has an alcohol problem, talk to someone else who has endured a similar situation (that's why groups like Al-Anon exist). If you're unfamiliar with the grant-application process for a particular foundation, talk to someone who has previously navigated the process.

Sam Walton made a habit of sniffing around his competitors' stores, looking for ideas that were better than his. Today, his style of eager competitive analysis has become conventional wisdom for most executives. They've long since learned to "benchmark" competitors and absorb industry "best practices." While these habits are useful, they are rarely transformative. Good ideas are often adopted quickly. When all retailers adopt centralized checkout as a "best practice," it's no longer a competitive advantage for anyone.

In other cases, practices that work for one organization may be incompatible with another, like an organ transplant that is rejected. (Imagine if McDonald's, inspired by movie theaters, started trying to hawk $12 Cokes.) That's why we shouldn't forget, when hunting for new options, to look inside our own organizations. Sometimes the people who have solved our problems are our own colleagues. That's what was discovered by the leaders of Kaiser Permanente, an HMO with almost 9 million members, making it one of the largest in the country.

In early 2008, Alan Whippy (her first name is pronounced uh-LANN), the medical director of quality and safety at the Permanente Medical Group in northern California, was staring at a set of data that astonished her. To continue pushing their hospitals to get better, Whippy and her team had asked the leaders of the 21 Kaiser Permanente hospitals in Northern California to do detailed case studies of the last 50 patients who had died at each of their hospitals. One problem their hospitals had addressed aggressively—heart attacks—accounted for 3.5% of the deaths. But almost 10 times as many deaths came from another cause that was barely on the radar screen at Kaiser Permanente or most of the other hospitals they knew: sepsis.

Dr. Whippy explained sepsis with an analogy: "If you have an infection on your skin, it gets inflamed—red and hot and swollen. The infection itself doesn't turn the skin red, that's the body reacting to the infection." Sepsis is a similar reaction to an infection in the bloodstream. The body's inflammatory reaction spreads to the whole body, even to parts far away from the infection—a case of pneumonia, for instance, can trigger kidney failure or even brain damage.

What Dr. Whippy and her team realized was that physicians were paying careful attention to the infections, like pneumonia, but they weren't aggressively treating the associated sepsis, which was often the true cause of a patient's death.

Freeze there. Whippy had a problem on her hands: She needed options for improving Kaiser Permanente's treatment of sepsis. Where could she find those options?

She located one critical connection within Kaiser: Dr. Diane Craig, a physician at Kaiser Permanente Santa Clara. Craig and her colleagues had spent several years working on sepsis and had already shown some reduction in their hospital's sepsis death rate. They were frustrated that progress was not quicker, though—especially since the "recipe" for managing sepsis was known. In 2002, a provocative article had appeared in the *New England Journal of Medicine* showing that patients were substantially less likely to die from sepsis if they received quick and intensive treatment shortly after they were diagnosed.

It was easier said than done, however. As Craig knew from personal experience, the quick and intensive treatment was difficult to implement for two reasons. First, sepsis is hard to detect. A patient might look fine in the morning but plunge into crisis by lunchtime, and by then it is often more difficult to correct the cascade of internal damage. Second, the protocol recommended by the article for treating sepsis—which involves administering large quantities of antibiotics and fluids to the patient—carries its own risks.

As Craig said, "It takes a while for people to get comfortable saying, 'This patient looks good but I'm going to put a large central IV catheter in their neck and put them in the ICU and pump them full of liters and liters of fluids. And we'll do all this even though they look perfectly fine at the moment.'" The research supports this early intervention. The risks are worth it. But it was difficult for doctors, with their "Do no harm" ethos, to move as quickly and forcefully as the research said they should.

Craig and Whippy realized that, to fight sepsis, they had to overcome these two problems by making sepsis easier to detect and by demonstrating to staff the risk of *inaction*.

With Whippy's support, Craig and her team began to incubate new approaches to the problem at Santa Clara. One idea was simple but powerful: Whenever physicians ordered a blood culture—a sign they were worried about a blood-borne infection—a test for lactic acid was automatically added to their orders. (Lactic acid is a critical indicator of sepsis.) This allowed them to detect sepsis well before it began to influence the patient's vital signs.

Other changes were intended to make the Santa Clara staff more aware of sepsis. Posters and pocket cards were printed up that highlighted the symptoms of sepsis. A grid on the printed materials showed the mortality risk for different patient circumstances. "People could see that this patient, right in front of me, even though they look good—they have a 20% chance of mortality. It was very powerful," said Craig.

If the doctors and nurses spotted the symptoms of sepsis, they were asked to call a "sepsis alert," equivalent in urgency to the "code blue" called when someone is experiencing a cardiac arrest. The sepsis alert summoned a team that could assess the patient and, if appropriate, begin the intensive sepsis protocol.

These innovative solutions began to work. Sepsis deaths began to decline. Whippy, who'd been following the work, knew that the Santa Clara team was assembling a package of cultural interventions that she could spread to other hospitals. Meanwhile, other hospitals, which had been pursuing their own solutions, added other critical pieces of the puzzle, like a "pressure bag" that fit around an IV like a balloon, ensuring that sepsis patients would receive fluids quickly enough.

Within a matter of months, under Whippy's direction, the sepsis protocol was being actively implemented in other hospitals. By summer 2012, Kaiser Permanente Northern California, composed of 21 hospitals serving 3.3 million people, had driven down risk-adjusted mortality from sepsis to 28% below the national average.

This solution has astonishing potential. If all hospitals could match Kaiser Permanente's 28% reduction, it would be the annual equivalent, in lives saved, of saving every single man who dies from prostate cancer and every single woman who dies from breast cancer.

THE LEADERS OF KAISER make it a priority to study their own internal "bright spots"—the most positive points in a distribution of data.* For the treatment of sepsis, for instance, Dr. Craig's team represented a bright spot, because of its lower death rate.

Bright spots can be much more mundane, though. If you're trying to stick to a new exercise regimen, then your bright spots might be the four times last month that you made it to the gym. If you take the time to study and understand your bright spots—how exactly did you manage to get yourself to the gym on those four days?—then you can often discover unexpected solutions. Maybe you'd notice that three of the four occasions were during lunch, which tends to be the least complicated time for you. So you might make a point to avoid scheduling things at lunchtime, keeping that time free for future workouts.

The wonderful thing about bright spots is that they *can't* suffer from the rejected-transplant problem, because they're native to your situation. It's your own success you're seeking to reproduce.

Both bright spots and best practices, then, act as sources of inspiration. If you've got a dilemma and you need new options, you can look for new ideas externally, like Sam Walton, or internally, like Kaiser's leaders. Notice that in both situations the process is reactive: Your dilemma sparks the search. But there's a lot to be gained by taking the results of

---

*"Bright spots" is a term that we defined in *Switch*, which discusses how to spark change. It was a more central concept in that book—if you'd like to learn more, check out a free excerpt about bright spots at http://www.fastcompany.com/1514493/switch -dont-solve-problems-copy-success.

your search and recording them for future use—to turn a reactive search into a proactive set of guidelines.

To see what we mean, imagine a manager who has a talented and ambitious employee, one who's eager to advance and earn more responsibility. Unfortunately, there's no obvious way the manager can honor the employee's ambition—no clear promotion path, no easy way to boost compensation. How do you avoid dampening the person's enthusiasm or, worse, losing them altogether?

The search for options might lead the manager to search first for best practices. In a world with thousands of other organizations, someone has surely faced this problem before. Next, she might look for bright spots within her own organization, interviewing a couple of longtime managers to fish for their insights.

What if she took things a step further and actually encoded what she learned so that the next manager in a similar situation—whether a month or a year down the line—could consult her ready-made list of suggestions? Her list might include thoughts like these: *Is there a way you can delegate some of your own higher-level work to the employee? Can you carve out a project that they can lead? Try to find ways to ensure that the employee is recognized publicly for their work.*

By encoding the advice, she'd be creating a kind of "playlist" of managerial greatest hits: questions to ask, principles to consult, ideas to consider.

This playlist idea turns a reactive search—*Who has solved my problem?*—into a proactive step: *We've already found the people who have solved this problem, and here's what they said.*

Dion Hughes and Mark Johnson have used this playlist technique, to considerable success, in the advertising industry. They founded a firm, Persuasion Arts & Sciences, that acts as a relief pitcher for advertising agencies that have hit a creative roadblock. Hughes and Johnson often come in at the last minute to offer fresh ideas just before an important pitch.

Both men had worked previously in top-tier ad agencies. Johnson had been part of the team that developed the "ultimate driving machine" positioning for BMW, and Hughes had won awards for the "how to speak Australian" campaign for Foster's beer. (Sample billboard: A picture of a dagger is captioned, "Australian for dental floss." Next to it, a bottle of Foster's is captioned, "Australian for beer.")

Dion Hughes said, "We knew that creative people tend to be precious about their ideas and find the ones that they're passionate about and then invest a lot of emotion into them. And they spend most of their time diving deep into one or two ideas and not a lot of time spreading their wings. So we thought, well, why don't we do the opposite?" So when Hughes and Johnson are called in by creative directors, they try to send them a dozen possible directions within a week. (Notice the multitracking.)

To generate that volume of ideas, they come back to the same playlist of questions again and again. For example, they might ask, *What kind of iconography within the brand is useful and what could we build around it?* For a UPS project it might be the shield logo or the classic brown UPS driver uniform or the familiar, boxy shape of the delivery truck. Other questions in the playlist include:

- Is there a key color for the brand?
- What is the enemy of this product?
- What would the brand be like if it was the market share leader?
- What if it was an upstart?
- Can you personify the product?

In 2008, Persuasion Arts & Sciences was approached by a small mom-and-pop brand, Diana's Bananas, which sold only one product: frozen chocolate-covered bananas. Diana's had been founded by a Chicago woman who had subsequently passed away, leaving her husband with, as Hughes said, "a tiny little company and a tiny little factory with one shift of workers."

Hughes and Johnson, moved by the story, agreed to do a small project for Diana's. The owner had $80,000 to spend, and they had to gently tell him that his budget wouldn't support a major TV ad campaign. In brainstorming campaign ideas, the duo knew they needed to overcome two problems: First, few shoppers came to the grocery store with "frozen bananas" on their grocery lists, and, worse, impulse buys were unlikely, since Diana's lacked the budget to pay for good placement in the freezers. The packages tended to be stranded on one of the bottom shelves.

These problems got them thinking: *These bananas are mostly for kids, and we could count on them to beg their parents to buy them, but the kids don't know the product exists. So we've got to lead them to the right place. But how?*

As they worked through the playlist, they paused on one question: *What kind of iconography within the brand is useful and what could we build around it?* One character on the packaging was a baby monkey in diapers. They started thinking about the monkey and the bananas, and they thought, *Hmm, what if the monkey were eating bananas and leaving the peels behind, like a bread-crumb trail?*

Excited by the idea, they designed a series of decals—bright yellow banana peels—that could be stuck to the floor of the grocery store, creating a trail that led right to the freezer where Diana's was stocked. Kids immediately caught on to the game, following the trail like a treasure hunt.

After the trails had been installed in a chain of grocery stores, Hughes and Johnson called to see how the campaign was doing. The owner said, "We have had to put on a second and third shift to keep up with demand." The trail of banana peels had worked like a charm.

Hughes and Johnson's biggest success to date was for a client that they aren't allowed to name, a *Fortune* 100 company that had put its ad agency on notice. The agency was told that if it didn't come up with fresher material, the nine-figure account would be moving elsewhere. So the agency, in a panic, summoned a group of around 40 creatives to an airport hotel outside a major industrial city. Hughes and Johnson joined the group, which was sequestered in secrecy, like the jury on a high-profile murder case. Even the locals from the ad agency weren't allowed to go home during the days of the briefing.

"We are looking around the room," said Hughes, "thinking, 'There are a lot of talented people in this room. How can we win?'" Knowing that the other agencies would take a few days to generate one or two carefully curated ideas, Hughes and Johnson went back to their playlist of questions. They thought they could win with speed and quantity.

They resolved to meet with the creative director the very next morning. "We won't have any TV commercials to view or print ads to give out," Hughes said. "We will just say, 'Here are the big fat areas for this brief to go in.' We will put an idea on each of those squares so that we own that square. So that when finally his other creative teams come to him a week later, he'll look at their work and go, 'Sorry, I already got something like that from Dion and Mark.'"

The plan succeeded. In the end, the ad agency presented six "finalist" ideas to the client. Four of the six were created by Hughes and Johnson, as was the eventual winner. The playlist had triumphed.

THERE'S A BRUTE-FORCE ASPECT to the strategy used by Hughes and Johnson. They force themselves to consider prescribed questions, one at a time, to generate new options. A "canned" list of stimuli seems to spark fresh insights. What's particularly surprising is that this brute-force approach can work in advertising, a domain that prizes creativity and novelty. If a playlist can work for advertisers, chances are it can work for you.

Could you create your own playlist to help your colleagues discover options? Think about some of the common types of decisions that have been made historically in your organization. For example, one unpleasant but common type of decision is how to make budget cuts. What if the wisest minds in your organization had come up with a list of ready-made questions and issues that could help direct the budget cutter?

- Is it possible the budget can be cut by delaying planned expenditures rather than by paring existing expenditures?

- Have you exhausted other potential sources of income that might relieve the need for cutting?

- Resist the urge to cut everything by a fixed amount. Think about ways to be more strategic with cuts.

- Could you cut deeper than you need to in order to free up funds to invest in exciting new opportunities?

As with the Hughes and Johnson playlist, this would allow a manager to sort quickly through potential options. Let's say a county government official is struggling with the need to cut her library budget by 10%. Initially, the official might have considered two options: cutting hours by 10% across the board or closing one library branch entirely. The playlist helps her see a broader spectrum:

- *Is it possible the budget can be cut by delaying planned expenditures rather than by paring existing expenditures?* I can delay a few IT hires. That will help a little but not a lot.

- *Have you exhausted other potential sources of income that might relieve the need for cutting?* Not much promise here—we certainly can't raise taxes in this climate. We can try to attract corporate sponsors, but those efforts wouldn't pay off until next year.

- *Resist the urge to cut everything by a fixed amount. Think about ways to be more strategic with cuts.* It might be wise to be strategic about the hours we restrict. For instance, with the library near the college, we could leave the evening hours intact but move the opening time later. In the neighborhood that's full of retirees, we could open at the same time but close earlier.

- *Could you cut deeper than you need to in order to free up funds to invest in exciting new opportunities?* This might make a lot of sense. If we closed our least utilized branch *and* cut back hours, that would free up $2 million that we could invest in our online tools, which would allow everyone in the community to benefit 24-7.

Virtually every organization would benefit from decision aids like this. (What's the downside?) Playlists should be as useful as checklists, yet your organization has many checklists and probably zero playlists. A checklist is useful for situations where you need to replicate the same behaviors every time. It's prescriptive; it stops people from making an error. On the other hand, a playlist is useful for situations where you need a stimulus, a way of producing new ideas. It's generative; it stops people from overlooking an option. (*Don't forget to shine your spotlight over here . . .*)

Playlists also spur us to multitrack. In the last chapter, we discussed the value of shifting between the prevention and promotion mindsets. A playlist can force us to make that shift. Note that in the budget-cutting example above, the last sentence is an explicit prod to shift to the promotion mindset: "Could you . . . free up funds to invest in exciting new opportunities?" That's a useful stimulus, because most decision makers struggling with budget cuts are likely to be trapped in the prevention mindset (concerned with preventing harm).

Of course, playlists are no panacea. You'll never have a playlist for any decision that is novel, for instance, and given the relentless pace of change, those decisions will be all too frequent. So what if you have a choice to make where there's no playlist to review, no best practices to consult, and no bright spots to study?

Simply put, what if you get stuck?

2.

Kevin Dunbar set out to understand how scientists think. How do they solve problems? Where do their breakthroughs come from? His interest in scientific thinking was a neat fusion of his own work in science (five

years as an undergraduate in molecular biology) and thinking (as a professor of psychology).

Dunbar quickly realized that the tools of psychology were poorly
suited to studying the novel problem solving that characterizes real-world
science. In a typical psychology experiment, undergraduate students—
the lab rats of psychology—might be asked to spend 10 minutes working on a problem generic enough to be cracked by a 20-year-old with
no technical expertise. By contrast, science unfolds in months and years
rather than minutes, and scientists possess deep knowledge of their domains. Surely, thought Dunbar, creating quick tests for undergraduates
wasn't the way to study the minds of scientists.

So, like a war reporter embedding himself with an army unit, Dunbar spent a year alongside the scientists in four leading molecular-biology
laboratories, watching and recording their work. The focus of his observations was the research meeting, a gathering common to the four labs,
usually held weekly, in which one of the lab's doctoral or postdoctoral
students would talk about an ongoing project.

What Dunbar discovered, after countless hours of eavesdropping
and interviewing and synthesizing, was that one of the reliable but un-
recognized pillars of scientific thinking is the analogy.

When the scientists ran into problems with their experiments, a
common day-to-day experience, they would often benefit from a "local
analogy": a comparison to a very similar experiment with a similar organism. So if one scientist was bemoaning a failed experiment with the
phage virus, a colleague might share an example of how he tweaked an
experiment to overcome a similar problem. "This type of reasoning occurred in virtually every meeting I observed, and often numerous times
in a meeting," said Dunbar.

Other times, the scientists were struggling with a bigger problem—
not just one experiment that didn't work but perhaps a whole series of
experiments that were producing consistent but unpredicted results. In
those discussions, Dunbar found, the scientists often switched from local
analogies to what he called "regional analogies." These typically involved

another organism that had a family relationship with the organism being studied. A scientist trying to understand how a new virus replicates, for instance, might work through an analogy from a better-known virus such as smallpox.

Dunbar said, "The use of analogies is one of the main mechanisms for driving research forward." And the key to using analogies successfully, he said, was the ability to extract the "crucial features of the current problem." This required the scientist to think of the problem from a more abstract, general perspective, and then "search for other problems that have been solved." (*Find someone who has solved your problem.*)

Interestingly, the scientists were often unaware of the prominent role analogies played in their problem solving. When Dunbar interviewed them a few days after a particular lab meeting, they could recall the conclusion they'd reached but not the chain of analogies that had helped them get there. (Dunbar has since written articles encouraging science educators to teach new scientists how to tap the power of analogies more explicitly.)

One surprise in Dunbar's study was that while three of the labs made consistent use of analogies, the fourth never did. He explains the consequences:

> In the laboratory that did not make analogies, the scientists used a different strategy when they encountered problems in their research; they manipulated experimental variables such as raising the temperature, varying chemical concentrations, and so forth, to make things work. Thus, a problem that could have been solved by making an analogy to another similar experiment (local analogy) or to another organism (regional analogy) was not made, leaving some problems unsolved, either temporarily or over the long term.
>
> Indeed, very similar research problems were encountered in the other laboratories, but they were solved much faster through the use of local and regional analogies.

Notice the slow, brute-force approach that had to be used by the lab that didn't use analogies. When you use analogies—when you find someone who has solved your problem—you can take your pick from the world's buffet of solutions. But when you don't bother to look, you've got to cook up the answer yourself. Every time. That may be possible, but it's not wise, and it certainly ain't speedy.

DUNBAR FOUND THAT GRANULAR problems benefit from local analogies, and conceptual problems lend themselves to regional analogies. In fact, the more you are able to extract the "crucial features" of a problem, the further afield you can go. A separate study of a medical-plastics design group, conducted by Bo T. Christensen and Christian D. Schunn, found that the designers tapped a veritable circus of analogies, including zippers, credit cards, toilet paper, shoes, milk containers, Christmas decorations, waterwheels, picture puzzles, venetian blinds, and lingerie.

What we're seeing here is that, when you're stuck, you can use a process of "laddering up" to get inspiration. The lower rungs on the ladder offer a view of situations very similar to yours; any visible solutions will offer a high probability of success, since the conditions are so similar. As you scale the ladder, you'll see more and more options from other domains, but those options will require leaps of imagination. They'll offer the promise of an unexpected breakthrough—but also a high probability of failure. When you start looking for cross-fertilization between the medical-plastics domain and the world of lingerie, you're likely to find yourself at a lot of dead ends (or perhaps with a very hard and uncomfortable bra).

For an example of laddering up, let's imagine a junior-high principal, Mr. Jones, who wants to speed up the lunch line in the school cafeteria. He figures if students spend less time waiting in line, they'll have more time to go outside and get some activity before afternoon classes begin.

Given this goal, where can Jones look for options? The first answer, we know now, is that he should look locally. Are there bright spots in his own staff? Maybe one checkout line always seems to move faster than the others; Jones could study how that checkout clerk handles the process. (Perhaps, like the collectors at tollbooths, she counts out common configurations of change in advance.) Jones could spread her approach to the remaining cashiers.

If there are no obvious bright spots, he can ladder up a couple of rungs and benchmark the practices of other schools in his city. If he strikes out again, he could keep laddering up. The next step might be to expand his search to *any* organization with a checkout process, from convenience stores to community pools. (These rungs of the ladder are akin to a scientist's use of a "regional analogy"—learning from another organism that is similar to the one being studied.)

As he climbed, he would broaden the definition of the problem. Instead of looking for people who have pioneered creative checkout solutions, he might hunt down people who excel at managing the flow of crowds: managers of sports stadiums, amusement parks, or shopping malls. (Could you learn something from Disney's roller-coaster queues, for instance, that might be useful in a crowded lunchroom?)

Up and up Principal Jones could climb—with another rung he might seek inspiration from people with expertise in managing the flow of a resource through a fixed space, such as plumbers, electricians, and factory owners. You can see how, as you grow more and more abstract, you eventually ascend past the zone of creativity and into the realm of absurdity. (If you ever find yourself seeking inspiration from other galaxies, ladder back down and have a cup of coffee.)

Lexicon, the naming firm discussed in the previous chapter, excels at this process. In naming the processor that became the Pentium, the creative team wanted names that suggested "speed," so they laddered up past the domain of computer technology to consider any fast, high-performance product. One team, in fact, spent time studying the names of slalom race skis. (In the end, another analogy would prevail: the notion that the processor was a powerful "ingredient," an essential element of the computer. Note the "-ium" ending, which is familiar from the inhabitants of the Periodic Table of Elements.)

TO SEE HOW LADDERING up can generate a truly novel option, consider the story of Fiona Fairhurst, a designer hired in 1997 by Speedo. She was given a crystal-clear mission: to design a swimsuit that would make swimmers faster.

Traditionally, swimsuits had evolved to become smoother, tighter, and skimpier, but Speedo had grown interested in new design approaches. Fairhurst, a swimmer herself, was unimpressed with Speedo's early designs, so she began to seek out other sources of inspiration. "This is how my brain works," she told Dick Gordon in a June 2012 interview. "If I'm going to make something that goes fast, I tend to look at everything that goes fast and the mechanisms that make things go fast. So I started looking at man-made objects like boats, torpedoes, space shuttles, everything."

Fairhurst was laddering up. She'd redefined the problem from "a swimsuit that goes fast" to "anything that goes fast, especially in the water." And that got her interested in animals that seemed to move faster in water than they ought to. Shortly thereafter, she had a fateful day at the Natural History Museum in London:

> It was one of those "eureka moments." . . . [The guide from the museum] took me to the back rooms of the Natural History Museum. . . . It's not where the public is allowed. And he had this huge metal tank, and he lifted it open, and inside was a nine-foot shark. And he said to me, "Fiona, you need to touch his nose, touch his belly." . . . I was thinking, "What the heck am I doing?"

As I touched the nose, it was exceedingly rough, almost sharp. It's made of this material like enamel, like our teeth. It's called dermal denticle. . . . If you run your hand from nose to tail, it's smooth, but a bit like any fish scale; if you run your hand backward, it's sharp and it will cut your hand.

They sent a sample of the shark's skin to a lab, which returned images of its rough and microgrooved texture. The images sparked an insight for Fairhurst: "For years many people thought smooth fabric was the key [to speed], but if you look at sharkskin and how rough it is, *roughness* is the actual key to making a fast fabric." (Indeed, one Harvard scientist has conducted experiments showing that the shark's rough denticles reduce drag and increase thrust.) Inspired, Fairhurst and her colleagues sampled over a thousand different fabrics until they found one whose texture convincingly mimicked sharkskin.

Another, perhaps more important, change they made to the new swimsuit was inspired by an analogy to a man-made object, the naval torpedo. Unlike skimpy traditional suits, Fairhurst's swimsuit covered much of the body, like a second skin. It was tight and restricting, which struck some athletes as uncomfortable at first, but Fairhurst said the effects were profound: "By compressing all your lumps and bumps, you can make a more torpedolike shape through the water."

The Speedo team began to test the new suit with Olympic athletes. In one test leading up to the 2000 games in Sydney, Fairhurst worked with Jenny Thompson, an American swimmer who'd already won medals in the 1992 and 1996 games. As Thompson's coach timed her, she swam 50 meters, once with her own suit and once with Fairhurst's new creation.

As Fairhurst recalled, when Thompson emerged from the pool, she said, "I hate this suit; it feels horrible." Meanwhile, her coach, staring at the timer, was incredulous. Thompson's time with the suit had been close to her world-record pace, even though she had started her swim by merely pushing off the wall with her feet rather than by diving in at full speed. He told her, "A world record isn't easy . . . so don't rule out the suit!"

In test after test, the new suit, which came to be called the Fastskin, consistently outperformed its predecessors. Next came a regulatory hurdle: For the suit to be used by swimmers in the Olympics, it had to be approved by the Fédération Internationale de Natation (FINA), the international governing body for the sport of swimming. Fairhurst was surprised when FINA officials objected to the suit on aesthetic grounds. "One of the things that they felt gave them very good TV coverage was the fact that it was beautiful people in swimsuits . . . a bit like the *Baywatch* mentality." FINA's leaders were worried that her suit was hiding too much flesh!

To her relief, FINA overcame these anxieties and approved the suit, and the Fastskin debuted at the 2000 Sydney Olympics. Its impact was immediate and dramatic: An astonishing 83% of swimming medals were won by swimmers who wore it.

The very success of the Fastskin inspired controversy. Critics, including some Olympic swimmers, questioned whether the suits were giving athletes an unfair advantage.

Later evolutions of Fairhurst's original swimsuit—the successors to Fastskin—kept boosting swimmers' performance, until finally FINA balked, banning certain fabrics and styles beginning in 2010.

Fairhurst's laddering had produced a competitive advantage so strong that it had to be banned to keep the playing field level.

IN THIS SECTION, WE'VE been looking for ways to evade a narrow frame, the tendency to unduly restrict our own options. It's not just teenagers and business executives who fall into this trap; it's all of us.

In interviews we conducted for this book, we had conversations with three people who were facing similar dilemmas. Two were wondering whether to quit their jobs, and the third was wondering whether to quit her relationship. All three of them, asked to state their options, saw only a binary choice: *I'm trying to decide whether or not I should leave.* (Here's hoping the "whether or not" phrase made you roll up your decision-adviser sleeves.)

Incredibly, none of these people were considering the obvious third option: to try to change their situation! *Couldn't you talk to your boss about a different set of duties? Couldn't you talk to your partner about ways to improve your relationship?* Two of the three, when pressed about this, had a head-slapping "duh" moment. (The third felt his dilemma was discussion proof.) These were smart people who were trapped in a kind of cognitive bubble.

Yet what makes narrow framing remarkable, among the four villains of decision making, is how easy it is to correct. The lightest prick often bursts the bubble. We've encountered a handful of techniques for doing just that—for Widening Our Options. One of them was the Vanishing Options Test: *What if you couldn't do any of the things you're considering—what else might you try? What if you were forced to invest your time or money in something else—what would be the next-best pick?*

We also saw that multitracking—thinking "AND not OR"—is a powerful way to compare options and that we can create more "balanced" options by toggling between the prevention and promotion mindsets.

Finally, if we get stuck, we should find someone who has already solved our problem. To find them, we can look inside (for bright spots), outside (for competitors and best practices), and into the distance (via laddering up).

When we Widen Our Options, we give ourselves the luxury of a real choice among distinct alternatives. Often the right choice won't be obvious at first glance, though we may have a hint of a preference. So, to inform our decision, we'll need to gather more information. But we've already encountered the villain that tends to thwart these efforts: the confirmation bias, which tempts us to collect only the information that supports our gut-level preference.

Unlike narrow framing, the confirmation bias is not easily disrupted. Even the smartest psychologists, who have studied the bias for years, admit that they can't shake it. It can't be wiped out; it can only be reined in. To see how we can hold our own against this tenacious foe, continue on to the next chapter, and get ready to Reality-Test Your Assumptions.

CHAPTER FOUR IN ONE PAGE
Find Someone Who's Solved Your Problem

1. When you need more options but feel stuck, look for someone who's solved your problem.

2. Look outside: competitive analysis, benchmarking, best practices.
   - *Sam Walton discovered an ingenious checkout solution by scoping out another store.*

3. Look inside. Find your bright spots.
   - *Kaiser's leaders found and scaled a solution for sepsis pioneered by one of Kaiser's own hospitals.*
   - *What can you learn from your own bright spots (e.g., the four days you went to the gym last month)?*

4. Note: To be proactive, encode your greatest hits in a decision "playlist."
   - *A checklist stops people from making an error; a playlist stimulates new ideas.*
   - *Advertisers Hughes and Johnson use a playlist to spark lots of creative ideas quickly.*
   - *A playlist for budget cuts might include a prompt to switch between the prevention and promotion mindsets: Can you cut more here to invest more there?*

5. A third place to look for ideas: in the distance. Ladder up via analogies.
   - *Kevin Dunbar: Analogies are a pillar of scientific problem solving. Scientists make progress through analogies to similar experiments and similar organisms.*
   - *Ladder up: Lower rungs show close analogies (low risk and low novelty), while higher rungs reveal more distant solutions (higher risk and higher novelty).*
   - *Fiona Fairhurst designed a speedier swimsuit by laddering up and analyzing "anything that moves fast," including sharks and torpedoes.*

6. Why generate your own ideas when you can sample the world's buffet of options?

Widen Your Options

Reality-Test Your Assumptions

Attain Distance Before Deciding

Prepare to Be Wrong

5

Consider the Opposite

1.

It is an unwritten law of the stock market that corporations must keep growing, year after year, and for the executives of a company straining to meet these growth expectations, buying another company can look like an awfully attractive shortcut. But it's an expensive shortcut. For public companies, the average premium paid in an acquisition is 41%, which means that if the target company is valued by the stock market at $100 million, the acquirer will bid $141 million for it. Or, to translate that into human terms, the acquiring CEO is basically saying to the target CEO, "I can run your company at least 41% better than you can."

As you might imagine, this self-confidence often proves unwarranted. Warren Buffett said, "In the past, I've observed that many acquisition-hungry managers were apparently mesmerized by their childhood reading of the story about the frog-kissing princess. Remembering her success, they pay dearly for the right to kiss corporate toads, expecting wondrous transfigurations." Unfortunately, said Buffett, "We've observed many kisses but very few miracles."

Two business-school professors, Mathew Hayward and Donald Hambrick, were puzzled by this phenomenon. Why do CEOs keep making pricey acquisitions that rarely pay off? The answer, they suspected, might have more to do with human flaws than with financial miscalculations. They theorized that the acquiring CEOs were being led astray by their own hubris.

Hubris is exaggerated pride or self-confidence that often results in a comeuppance. In Greek mythology, a hubristic protagonist often suffers humiliation. When Icarus ignored advice not to fly too close to the sun, his wax wings melted and he fell to his death. (By contrast, in American business, hubris is less damning. If Icarus had been a bank CEO, he'd have escaped with a $10 million golden parachute.)

Hayward and Hambrick speculated that executives' hubris—their confidence that they could work magic with their acquisitions—would lead them to overpay for their targets. The researchers tested this theory by analyzing every large acquisition ($100 million or more) conducted in the public markets during a two-year period, a sample that contained 106 transactions. What they wanted to see was whether the price paid in the acquisition was influenced by three particular factors, all of which would tend to inflate the ego of the acquiring CEO:

1. Praise by the media

2. Strong recent corporate performance (which the CEO could interpret as evidence of his/her genius)

3. A sense of self-importance (which was measured, cleverly, by looking at the gap between the CEO's compensation package and the next-highest-paid officer—a CEO must think a lot of himself if he's paid quadruple the salary of anyone else)

Hayward and Hambrick were right on all counts. As each of these three factors increased, so did the tendency of a CEO to pay a higher premium for an acquisition.

As one example, they found that for every favorable article written in a major publication about the CEO, the acquisition premium paid went up by 4.8%. That's a $4.8 million boost on a $100 million acquisition! Because of one flattering article! And a second article would inflate it by another $4.8 million.

The authors wrote, "It seems some CEOs who pay extremely large acquisition premiums . . . come to believe their own press." (The lyrics of an old Mac Davis song come to mind: "Oh Lord, it's hard to be humble / when you're perfect in every way. / I can't wait to look in the mirror / 'cause I get better looking each day.")

All of this suggests an important lesson for entrepreneurs: If you're looking to sell your company, definitely call the person on the cover of *Forbes*.

HAYWARD AND HAMBRICK ALSO discovered an antidote to hubris: disagreement.

They found that CEOs paid lower acquisition premiums when they had people around them who were more likely to challenge their thinking, such as an independent chairman of the board or outside board members who were unconnected to the CEO or the company. Unfortunately, these independent viewpoints weren't always present. Remember the former CEO of Quaker who said that there was *no one* inside the firm arguing against the Snapple acquisition?

To make good decisions, CEOs need the courage to seek out disagreement. Alfred Sloan, the longtime CEO and chairman of General Motors, once interrupted a committee meeting with a question: "Gentlemen, I take it we are all in complete agreement on the decision here?" All the committee members nodded. "Then," Sloan said, "I propose we postpone further discussion of this matter until our next meeting to give ourselves time to develop disagreement and perhaps gain some understanding of what this decision is about."

Few of us are stuck in a bubble of power like a CEO, and our hubris levels are mercifully lower, but we do have something in common with them: a bias to favor our own beliefs. Our "bubble" is not the boardroom; it's the brain. The confirmation bias leads us to hunt for information that flatters our existing beliefs.

Imagine that a new restaurant has just opened near you. It serves your favorite kind of food, so you're excited and hopeful. You search the restaurant's reviews online, and the results show a handful of good reviews (four out of five stars) and a handful of poor ones (two stars). Which reviews would you read?

Almost certainly, you'd read more of the positive reviews. You really want this restaurant to be great. A recent meta-analysis of the psychology literature illustrated how dramatic this effect is. In reviewing more than 91 studies of over 8,000 participants, the researchers concluded that we are more than twice as likely to favor confirming information than disconfirming information. (So, scientifically speaking, you'd probably read twice as many four-star reviews as two-star reviews.)

The meta-study found that the confirmation bias was stronger in emotion-laden domains such as religion or politics and also when people had a strong underlying motive to believe one way or the other (as in Upton Sinclair's observation, "It is difficult to get a man to understand something when his salary depends on his not understanding it!"). The confirmation bias also increased when people had previously invested a lot of time or effort in a given issue.

In the previous section, we saw that it's crucial to Widen Our Perspective in order to break out of a narrow frame; by doing that, we expand the number of options open to us. In this section we ask, what's the best way to *assess* those options?

We know that the confirmation bias will skew our assessment. If we feel a whisker's worth of preference for one option over another, we can be trusted to train our spotlight on favorable data. So how can we learn to overcome the confirmation bias and Reality-Test the Assumptions we're making?

The first step is to follow the lead of Alfred Sloan, the former GM CEO, and develop the discipline to consider the opposite of our initial instincts. That discipline begins with a willingness to spark constructive disagreement.

IN MOST LEGAL SYSTEMS, disagreement is baked into the process. Judges and juries will never find themselves in a CEO-style information bubble, since they are forced to consider two opposing points of view.

The justice system isn't alone in using a balanced process. For centuries, the Catholic Church made use of a "devil's advocate" in canonization decisions (i.e., in deciding who would be named a saint). The devil's advocate was known inside the church as the *promotor fidei*—the "promoter of the faith"—and his role was to build a case *against* sainthood.

John Paul II eliminated the office in 1983, ending 400 years of tradition. Since then, tellingly, saints have been canonized at a rate about 20 times faster than in the early part of the twentieth century.

In our individual decisions, how many of us have ever consciously sought out people we knew would disagree with us? Certainly not every decision needs a devil's advocate—"I *strenuously object* to your purchasing those slacks!"—but for high-stakes decisions, we owe ourselves a dose of skepticism. If you have teenagers, they may be a good resource here. Our typical tendency is to flee these skeptical conversations rather than embrace them, but that reflects short-term thinking. We want to avoid the momentary discomfort of being challenged, which is understandable, but surely it's preferable to the pain of walking blindly into a bad decision.

How can we plan for disagreement inside organizations? Some have created devil's advocate–style traditions. The Pentagon used a "murder board," staffed with experienced officers, to try to kill ill-conceived missions. In the era when Disney was churning out hits such as *The Lion King* and *Beauty and the Beast*, its senior leadership team used a *Gong Show* format that allowed many people to pitch ideas for movies or theme-park rides—but the leaders brought the curtain down quickly on bad ideas.

It might be tempting to think about hiring a formal devil's advocate, someone who could inject criticism into a complacent organization. However, it's too easy to imagine the position being marginalized and, beyond that, offering an excuse for others to pull back their own criticism. ("I know the devil's advocate will give this deal a thorough going-over, so I don't need to worry about it.")

The most important lesson to learn about devil's advocacy isn't the need for a formal contrarian position; it's the need to interpret criticism as a noble function. An effective *promotor fidei* is not a token argumentative smarty-pants; it's someone who deeply respects the Catholic Church and is trying to defend the faith by surfacing contrary arguments in situations where skepticism is unlikely to surface naturally. (Who wants to argue *against* someone who's lived a life so admirable that they merit consideration as a saint?)

There are many ways to honor that spirit of values-based opposition. In some organizations, the executive in charge might assign a few people on the executive team to prepare a case against a high-stakes proposal. (What if the Quaker CEO had assigned a team to make a case against the Snapple purchase?) That's a wise idea. It puts the team members in the role of "protecting the organization," and it licenses their skepticism. Another alternative is to seek out existing dissent rather than creating it artificially. If you haven't encountered any opposition to a decision you're considering, chances are you haven't looked hard enough. Could you create a safe forum where critics can air their concerns?

THE DOWNSIDE OF PROVOKING disagreement is that it can curdle into bitter politics. Roger Martin, the dean of the Rotman School of Business and the author of *The Opposable Mind* and other well-regarded business books, said that people often complain to him that their strategy meetings "descend into adversarial position-taking." In his judgment, that's the single biggest barrier to creating effective strategies.

Martin believes that overcoming this problem is easier than you might think. The solution is a practice that he improvised in a difficult moment early in his career.

In the mid-1990s, Martin, a recent business-school graduate, was working for the Monitor Group, a consulting firm. One of Monitor's clients was Toronto-based Inmet Mining, whose executives were debating the fate of Copper Range, a struggling copper mine in the upper peninsula of Michigan. The mine, which in its glory days had been one of the largest copper mines in America, was losing money fast. To discuss the situation, a critical meeting was set in Rhinelander, Wisconsin. The mine managers drove three hours to be there, and the corporate executives flew in from Toronto. They met in a nondescript hotel conference room near the airport.

The meeting was tense. The Inmet VP of treasury, Richard Ross, came into the meeting suspecting that the right option was to close the mine. "Metal prices were coming down and we were getting squeezed," he said. "We had invested a lot and there was no dividend in sight. Eventually it becomes clear you're not going to turn a sow's ear into a silk purse."

But closing the mine would have harsh consequences. Copper Range employed over a thousand people, and it was the only major business in its region, so the ripple effects on the local economy would be devastating. The shutdown would also be costly for the executive team's reputation—they'd only recently acquired the mine and had chosen to invest millions in it. If they shut it down so soon, what would shareholders think of their judgment?

There were several options other than closing the mine. One alternative was to close down the existing smelter, which was on its last legs, and ship the ore to Canada to be refined in a more modern smelter. Another was to supplement the dwindling supply of ore in the current mine by expanding to the north, toward an area that was thought to have an untapped vein of ore.

As the discussion progressed, the two sides settled into their predictable roles: The executives were leaning toward closing the mine, and the mining managers opposed it. People were talking past one another. Roger Martin describes the initial discussion as "all over the map."

"I remember we'd been there probably a couple of hours," said the treasurer, Ross. "And there was this sense of frustration. *There's a lot here to talk about. How do we work through it?*"

"I could tell it was going nowhere," said Martin. At the point of impasse, he said, "an idea popped into my head."

He issued the group a challenge: Let's stop arguing about who is right, he said. Instead, let's take each option, one at a time, and ask ourselves: *What would have to be true for this option to be the right answer?*

Surely it's possible, he said, to imagine a set of evidence that would persuade us to change our minds. Let's talk about what that evidence would look like.

Ross said that after Roger Martin posed his challenge, "the lights went on for everyone." Participants switched from arguing to analyzing, discussing the logical underpinnings of each option.

The executives, asked to specify the conditions under which it would make sense to keep the mine open, started talking about production targets that would make it viable. The mine managers, asked to contemplate a scenario where closing the mine might be the best option, agreed that if copper prices didn't recover, it would be hard to recommend continued operations.

The tenor of the discussion changed. There was still tension in the room, but it was productive tension. Martin's reframing of the meeting had changed adversaries into collaborators.

"It was magic," said Martin. "By the end of the day, we had the group's agreement on what had to be true for each of the five options for it to be the very best choice."

After the meeting wrapped up, the parties began to gather the information they'd agreed would be needed. They experimented with the idea of shipping the ore to Canada, but that turned out to be more costly than anyone had predicted, so they crossed that option off the list.

They also explored the option of expanding the mine but ended up running into a wall, literally. There was an unexpected structural constraint in punching through the rock to get to the new vein. John Sanders, the general manager of the mine at the time, said that you can imagine the old mine and the potential new mine as two shopping centers side by side underground. "Then you discover that, in fact, you can only get one small door, the size of a washroom door, open between the two shopping centers and all the traffic would have to walk through this little door. You just can't do this."

By the time of the next board meeting, they'd arrived at an answer: There were no compelling options for keeping the mine open. Even John Sanders, in his role as general manager of the mine, was convinced. He stood up in front of the board and reluctantly endorsed the closure.

ROGER MARTIN SAYS THE "What would have to be true?" question has become the most important ingredient of his strategy work, and it's not hard to see why. The search for disconfirming information might seem, on the surface, like a thoroughly negative process: We try to poke holes in our own arguments or the arguments of others. But Martin's question adds something constructive: *What if our least favorite option were actually the best one? What data might convince us of that?*

Martin said, "If you think an idea is the wrong way to approach a problem and someone asks you if you think it's the right way, you'll reply 'no' and defend that answer against all comers. But if someone asks you to figure out what would have to be true for that approach to work, your frame of thinking changes. . . . This subtle shift gives people a way to back away from their beliefs and allow exploration by which they give themselves the opportunity to learn something new."

This technique is particularly useful in organizations where dissent is unwelcome, where people who challenge the prevailing ideas are accused of failing to be "team players." Martin's question makes dissenters seem less like antagonists and more like problem solvers.*

What makes Roger Martin's technique so effective, in short, is that it allows people to disagree without becoming disagreeable. It goes beyond merely exposing ourselves to disconfirming evidence; it forces us to imagine a set of conditions where we'd willingly change our minds, without feeling that we "lost" the debate.

2.

We are all pretty good at digging up disconfirming information to respond to a sales pitch. When a time-share salesman raves about a "once in a lifetime" deal, our shields go up and we become implacably logical, picking apart his exaggerated claims. ("Er, if your resort is so popular that I risk losing a unit if I don't buy it right now, then why do you seem so desperate? And why did you have to bribe me to be here?")

The problem comes, of course, when *we sort of want to be sold*. At dinner, the waiter approaches with a dessert tray featuring a chocolate lava cake large enough to have its own ZIP code, and, as your mouth starts to salivate, you ask hopefully, "Is it good?" Not exactly a tough stand.

Sometimes we think we're gathering information when we're actually fishing for support. Take the tradition of calling people's references when

---

*Another technique for dissenters that we'll explore later is setting a tripwire, à la David Lee Roth. A tripwire specifies the circumstances when the team would reconsider a decision. So if you're skeptical of a decision but lack the power to change it, encourage your colleagues to set a tripwire. ("If X happens, we'll take another look at this.") This will be easy for them to accept, since most people are overconfident and will underestimate the chances of hitting the tripwire. Meanwhile, you've made it possible to reconsider the decision at a later date without seeming like the person who said, "I told you so."

you want to hire them. It's an exercise in self-justification: We believe someone is worth hiring, and as a final "check" on ourselves, we decide to gather more information about them from past colleagues. So far, so good. Then *we allow the candidate to tell us whom we should call*, and we dutifully interview those people, who say glowing things about the candidate, and then, absurdly, we feel more confident in our decision to hire the person. (Imagine if we bought a time-share because the salesman had three *awesome* references.)

In some organizations, hiring managers have become smarter about reference calls. Some ask the references for additional people to contact who weren't on the original list. Those secondary interviews will tend to yield more neutral information. Other people have reconsidered the kinds of questions they ask in reference calls. Rather than ask for an *evaluation* of the candidate ("Would you say Steve's performance was closer to 'stunning' or 'breathtaking'? Be honest."), many firms now seek specific factual information. For example, Ray Rothrock, a venture capitalist with Venrock, says that one of the best diagnostic questions he's discovered in assessing entrepreneurs is "How many secretaries has this entrepreneur had in the past few years?" If the answer is five, chances are you've got someone with some issues.

This same strategy of fishing for specific information was endorsed in a brilliant article called "On Being a Happy, Healthy, and Ethical Member of an Unhappy, Unhealthy, and Unethical Profession," published in 1999 by U.S. District Court judge Patrick J. Schiltz. In the piece, Schiltz urges law students to ask tough, disconfirming questions before taking a job with a big corporate law firm:

> Every big firm claims that it is different. Every big firm denies that it is a sweatshop. Every big firm insists that, although its attorneys work hard, they lead balanced lives. This is almost always false. It *has* to be. There is no free lunch. . . .
>
> Ask tough questions of the lawyers you meet. When you are at a recruiting dinner with a couple of lawyers from the firm, don't

just ask them, "So, do you folks have any kind of life outside of work?" They will chuckle, say "sure," and ask if you want more wine. Instead, ask them how many times last week they had dinner with their families. And then ask them what time dinner was served. And then ask them whether they worked after dinner.

Ask them what their favorite television show is or what is the last good movie they saw. If they respond, respectively, *Welcome Back, Kotter* and *Saturday Night Fever*, you will know something's wrong. . . . When a lawyer tells you that he gets a lot of interesting assignments, ask for examples. You may be surprised at what passes for "interesting" at the firm. And when a lawyer tells you that associates are happy at the firm, ask for specifics. How many associates were hired five years ago? How many of those associates remain at the firm? Who were the last three associates to leave the firm? What are they doing now? How can you contact them?

Asking tough, disconfirming questions like these can dramatically improve the quality of information we collect, as illustrated in a study titled "There *Is* Such a Thing as a Stupid Question," authored by three Wharton researchers, Julie A. Minson, Nicole E. Ruedy, and Maurice E. Schweitzer.

In the study, participants acted as the seller in a role-played negotiation over an iPod. As sellers, they knew everything about the iPod: It was relatively new, had a spiffy cover, and was filled with an impressive collection of songs. On the other hand, it had frozen up twice in the past, forcing a reset that resulted in all the music being deleted.

The researchers wondered what it would take for the sellers to disclose the freezing problem. The buyers in the negotiation, who were cronies of the researchers, tried three different strategies. When the buyers asked about the iPod, "What can you tell me about it?," only 8% of the sellers disclosed the problem. The question "It doesn't have any problems, does it?" boosted the disclosure to 61%.

The best question to ask, in hopes of discovering the truth, was this one: "What problems does it have?" That prompted 89% of the sellers to come clean.

The researchers explain that probing questions signal confidence and experience in the asker. The seller knows she isn't likely to pull one over on you. There's a similar signaling effect with Judge Schiltz's questions. A law student is likely to get straight answers to the questions "How many associates were hired five years ago?" and "How many of those associates remain at the firm?"

THIS PRACTICE OF ASKING probing questions is useful when you are trying to pry information from people who have an incentive to spin you: salesmen, recruiters, employees with agendas, and so on. On the other hand, it can backfire in situations where there's a clear power dynamic, as between a doctor and a patient. Here's why: Tough questions work in the iPod situation because they signal confidence and experience in the asker, but when the asker is already the clear "expert," as the doctor is in the doctor/patient situation, then asking aggressive questions will only reinforce the doctor's dominance. That can cause patients to clam up or to follow the doctor's lead too eagerly, even if it isn't the most productive direction.

So, for doctors to gather trustworthy information, they've got to be diligent about asking open-ended questions—much more like the generic iPod question, "What can you tell me about it?" That kind of question was ineffective in the iPod situation, but it works wonders with patients.

The late Dr. Allen Barbour, the chief of the Stanford Diagnostic Clinic at the Stanford University School of Medicine, was a master of open-ended interviewing. In his book *Caring for Patients*, he recalls seeing a patient named Joseph H., whose ailment had puzzled other doctors for months.

Joseph, 67, had first come to his regular doctor (not Dr. Barbour) reporting feeling "lightheaded, dizzy." His doctor knew that many diseases might be producing these symptoms, so to diagnose Joseph accurately, the doctor and his colleagues ordered a laundry list of tests: "EKG, EEG, aortic arch and cerebral arteriography, consultations in neurology and ENT with electronystagmography, audiometry, and other special tests." All the tests came back negative.

So the doctor tried a portfolio of pharmaceuticals: Hydergine, vasodilators, the "anti-vertigo" antihistamines, and anticoagulants. Nothing worked. Joseph's ailment was a mystery.

Frustrated, the doctor referred Joseph to Dr. Barbour. In their first meeting, Dr. Barbour asked Joseph to describe in depth what he meant by "feeling dizzy" and how often he felt that way. Joseph responded:

> "Doctor, I feel dizzy nearly all the time since my wife died. I don't know what to do with myself. I'm confused. I watch TV, but I'm not interested. I go outside, but there's no place to go."
>
> He looked sad indeed as he told of the emptiness of his life. He had moved to California with his wife after retirement. He had no children, no close friends, no special interests.

Suddenly the real problem became clearer to Dr. Barbour. "Dizzy" was Joseph's way of expressing his confusion. He was a lonely man, overcome with grief, who hadn't yet learned to develop a new life.

Before Dr. Barbour, none of Joseph's doctors had thought to ask him what he meant by "feeling dizzy." They had never considered that the cause might be emotional rather than physical.

Dr. Barbour argues that doctors are trained to be expert disease detectors, taught to diagnose patients based on fragments of information: a fever, an odd pain, a spell of disorientation. But this disease hunt can backfire, tempting them to lock on to a possible diagnosis prematurely. Dr. Barbour shared the transcript of an interview that illustrates this:

RESIDENT: What's troubling you?

PATIENT: I have this pain in my stomach (indicating with his hands the entire abdomen).

RESIDENT: Where is it?

PATIENT: Pretty much all over.

RESIDENT: Is it here (pointing to the patient's epigastrium)?

PATIENT: Yes, I feel pain there.

RESIDENT: When do you get it?

PATIENT: A lot of the time.

RESIDENT: Before meals?

PATIENT: Yes, before meals, but I get it any old time.

Barbour pointed out how quickly the doctor takes over the interview—and how he prematurely localizes the patient's complaint by asking, "Is it here?" (If the pain is "pretty much all over," then, yes, it's probably in that spot but also many others.) Meanwhile, the patient has been trained not to volunteer information. After a very brief exchange, the doctor develops a tentative diagnosis of peptic ulcer disease and orders the related tests. The tests prove him wrong.

Barbour's assessment of this interview was damning: "Though [the resident] regards himself as objective and scientific, he manipulates the data to fit his concept of disease, but is not aware that he does so. He does not discover a pattern; he generates one."

Unfortunately, the speed with which the doctor took over the interview in the case above may not be unusual. One study of patient interviews revealed that it took only 18 seconds, on average, for a doctor to interrupt a patient.

Barbour recommends a process that is better equipped to dodge the confirmation bias. When the doctor starts asking questions, she should start broad and open-ended: "What was the pain like? How did you feel?" Then she can move slowly and cautiously toward more directed questions: "Was it sharp or dull?" "Were you sad?" In this way, the doctor can avoid unwittingly biasing the interview.*

How do you know whether to ask probing questions or open-ended ones? A good rule of thumb is to ask yourself, "What's the most likely way I could fail to get the right information in this situation?" Generally, it will be obvious what the answer is: If you're buying a used car, you're most likely to fail by not discovering a flaw of the vehicle, or if you're a vice president seeking feedback from factory workers, you're most likely to fail by not uncovering what they really think. You can tailor your questions accordingly—more aggressive in the used-car negotiations and more open-ended with the factory worker.

3.

When we want something to be true, we gather information that supports our desire. But the confirmation bias doesn't just affect what information people go looking for; it even affects what they notice in the first place. Think of a couple in a troubled marriage: If one partner has labeled the other's shortcoming—for instance, being "selfish"—then that label

---

*Of course, there are also times when doctors need more aggressive questions. Consider a situation where a patient's blood test seems to indicate that she is not taking a critical medication. A broad question like "Are you keeping up with your medication?" is unlikely to work, because many patients may answer "yes" out of fear or embarrassment. A more probing question such as "When was the last time you took your medication?" or "Roughly how many pills do you have left?" will be more effective.

can become self-reinforcing. The selfish acts become easier to spot, while the generous acts go unnoticed.

In situations like this, the therapist Aaron T. Beck, the founder of cognitive behavioral therapy, advises that couples consciously fight the tendency to notice only what's wrong. To avoid that trap, he advises couples to keep "marriage diaries," chronicling the things their mates do that *please* them.

In his book *Love Is Never Enough*, he describes a couple, Karen and Ted, who kept such a diary. One week, Karen noted several things that she appreciated about Ted: *He sympathized with me about some bad behavior by one of my clients. He pitched in to help clean up the house. He kept me company while I was doing laundry. He suggested we go for a walk, which I enjoyed.*

Beck said, "Although Ted had done similar things for Karen in the past, they had been erased from her memory because of her negative view of Ted." The same effect held true for Ted's memory of the nice things Karen had done.

Beck cites a research study by Mark Kane Goldstein, who found that 70% of couples who kept this kind of marriage diary reported an improvement in their relationship. "All that had changed was their *awareness* of what was going on," Beck wrote. "Before keeping track, they had underestimated the pleasures of their marriage."

As in the marriage situation, our relationships at work are sometimes corrupted by negative assumptions that snowball over time. A colleague speaks out against our idea in a meeting, and we think, *He's trying to show off in front of the boss.* If this happens another time or two, we might conclude he's a "brown-noser," a label that will become self-sustaining, as in the marriage situation.

To interrupt this cycle, some organizational leaders urge their employees to "assume positive intent," that is, to imagine that the behavior or words of your colleagues are motivated by good intentions, even when their actions seem objectionable at first glance. This "filter" can be extremely powerful. Indra Nooyi, the chairman and CEO of PepsiCo, cited it to *Fortune* as the best advice she ever received. (She learned it from her father.)

She said, "When you assume negative intent, you're angry. If you take away that anger and assume positive intent, you will be amazed. . . . You don't get defensive. You don't scream. You are trying to understand and listen because at your basic core you are saying, 'Maybe they are saying something to me that I'm not hearing.'"

A blogger named Rochelle Arnold-Simmons uses the "assume positive intent" principle with her husband: "When your husband does something and you immediately go to a negative place, ask yourself, 'What are other possibilities that may be more positive than what you are thinking?' Assume he is trying to help, assume he does not need to be reminded, assume it is not his fault. I try to always ask the question, 'What's another possibility?'"

Pittsburgh-area Industrial Scientific had to give its employees a crash course in assuming positive intent when it added a French subsidiary to its existing operations in the United States and China. The cultural differences played themselves out in many subtle ways. For example, French employees were very chatty in e-mails, while the Chinese were direct. Each saw the others' e-mails as a little disrespectful. Chairman Kent McElhattan said in an interview that his employees need to be reminded, about their colleagues, that "they are interested in the same things you are. Assume that."

ASSUMING POSITIVE INTENT AND keeping a marriage diary are two examples of what psychologists call "considering the opposite." *I think my spouse is selfish—but perhaps I should keep track of situations where he's looking out for me. I think my colleague is being rude and abrupt—but what if he's not being abrupt and is just trying to respect my time? (Oops, and what if he thinks I'm disrespecting his time when I try to chat?)* This simple technique of considering the opposite has been shown, across multiple studies, to reduce many otherwise thorny cognitive biases. (See endnotes for more.)

The ultimate form of "considering the opposite" might be what Paul Schoemaker did when he convened his colleagues at DSI—Decision Strategies International, the management consulting firm he'd founded—to discuss an important matter of business. He wanted them to make a mistake.

Schoemaker, a decision researcher and consultant, was dead serious. He wanted his colleagues to help him plan and execute a deliberate mistake, as a way of testing their assumptions about DSI's business.

"Everyone at our firm was willing to believe that some of our beliefs were flawed and we should subject them to a test," Schoemaker said, "but as soon as we got concrete about it, people kind of thought it was not very wise or even silly. So as a leader I stepped in and said, 'I'll take the blame for it.' After all, leaders always say, 'I learned the most from my mistakes.' Well, why leave the mistakes to serendipity? Why not take some control of the process and make mistakes that you're most likely to learn from?"

As he describes in his book, *Brilliant Mistakes*, his team started by listing some of the key assumptions underlying their efforts, an exercise that surfaced the "conventional wisdom" that, in most organizations, is never articulated or questioned.

After they'd identified ten key assumptions, they whittled the list down to three—those they were least confident about and that, if proven wrong, had the highest potential payoff for the business:

1.   Young MBAs don't work well for us. We need experienced consultants on the team.

2.   The firm can be successfully run by a president who is not a major-billing senior consultant.

3. It is not worthwhile to respond to RFPs. Clients who use RFPs are usually price shopping or are going through the motions to justify a choice they have already made. [RFPs are requests for proposals. Customers send out RFPs to attract vendors to bid on their business.]

A further round of assessment led them to select number 3 as "having the highest potential of benefiting from a strategy of deliberate mistakes." Now they were ready to make their mistake.

The firm's policy had been never to respond to an RFP, but they resolved to respond to the next one that came over the transom, which, as it happened, came from a regional electric utility. The DSI team submitted a proposal with a budget of about $200,000, a price that reflected their normal fees but that they suspected would be well out of the client's league. Schoemaker said, "To our surprise, the electric utility invited our firm to visit with the CEO and the senior management team to explore not only the project in question but others as well."

DSI would eventually land over $1 million in consulting business from the utility. "Not a bad return for making a small mistake," said Schoemaker.

WHY COULDN'T YOU RUN Schoemaker's game plan in your organization? Could you create a "Mistake of the Year" program? To be clear, you shouldn't do it expecting a million-dollar surprise to pop out. Most of your "deliberate mistakes" will fail, and in fact that failure should be encouraging, because it means you've been making the right assumptions all along. Beyond the mistake itself, the willingness to test your assumptions has its own value. It signals to your colleagues that your work will be conducted based on evidence, not folklore or politics.

That cultural reinforcement is precious, because it helps to correct for our natural inclination to avoid this work. Reality-Testing Our

Assumptions is difficult. We'll rarely do it instinctively. That's the whole point of the confirmation bias—deep down, we never really want to hear the negative information. (When's the last time you earnestly "considered the opposite" of one of your political views?) That's why we are advocating so strongly in this book for the use of a process, something that becomes habitual. Otherwise it will be too easy to discard this advice in the heat of the moment.

If you are an overachiever—and single—you might even consider applying this "consider the opposite" principle to your dating life. One research team, interested in why some people find someone to marry and others don't, interviewed women who were exiting the office where they'd just received their marriage license. To their surprise, 20% of the women reported *not liking* their spouse-to-be when they first met. (This also implies that there are millions of other people who *met their future spouse and then walked away* because their gut instinct led them to abandon the interaction too early.)

The researcher who led that study, John T. Molloy, reported that some of the single women on his research team were surprised and intrigued by this result. Almost all of them could think of men whose interest they'd rejected—and some of these men were continuing to express their interest (in acceptable, non-stalkerish ways). Now the women wondered if these men might be overlooked potential mates. So they decided to try their own version of a "deliberate mistake" strategy, accepting a date with a guy they'd turned down multiple times in the past.

Molloy said that "most women decided they were right the first time." But one of his team members liked the first date enough to go on a second, and a third, and a fourth. She ended up marrying the guy! (*By the power vested in me, I now pronounce you Mistake and Wife.*) And not only did she find a spouse, but she also scored an inspiring victory over the confirmation bias.

. . .

SO FAR, WE'VE REVIEWED three approaches for fighting the confirmation bias: One, we can make it easier for people to disagree with us. Two, we can ask questions that are more likely to surface contrary information. Three, we can check ourselves by considering the opposite.

There's a different strategy for helping people Reality-Test Their Assumptions that involves knowing where to go looking for the right information: If your boyfriend is considering the hot new "Caveman Diet," how should he assess it? If your boss wants to cut the amount of inventory you hold, how would you determine whether that's a good idea?

The answer will force us to embrace a certain cosmic humility. From the perspective of our brains, we are unique. Our challenges and opportunities feel particular to us. From the perspective of the universe, though, we are utterly typical. And as we'll see in the next chapter, when our predictions and opinions clash with the universe's averages, the universe usually wins.

CHAPTER FIVE IN ONE PAGE
Consider the Opposite

1. Confirmation bias = hunting for information that confirms our initial assumptions (which are often self-serving).

   - *The hubris of CEOs can be counteracted by disagreement. We need the same disagreement to counteract our confirmation bias.*

2. We need to spark constructive disagreement within our organizations.

   - *The devil's advocate, murder boards, and* The Gong Show *all license skepticism. How can we?*
   - *Roger Martin's brilliant question: "What would have to be true for this option to be the very best choice?"*

3. To gather more trustworthy information, we can ask disconfirming questions.

   - *Law students: "Who were the last three associates to leave the firm? What are they doing now? How can I contact them?"*
   - *iPod buyers: "What problems does the iPod have?"*

4. Caution: Probing questions can backfire in situations with a power dynamic.

   - *Doctors are wiser to use open-ended questions. "What do you mean by 'dizzy'?"*

5. Extreme disconfirmation: Can we force ourselves to *consider the opposite* of our instincts?

   - *A marriage diary helps a frustrated spouse see that his/her partner isn't always selfish.*
   - *"Assuming positive intent" spurs us to interpret someone's actions/words in a more positive light.*

6. We can even test our assumptions with a deliberate mistake.

   - *Schoemaker's firm won $1 million in business by experimenting with the RFP process.*
   - *One woman actually married her "mistake."*

7. Because we naturally seek self-confirming information, we need discipline to consider the opposite.

6

Zoom Out, Zoom In

1.

The photos on the Web site of Myrtle Beach's Polynesian Resort depict a beach paradise, a landscape of golden sand and palm trees and colorful umbrellas. People recline on lounge chairs; a catamaran sails in the distance. It looks like just the kind of place you might want to take your family on a summer vacation.

By the time you're reading this, it might indeed be a lovely place. But in 2011, when we saw the Web site, the Polynesian Resort had a nasty secret—it had been named by TripAdvisor, a travel advice Web site, as one of 2011's Top 10 Dirtiest Hotels in the United States.

Many of the hotel's past guests have shared their opinions of the experience on TripAdvisor; their commentaries are often scathing and hilarious:

Terri B (7/24/12): We checked in on July 21st and left in 10 minutes. I cannot put into words the horror.

Fetters26 (6/7/2011): My dog was at a kennel and his accommodations were much cleaner and more plush than the Polynesian!

Jackie503 (6/30/2011): The floors have not been mopped or vacuumed since Moses parted the Red Sea. The beds were old and the sheets were itchy . . .

4q2 (1/27/11): Many reviews compared this property to a dump. That just isn't fair to the dumps of the world.

Thanks to sites like TripAdvisor, it's easier for us to avoid making a hotel choice we'll regret. We can ignore the glossy pictures and simply look at the reviews. In the case of the Polynesian Resort, 67% of the reviews rated the experience as "Terrible," compared with a mere 4% who said "Excellent." (One of those "Excellent" reviews cites the place as perfect for a debaucherous spring break, if you don't mind the "filthy rooms.")

Many people have come to take this kind of review shopping for granted. We hunt routinely for the rating of a book on Amazon or a restaurant on Yelp or a digital camera on CNET. It's an obvious thing to do, right? But this "obvious" behavior shows wisdom. Because when we make decisions based on reviews, we are acknowledging two things: (1) Our ability to glean the truth about a product is limited and subject to distortion by the company that makes it; and (2) For that reason, we are smarter to trust the averages over our own impressions.

Often in life, though, we do the opposite: We trust our impressions over the averages. For example, many people will accept a new job without consulting a sample of people who currently or formerly held the same title. Shouldn't their "reviews" be as valuable as a stranger's assessment of a hotel room or restaurant?

Strange to think that when we make critical decisions, we do less objective research than when we're picking a sushi joint.

Psychologists distinguish between the "inside view" and "outside view" of a situation. The inside view draws from information that is in our spotlight as we consider a decision—our own impressions and assessments of the situation we're in. The outside view, by contrast, ignores the particulars and instead analyzes the larger class it's part of. So in deciding whether to book a reservation at the Polynesian Resort, the inside view relies on our own assessment: *Does this look like the kind of place where I would enjoy staying?* The outside view trusts the TripAdvisor reviews: *How much did people, in general, enjoy staying there?*

The outside view is more accurate—it's a summary of real-world experiences, rather than a single person's impressions—yet we'll be drawn to the inside view. To see why, imagine a restauranteur, Jack, who is deciding whether to take out a loan to start a Thai restaurant in downtown Austin. What's in the spotlight, for him, will be all the factors going for him: *I'm a wonderful Thai cook. The location on 4th Street would be perfect. The foot traffic in that area is huge. There's no other Thai restaurant close by.* From the inside view, the opportunity looks pretty good.

By contrast, the outside view does not treat Jack's situation as unique. It looks for the averages: Are there other people who've faced a similar situation, and if so, how did they fare? This involves looking for, in statistics terminology, some "base rates" on the situation—data showing the record of other people in similar circumstances. Jack might learn, for instance, that 60% of restaurants fail in their first three years. From the outside view, the restaurant looks pretty risky.

Yet notice how different this feels from the TripAdvisor situation. It is *intuitive* for us to accept that we're likely to have a bad experience at the Polynesian Resort, but it's not intuitive for Jack to accept that he's likely to fail. Why?

The outside view ignores everything that is special about our situation. All entrepreneurs have reason to believe, at the beginning, that they will succeed. Jack, for instance, would surely scoff at the base-rates data, saying, "I know Thai food, and I know Austin, and I know this will work. You can't lump me in with a guy who sells corn dogs at the mall." But he'd be wrong. There are enough commonalities among restaurants that their experiences are likely to be more similar than different. He should trust the base rates on restaurant success almost as much as he trusts the base rates on staying at the Polynesian Resort.*

Mind you, for Jack to take the outside view—and accept those bleak odds of restaurant success—does not demand that he give up on the idea. It may be that a successful restaurant would be so lucrative that the risk is worth taking. Or he may consider the restaurant a good investment in his career, even if it fails. The outside view doesn't require defeatism, but it does require respect for the likely outcomes. Put it this way: If he bets his kids' college money on the venture, he's nuts.

Your friends and colleagues will suffer from this same stubbornness: the tendency to trust their own impressions too much. They'll be trapped in the inside view, but you'll have an easier time seeing the outside view. Be forewarned, though: Sometimes people can have access to the perfect set of data—and still manage to ignore it.

This was something Daniel Kahneman, the Nobel Prize–winning psychologist, experienced himself early in his career. He and his colleagues were exploring the idea of writing a high-school textbook on the subject of judgment and decision making. They would be the first to develop curricula on those subjects, so they roped in the dean of the School of Education, who was a curriculum expert, to work with them. The team began to write some sample chapters, and they met every Friday to review their progress. One Friday, they were discussing research about how groups think about the future, and it occurred to Kahneman that they should take their own advice. He said, "Let's see how we think about the future."

He asked his colleagues to write down the date when they thought

---

*Why "almost"? To be fair, Jack has some control over the situation in a way that the Polynesian Resort's guests don't: His experience and his cooking and his business savvy do matter. The point is that *these differences are all he sees*, so the spotlight effect will lead him to overweight them. He will tend to forget that he can't affect the macro Austin environment for restaurants any more than a guest can affect the cleanliness of the Polynesian Resort. So while the factors he controls may *adjust* the odds in his favor, they're unlikely to *transform* the odds.

the textbook would be completed. The range of estimates was quite narrow—everyone's projections, including Kahneman's and the dean's, ranged from 1.5 to 2.5 years into the future. Then Kahneman suddenly recalled the idea of base rates from his statistics training, so he asked the dean whether he could recall other groups similar to theirs that had written a new curriculum from scratch. The dean said, yes, he could remember quite a few of them. Kahneman asked him to quantify the base rate: *How long did it take them to finish?*

After some back-and-forth, two disturbing facts had surfaced. One: According to the dean, 40% of the groups never finished writing the curriculum. Two: Of the groups that did finish, all of them took seven to ten years. Then Kahneman asked the dean, "How does our group compare to the others?" (Note that he's trying to see whether there's any reason to adjust their prediction up or down from the base rate, based on the group's skill.) The dean replied, "Below average, but not by much."

The curriculum took eight years to write.

LIKE JACK THE RESTAURANTEUR, Kahneman and his colleagues were optimistic when they took the inside view. The puzzle here is the dean's behavior. He *knew* the base rates for developing a new curriculum, but his spotlight stayed trained on the group's unique circumstances. From the inside view, it looked like they could wrap it up in two years. "There was no contact between something he knew and something he said. . . . He had all the information necessary to conclude that the prediction he was writing down was ridiculous," said Kahneman.

This brings us to a critical point about experts. Perhaps the simplest and most intuitive advice we can offer in this chapter is that when you're trying to gather good information and reality-test your ideas, go talk to an expert. If you're considering filing an intellectual-property lawsuit against a competitor, talk to a top IP lawyer.

An expert doesn't have to be a heavily credentialed authority, though. The bar is actually far lower than that: An expert is simply someone who has more experience than you. If your son wants to be a carpenter, go talk to a carpenter. Any carpenter. If you're thinking about relocating your business to South Carolina, call up someone, anyone, who has relocated their business to South Carolina.

Here's what is less intuitive: Be careful what you ask them. As we'll see in the next chapter, experts are pretty bad at predictions. But they are great at assessing base rates.

As an example, imagine that you are indeed consulting an IP lawyer about a potential patent-infringement suit. The right kinds of questions to ask him are "What are the important variables in a case like this?," "What kind of evidence can tip the verdict one way or the other?," "In percentage terms, how many cases get settled before trial?," and "Of those that go to trial, what are the odds that the plaintiff prevails?" If you ask questions like that—questions about past cases and legal norms—you will get a wealth of trustworthy information.

On the other hand, if you ask a predictive question—"Do you think I can win this case?"—it will trigger the lawyer to slip into the inside view. Like the curriculum-writing dean, your lawyer will tend to be too optimistic about the chances of success.

We don't want to overstate the case here—a good IP lawyer will surely know the difference between a slam-dunk case and a long shot. The point is that the *predictions* of even a world-class expert need to be discounted in a way that their *knowledge of base rates* does not. In short, when you need trustworthy information, go find an expert—someone more experienced than you. Just keep them talking about the past and the present, not the future.

2.

What we've seen so far is a very simple rule for analyzing your options: Take the outside view. You should distrust the inside view—those glossy pictures in your head—and instead get out of your head and consult the base rates. Sometimes those numbers are readily available, as on Trip-Advisor or Yelp. Sometimes you might have to cobble them together yourself. If neither of those options is possible, try consulting an expert for their estimates of the base rates.

In our experience, people fall into two camps about the outside view. Some people buy into the idea immediately, but others feel a bit dissatisfied. Should we really be willing to trust a set of data over our own antennae? Isn't that dehumanizing somehow? Overly analytical?

The advice to trust the numbers isn't motivated by geekery; it's motivated by humility. We can't lose sight of what the numbers represent: A lot of people like us—people full of passion for their opportunities—spent their time trying something very similar to what we're contemplating. To ignore their experience isn't brave and romantic—"I'm not going to let some *analysis* stand in the way of doing what I believe." Rather, it's egotistical. It's saying, *We set ourselves apart from everyone else. We're different. We're better.*

The humble approach is to ask, "What can I reasonably expect to happen if I make this choice?" Once we accept the answer—and trust it to make our decision—*then* we can turn our attention to fighting the odds. That, in essence, is the story of Brian Zikmund-Fisher, who as a young man was forced to make a life-or-death choice.

In early 1998, Zikmund-Fisher, a 28-year-old graduate student in the Social and Decision Sciences group at Carnegie Mellon University in Pittsburgh, was playing racquetball with a friend. At one point, he made an overeager swing of the racket and hit himself in the left arm.

An hour later, he had a bruise that started at his shoulder and ended at his wrist.

Brian was disturbed but not shocked. He had a history of blood problems that had begun 13 years earlier, when he was a junior in high school. At the time, he was traveling with his mother, visiting universities, when he got an urgent message from his doctor, whom he'd seen recently for a checkup. Brian called him back, and the doctor sounded tense.

"Are you okay?" said the doctor.

"Yes, why?" said Brian.

"We'd like you to retake your blood test when you can. As soon as possible," said the doctor.

The second test confirmed what had spooked the doctor: Brian's blood platelet count was 45, a disturbingly low number. (To be more accurate, that's 45×10^9 per liter. Platelets play an important role in clotting, and the platelet count is also a good diagnostic for the health of a person's blood supply and immune system.) Normal counts are between 150 and 450. By way of comparison, patients aren't allowed to undergo surgery when they're below 50, and at about 10, there's a risk of spontaneous bleeding and hemorrhaging.

After some treatment, Brian's count climbed back up to 110. His doctors warned him that he'd need to be checked at least every six months for the rest of his life.

Until the racquetball game, it had been years since he'd had a problem. But when the bruise took over his arm, Brian knew what was happening. He went to the doctor and, as he suspected, his platelet count was shockingly low—19, in fact.

The doctors, after further testing, diagnosed Brian with a life-threatening disease called myelodysplastic syndrome (MDS). The hallmark of MDS is that a person's bone marrow stops producing blood cells effectively. Brian's doctors told him that eventually, not even the platelet transfusions he was receiving (every eight days) would be enough to keep him from bleeding to death.

Brian said, "The message was that I didn't have to do anything immediately. But I did not have 10 years; I had maybe 5."

The only potential cure for MDS was a complete bone-marrow transplant, a complex and dangerous procedure. The treatment typically begins with radiation and chemotherapy, a combination that demolishes the patient's immune system.

The goal is for the patient to start over with a completely new immune system, transplanted from a donor who is a good genetic match.

Unfortunately, there is no guarantee that the patient's body will accept the transplant, and in Brian's case, finding a compatible donor would be tricky. The best matches for bone marrow come from siblings, and Brian was an only child.

During the year or more that it takes the transplant to take hold, the patient operates without a well-running immune system, so *any* infection—even a basic cold—can be life threatening.

The transplant, then, was a cure fraught with peril. The doctors told Brian that, if he chose to get a transplant, he had a one in four chance of not surviving the year. If he did survive, though, he would likely enjoy a long life.

He faced a brutal choice: Refuse the transplant and live another five or six years of relatively normal life, until the inevitable collapse. Or endure a devastating procedure that could cure him for good—or leave him dead within a year.

What made the choice harder still was that Brian's wife was six months pregnant with their first child.

BRIAN WAS DESPERATE FOR information that could help him make the decision, but it wasn't always clear how to interpret what he found. He could locate relevant journal articles and books online, but he wondered whether the base rates in the study were relevant to him. "Most people with my diagnosis are much older than me. So I looked through the studies—the population is 60-year-olds and I'm 28. I'm like, 'Okay, is this going to apply to me? Is this not going to apply to me? How do I know?'"

For answers, he turned to a friend who was a hematologist. She advised him that he should take the average outcomes in the journals seriously, but since his youth and vigor would help him survive the procedure, his odds were probably a little better than the averages. She also highlighted another variable that was critical: the experience of the hospital doing the procedure. In picking an institution, she counseled, don't just seek out a well-known hospital like the Mayo Clinic; look for a place that specializes in bone-marrow transplants, such as the Fred Hutchinson Cancer Research Center in Seattle or the MD Anderson Cancer Center in Houston. He should trust his health to a hospital doing 300 transplants per year rather than 30.

Brian wanted to understand, too, what kinds of complications the transplant would entail. To his frustration, he found that when he asked about the risks of various side effects, doctors gave vague answers. He wanted hard numbers, but they were reluctant. "To overcome the reluctance of doctors to give estimates, I've taken to asking questions that may sound almost ridiculous. . . . 'Are we talking about a 50% chance? A 5% chance? A five-in-a-thousand chance? A five-in-a-million chance?' And you make it obvious that you're not asking for them to be precise. It just puts them at ease."

Brian and his wife, Naomi, sought out contact with other transplant patients and their families, so they could learn how they'd coped with the process. "We didn't have fancy online communities back then," said Brian. "We had a Listserv, an e-mail distribution list. We started following the list and tracking particular people. . . . They would talk about all kinds of medical topics, like dealing with chemotherapy nausea, but some of the most useful topics for us had nothing to do with medicine. . . .

"One of our big questions up front was, How much will Naomi have to be with me? And with a one-year-old, how do we arrange that? It became very clear that we needed to have a third adult, in the same place, to manage the child care. There would be times when Naomi would need to be with me to ask the questions I was mentally or physically unable to ask, and those moments might arise unexpectedly, and they might be at feeding or nap time. She couldn't ask the right questions and hear the answers if she's watching a one-year-old."

After hearing about the need for a "third adult," Brian's parents offered to relocate with Brian and Naomi if they decided to have the procedure done outside Pittsburgh. That allowed them to consider the high-volume transplant centers in other parts of the country.

Naomi and Brian's parents were strongly in favor of the transplant, and he was leaning that way as well, but he didn't find the decision as easy as they did. One night, he talked to Naomi and shared his fear that, if he didn't survive the transplant, his daughter would not have any memories of him. If he avoided the transplant, at least he'd have the luxury of a few years with her. When he was gone, she'd remember him.

Naomi acknowledged that this was true but said gently, "What she'll remember about you is that her daddy was always in the hospital getting transfusions and lying in hospital beds. That will be the memory that she has of you."

"I remember that moment," said Brian. "I thought, 'Damn, she's right.' And I knew."

HE MADE THE DECISION to have the transplant done under the care of the Fred Hutchinson Cancer Research Center, one of the centers most experienced with the procedure. That choice required him and Naomi to relocate from Pittsburgh to Seattle along with their new baby, Eve. His parents also joined them in Seattle, as they'd promised, to provide support for the weeks around the procedure.

Meanwhile, Brian had embarked on a self-imposed training regimen. After hearing on the Listservs how difficult the recovery was, even for young people, Brian was determined to stack the odds as far in his favor as he could. "I realized, *I need to train for this*," said Brian. "I intentionally tried to do more exercise to get into the best possible physical shape before the transplant."

After 40 potential marrow matches that didn't pan out, doctors finally located a promising genetic match, and Brian was approved for a transplant.

The process began with six days of intensive chemotherapy. "They hit your body hard and fast," said Brian. His old defective bone marrow was destroyed, and his body was ready to start over with the transplant. The transplant procedure itself was a bit of an anticlimax. "You sit there and they drip your new blood cells into your body through an IV drip," he said.

In the anxious 30 days following the transplant, Brian couldn't leave the hospital. His daughter, Eve, had her first birthday during this period. They have pictures of her eating birthday cake on Brian's hospital bed.

The recovery process proved as challenging as he had anticipated. Knowing that exercise was critical to ward off complications, he pushed himself to fight his nausea and fatigue and keep moving by doing laps around the hospital ward. "I don't think I would have kept going without having heard other people's experiences and knowing in advance how difficult it would be," he said.

After a month in the hospital and two more months recovering nearby in Seattle, he returned home to Pittsburgh. It was 18 months before he could work consistently, because the fatigue and nausea were so intense and unpredictable. But he was steadily recovering.

He was one of the lucky ones. Of the six people he'd grown close to at the transplant center, three died before the end of the first year.

Thirteen years after his transplant, Brian is thriving. He is now a professor at the School of Public Health at the University of Michigan and has become known among his colleagues for his research on medical decision making and among his students for his patient-centered lectures.

He recently helped his daughter Eve, now 14, make a tough decision about which high school she'd attend.

BRIAN WAS A SICK patient facing one of the hardest choices imaginable: the guarantee of a short life or the chance at a longer one. As a decision-making expert, he was also a man determined to use every scrap of his expertise to make that choice. And if you replay the story, what you'll notice is that he was constantly taking the outside view and pushing for base rates.

After reading the journal articles, he wondered which base rate he should be consulting: Was the evidence derived from older patients applicable to him? So he talked to an expert, the hematologist, who told him to take the odds of success seriously but to adjust them upward a little because of his youth and health. She also suggested a different base rate to consult: the success rates of different hospitals, which hinged on the volume of transplants they performed. (He didn't ask the expert to predict *what would happen in his case.* Experts are great with base rates and mediocre at predictions.)

Concerned about side effects, he pumped doctors for base-rate information: *Are we talking about a 50% chance? Or a 5% chance? Or a five-in-a-million chance?*

Notice, however, that knowing the base rates did not make the choice easy for Brian. He agonized about it for months, and it actually took a moment of intense emotion—his wife's comment about how his daughter would remember him—to clinch his decision. This foreshadows what we'll encounter in the next section, which is that the right kind of emotion can be exactly what we need to make a wise choice.

There's one aspect of Brian's decision-making process, though, that looks nothing like base-rate thinking: He sought out the stories of other transplant patients, eager to learn from their experiences. What he learned led to a few choices that almost certainly increased his odds of success, including his self-imposed exercise regimen and the decision of his parents to accompany him to Seattle.

These insights didn't arise from asking doctors about base rates. Nor did they come from a flawed "inside view" approach—he was not simply trusting his own impressions; he was diligently gathering evidence. What, exactly, was his strategy?

Brian wanted more textured information, more color. He wanted to see, with his own eyes, what life was like for these patients. And that's what we'll see next: In assessing our options, the best complement to the big picture is often a close-up.

3.

This mixture of the big-picture view and the close-up was the signature strategy of President Franklin D. Roosevelt, whom historians consider a master of information collection. FDR's family physician, asked to describe the president, said, "He loved to know everything that was going on and delighted to have a finger in every pie."

Like all presidents, FDR was concerned about the quality of information that reached him, worried that it would be polluted by the agendas of the people passing it along. Hungry for trustworthy data, FDR became the first president to make heavy use of polling to keep tabs on public opinion.

He was also aggressive about developing sources of "ground truth," cultivating a network of sources outside the federal government, such as businessmen, academics, friends, and relatives. They served as his eyes and ears outside of the bureaucracy. "Go and see what's happening," he told one. "See the end product of what we are doing. Talk to people; get the wind in your nose."

He had an able collaborator in the First Lady, Eleanor Roosevelt, who would often visit projects unannounced so she could avoid "stage-managed" situations. Once on-site, she'd interview the directors and staff and compile detailed reports for FDR. "As the years went by I became a better and better reporter and a better and better observer," she said, "largely owing to the fact that Franklin's questions covered such a wide range. I found myself obliged to notice everything."

FDR was known for cultivating relationships with lower-level staffers, bypassing his own department heads, which made them furious. In his memoirs, FDR's secretary of the interior, Harold Ickes, complained indignantly about the president's penchant for calling on members of

Ickes's staff without consulting him first. During the lead-up to World War II, Roosevelt consistently circumvented Secretary of State Cordell Hull, developing a close relationship with his undersecretary Sumner Welles and even hiring his own personal liaison to Winston Churchill, so that he didn't have to rely exclusively on Secretary Hull's reports.

One of the White House staffers reflected on Roosevelt's mastery of the flow of information: "He would call you in and he'd ask you to get the story on some complicated business, and you'd come back after a couple of days of hard labor and present the juicy morsel you'd uncovered under a stone somewhere, only to find out he knew all about it, along with something else you didn't know. . . . After he had done this to you once or twice, you got damn careful about your information."

Much more than prior presidents, Roosevelt used the mail as a strategic source of information. In his fireside chats, he encouraged Americans to send him their views, and they responded: The White House averaged 5,000 to 8,000 pieces of mail per day. If the volume of mail dipped, he groused to his advisers about it. Roosevelt insisted that the mail be analyzed scientifically; he had it sorted by category and by stance, and these statistical breakdowns were delivered to him as "mail briefs." These briefs provided ready-made base rates on the public's point of view.

FDR went a step further; he pushed beyond the base rates and reviewed a sample of the actual letters. What the letters added was texture. It's one thing to know, in statistical terms, how people feel about an issue. But what's their temperature? Are they concerned, or irritated, or angry, or violently incensed? The numbers can conceal the nuance.

This is why we need to add the "close-up" to our tool kit. Base rates are good at establishing norms: *Here are the outcomes we can expect if we make this decision.* Close-ups, though, create intuition, which can be just as important.

Imagine that you're craving Mexican food for dinner, so you look on Yelp for a restaurant, and you find a nearby spot that garnered a 3.5-star rating, which is good but not great. Ordinarily you'd hold out for 4 stars, but in this case you decide to read a sample of the reviews, and what you find is that most people rave about the food but there's a subset of people who are irritated about the high prices. Well, now you're untroubled, because you're a high roller! A Mexican-food connoisseur! You have no problem paying a high price for a truly tasty plate of enchiladas. The base rates obscured the texture of the reviews, but the close-up view revealed it.

SOME ORGANIZATIONAL LEADERS HAVE caught on to the wisdom of this close-up approach. One of them was Anne Mulcahy, who as CEO of Xerox orchestrated one of the most dramatic turnarounds in recent business history. When she took the reins in 2001, the company was $19 billion in debt and had almost no cash in the bank. Its stock price had dropped by 90% the year before. On the day Mulcahy was named CEO—as a 45-year-old, little-known executive—investors welcomed her with an additional 15% plunge in the share price. Six years later, Mulcahy had cut the debt in half and made the stock four times more valuable.

One of the many challenges Mulcahy faced was that her executive team had lost touch with the company's most important customers. In response, she created a program called Focus 500, which was designed to provide a close-up view of Xerox's customers and their challenges. In the program, Xerox's top 500 clients were each matched with a top executive. Every senior executive—including the chief accountant and the general counsel—was responsible for working with at least one customer.

In addition, Mulcahy announced that executives, on a rotating basis, would have to serve as the customer officer of the day. The customer officer would have to deal with every customer complaint that came into corporate headquarters that day. Mulcahy said, "It keeps us in touch with the real world. It grounds us. It permeates all of our decision making."

This program created perhaps the world's most expensive customer-support department. But it also helped a group of top executives reconnect with the customers who were the lifeblood of the company.

Another variety of close-up involves going to the *genba*, a Japanese term meaning "the real place" or, more loosely, the place where the action happens. Japanese detectives, for instance, call the crime scene the *genba*. In a manufacturing firm, the *genba* would be the factory floor, and for a retailing company it would be the store. Practitioners of Total Quality Management encourage leaders to "go to the *genba*" to understand problems. If a problem occurs on a factory floor, for example, engineers should go see it firsthand, assessing the situation and talking directly to the people involved. The best ideas, it's believed, come from this kind of close-up sensory investigation of the situation; how can you improve something you don't fully understand?

So engineers diagnosing problems in a factory find it useful to have a close-up view of the relevant process, and Mulcahy found it useful to give her leadership teams a close-up view of how Xerox was treating its customers. A consumer research director at Procter & Gamble (P&G) named Paul Smith used a similar technique to give his colleagues a close-up view of their competitors.

For consumer products, such as paper towels or dishwashing soap or toothpaste, the competition is fierce, dominated by several multinational companies that wrestle one another for market share. The competitors understand one another's products mind-bogglingly well at a technical level. In the labs at P&G, for instance, here are some of the scientific tests that paper towels are subjected to:

- *The Caliper Test:* A micrometer presses down on a single sheet to a set pressure and measures its thickness in thousandths of an inch. (thicker = better)

- *Rate of Absorbency Test:* Allow the center of a sheet to touch a pool of water for a fixed amount of time. Measure the rate at which the water is absorbed in grams per second. (faster = better)

- *The Tensile Strength Test:* Put the paper towel in clamps and pull from both ends until it tears; measure how many grams per inch of pressure it takes to rip. (tougher = better)

By conducting these tests in the lab—or, as we call it, the paper-towel torture chamber—the scientists can pinpoint the strengths and weaknesses of competitors' products.

The precision of these numbers, though, can cloud a real understanding of the products. What do you really understand about your competitor's paper towel when you know its tensile strength? So Paul Smith decided to arrange a close-up for his colleagues. He began stocking the competitors' products in their office: paper towels, toilet paper, and facial tissue.

"We collect consumer reactions from thousands of consumers a year, but I wanted the people in my building to have a personal, visceral understanding of how good (or bad) our competitors' products were," Smith said. "The typical marketer thinks, 'I've been working here for three years and I think my product is the best thing since sliced bread.' Well, of course you do, because it's your product. But if you actually try your competitors' products yourself, it gives you a different kind of understanding."

Initially, the presence of the competitors' products was greeted with all the enthusiasm of Whoppers being served at a McDonald's company picnic. The competitive chest puffing eventually yielded to another reaction, which Smith characterizes as "Holy crap, my competitors' products are much better than I thought!"

One brand manager said, "I was really surprised. I liked the other brand a lot more than I thought I would! I didn't think product performance was an area I needed to worry about much. Now I do."

Others found that the close-up revealed important competitive advantages. One member of the Bounty team said, "I used the other paper towel to wipe off the sink in the bathroom after I washed my hands, but all it did was push the water around. I had to use two sheets to get the job done quickly." As a result, the marketer began to brainstorm about ways to highlight Bounty's advantage in advertisements.

By staging a close-up for his team, Paul Smith helped reveal important nuances that weren't visible in the numbers.

· · ·

WHEN WE ASSESS OUR choices, we'll take the inside view by default. We'll consider the information in the spotlight and use it to form quick impressions. *The Polynesian Resort looks great. My Thai restaurant is a sure thing.* What we've seen, though, is that we can correct this bias by doing two things: zooming out and zooming in.*

When we zoom out, we take the outside view, learning from the experiences of others who have made choices like the one we're facing. When we zoom in, we take a close-up of the situation, looking for "color" that could inform our decision. Either strategy is helpful, and either one will add insight in a way that conference-room pontificating rarely will.

When possible, we should do both. In interpreting the sentiments of Americans, FDR created statistical summaries *and* read a sample of real letters. In assessing the competitors' products, Paul Smith's colleagues relied on scientific data *and* personal experience. In making a high-stakes health decision, Brian Zikmund-Fisher trusted both the base rates *and* the stories of actual patients.

Zooming out and zooming in gives us a more realistic perspective on our choices. We downplay the overly optimistic pictures we tend to paint inside our minds and instead redirect our attention to the outside world, viewing it in wide-angle and then in close-up.

---

*We use the phrase "zooming out and zooming in" because it provides a simple summary of the chapter, but we want to highlight one aspect of the phrase that's not ideal. "Zooming out" is synonymous with taking the outside view, but zooming in is *not* synonymous with taking the inside view. The inside view is always *inside our heads.* When you think "zoom out, zoom in," think photography. You can't take a photograph inside your head; you point your camera at the world outside and zoom out and zoom in to capture it.

CHAPTER SIX IN ONE PAGE
Zoom Out, Zoom In

1. Often we trust "the averages" over our instincts—but not as much as we should.

   - *We trust the horrible reviews of the Polynesian Resort. But we don't always seek reviews for our most important decisions (new job, college major).*

2. The inside view = our evaluation of our specific situation. The outside view = how things generally unfold in situations like ours. The outside view is more accurate, but most people gravitate toward the inside view.

   - *Jack knows his Thai restaurant will be a hit. Lumping himself with other restaurants feels wrong.*
   - *Kahneman's curriculum story: Even the dean, who knew the base rates, got stuck in the inside view.*

3. If you can't find the "base rates" for your decision, ask an expert.

   - *You might ask an IP lawyer: "What percentage of cases get settled before trial?" etc.*
   - *Warning: Experts are good at estimating base rates but lousy at making predictions.*

4. A "close-up" can add texture that's missing from the outside view.

   - *Brian Zikmund-Fisher studied the base-rate outcomes of patients with MDS, but he also sought a close-up (discovering the need for exercise and a "third adult").*
   - *FDR had his staff compile a statistical "mail brief," and he also read a sample of the letters.*
   - *More close-ups: Xerox's customer officer of the day. "Going to the genba." Using competitors' paper towels.*

5. To gather the best information, we should zoom out and zoom in. (Outside view + close-up.)

7

Ooch

1.

In 2006, John Hanks, a vice president at National Instruments (NI), a company that makes scientific equipment, was deciding whether to make a big bet on wireless sensors. The technology had a lot of promise: A wireless sensor might be installed in a coal mine, in lieu of a canary, to monitor methane levels. Or sensors could send information back from a rotating piece of equipment, like an oil drill head, where a wired solution would be impractical. (Picture spaghetti wrapping around a fork.)

Some of NI's customers were skeptical. Could you secure the data sent by the wireless sensors? How reliable would the sensors be when installed in tough environments? In light of this skepticism, Hanks didn't feel like he had enough information to make a wise decision.

What he needed to do, he realized, was ooch.

To ooch is to construct small experiments to test one's hypothesis. (We learned the word "ooch" from NI, but apparently it's common in parts of the South. Maybe it's a blend of "inch" and "scoot"?) Hanks said, "Part of the culture here is to ask ourselves, 'How do we ooch into this?' . . . We always ooch before we leap."

Hanks went looking for a good pilot customer—someone he could learn from, someone who had complicated technical needs. When he met Bill Kaiser, he knew he had the right guy. Kaiser, an electrical-engineering professor at UCLA, was working with some biologists to develop wireless sensors to be installed in the jungles of Costa Rica.

The mission of their project was to understand the flux of carbon dioxide (CO_2) in a jungle. To make those measurements possible, the NI team faced a demanding set of challenges: The sensors would have to be installed throughout the jungle. They'd need to be battery powered (since outlets are rare in jungles). They'd need to be resistant to the elements. Not to mention they'd need to take accurate measurements and send them reliably.

In trying to meet the biologists' needs, Hanks's team didn't bother building an elegant product. Elegance is expensive and time-consuming. Instead, they cobbled together a prototype using what they had on hand. Hanks compared the result to a "brick in a bucket."

The UCLA biologists wanted to measure CO_2 levels at different heights in the jungle, so the NI team helped them rig up zip lines between trees. The buckets slid along these cables, powered robotically, taking measurements as they moved. "It was like the ESPN football sports cam for the Costa Rican jungle," said Hanks.

The project gave Hanks a crash course in what it would take to serve a cutting-edge customer with sophisticated needs. If the sensors could work for the demanding UCLA project in the jungles of Costa Rica, then they could probably work anywhere.

The ooch boosted Hanks's faith in the technology, and after a few more experiments, he was ready to stop ooching and start leaping. He gained approval to begin developing wireless sensors, a multiyear project that he estimated would require an investment of $2–3 million. The experiments had allowed him to confirm his intuition about wireless sensors, and now he could proceed with greater confidence.

RATHER THAN JUMP HEADFIRST into the wireless market, Hanks and his colleagues decided to dip a toe in. Rather than choose "all" or "nothing," they chose "a little something." That strategy—finding a way to ooch before we leap—is another way we can reality-test our assumptions. When we ooch, we bring real-world experience into our decision.

Think about a student, Steve, who has decided to go to pharmacy school. What makes him think that's a good option? Well, he spent months toying with other possibilities—medical school and even law school—and he eventually decided pharmacy was the best fit. He's always enjoyed chemistry, after all, and he likes the idea of working in health care. He feels like the lifestyle of a pharmacist, with its semireasonable hours and good pay, would suit him well.

But this is pretty thin evidence for such an important decision! Steve is contemplating a minimum time commitment of two years for graduate school, not to mention tens of thousands of dollars in tuition and forgone income. He's placing a huge bet on paltry information. This is a situation that cries out for an ooch, and an obvious one would be *to work in a pharmacy for a few weeks.* He'd be smart to work for free, if need be, to get the job. (Certainly if he can afford several years of school without an income, he can afford to take a monthlong unpaid internship.)

Surely this concept—testing a profession before entering it—sounds obvious. Yet every year hordes of students enroll in graduate schools without ever having run an experiment like that: law students who've never spent a day in a law office and med students who've never spent time in a hospital or clinic. Imagine going to school for three or four years so you can start a career that never suited you! This is a truly terrible decision process, in the same league as an impromptu drunken marriage in Vegas. (Though maybe that's unfair to Vegas, since a hungover annulment might be preferable to a hundred grand in student debt.)

To correct this insanity, the leaders of many graduate schools of physical therapy have begun forcing students to ooch. Hunter College at the City University of New York, for instance, does not admit students unless they have spent at least a hundred hours observing physical therapists at work. That way, all incoming students are guaranteed a basic understanding of the profession they're preparing to enter.

Ooching is a diagnostic, then, a way to reality-test your perceptions. If you think the wireless-sensor market is promising, try it first. If you think you want to be a pharmacist, try it first.

The strategy is useful even for more subtle situations. Some therapists, for instance, have begun using a cousin of ooching to help people reduce anxieties about decisions in their personal and work lives. The therapists Matthew McKay, Martha Davis, and Patrick Fanning wrote about the case of Peggy, "a perfectionist legal secretary" who was terrified of making mistakes on the senior partner's documents. She would spend hours hunting for and correcting mistakes. Then she'd worry that her corrections might have inadvertently created other mistakes, so she'd start the review over again. After a long day at work, she'd take the documents home, spending hours trying to make them flawless.

It was inconceivable to Peggy that she could proof a document only once and be satisfied with her work. The stakes seemed too high. So, in conjunction with her therapists, she created a list of ooches—small, incremental steps that would allow her to reality-test her fears—to see whether the sky would really fall if she eased up on her proofing regimen. If she survived one ooch, she'd move on to the next. Here was the sequence she mapped out:

1.   Take brief home and do three extra passes through it.

2.   Take brief home and do two extra passes.

3. Take brief home and do one extra pass.

4. Stay up to one hour late and leave brief at work. No extra pass.

5. Leave brief at work and go home on time. No extra pass.

At each stage, she experienced intense anxiety, worrying about the dire consequences of her decision for the firm and her own job tenure. But after she completed each stage, she was surprised to discover that things worked out fine, which gave her just enough confidence to attempt the next one. Once she had completed stage five, she *really* pushed her comfort level:

6. Deliberately leave one punctuation error in brief.

7. Deliberately leave one grammatical error.

8. Deliberately leave one spelling error.

According to her therapists, Peggy "found that making small mistakes didn't cause the firm to lose cases, and also didn't get her fired. Nobody even noticed the errors."

She eventually eased her way into an editing routine that was strict but not obsessive. She'd ooched her way into making bolder decisions.

OVER THE PAST SEVERAL years, the notion of exploring options with small experiments has popped up in many different places. Designers talk about "prototyping"; rather than spending six months planning the perfect product, they'll just hack together a quick mock-up and get it in the hands of potential customers. That real-world interaction sparks insights that lead to the next prototype, and the design improves in an iterative fashion.

Meanwhile, health-care leaders advise using "small tests of change": piloting new processes or innovations on a small scale to see if they yield measurable results. For business executives, Jim Collins and Morten Hansen advocate a strategy they call "firing bullets then cannonballs," that is, running small experiments and then doubling down on the ones that work best. (This mirrors National Instruments' "ooch then leap.") Finally, for a book-length treatment of the ooching philosophy, see Peter Sims's book *Little Bets*.

The "ooching" terminology is our favorite, but we wanted to be clear that these groups are all basically saying the same thing: Dip a toe in before you plunge in headfirst. Given the popularity of this concept, and given the clear payoff involved—little bets that can improve large decisions—you might wonder why ooching isn't more instinctive.

The answer is that we tend to be awfully confident about our ability to predict the future. Steve, the budding pharmacy student, doesn't perceive himself to be in a state of confusion. Why would he waste his time getting a free internship when he *knows* pharmacy is for him? (If he drops out after a year, he'll say, "It just wasn't for me," as if that were something he never could have anticipated.) In the design world, the diva product designer just knows, in his gut, that the product is right. The idea of a "quick and dirty prototype" just makes him roll his eyes. *You don't prototype elegance.*

That diva-ish, "I just know in my gut" attitude is inside all of us. We won't want to bother with ooching, because we think we know how things will unfold. And to be fair, if we truly are good at predicting the future, then ooching is indeed a waste of time.

So the key question is: How good are we at prediction?

2.

Early in his career, Phil Tetlock, a professor of psychology and management at the University of Pennsylvania, served on a National Research

Council committee with a sobering mission: to assess what the social sciences might contribute to rescuing civilization from the threat of nuclear war. It was 1984, during the first term of Ronald Reagan, who in a speech the previous year had referred to the Soviet Union as an "evil empire." Political experts felt that the relations between the two nations were "precariously close to the precipice," said Tetlock.

Then, a year later, everything changed. Mikhail Gorbachev became general secretary of the Communist Party and ushered in an era of sweeping reforms. In a few short years, fears of nuclear war came to seem absurd. (A colleague even teased Tetlock about the alarmist report that the committee had produced, saying: "So the sky was not falling.")

To Tetlock's surprise, the experts who had utterly missed the rise of Gorbachev never admitted their failures. They'd say America had gotten lucky, or they'd maintain that their predictions about nuclear disaster "almost" came true (which Tetlock calls a "close-call counterfactual").

Exasperated, Tetlock resolved to design a study that would, for the first time, hold experts' feet to the fire. He recruited 284 experts, people who made their living by "commenting or offering advice on political or economic trends." Almost all of them had a graduate degree and over half had a PhD. Their opinions were eagerly sought; 61% of them had been interviewed by the media.

They were asked to make predictions in their area of expertise. Economists were asked questions like this one:

> With respect to economic performance, should we expect, over the next two years, growth rates in GDP to accelerate, decelerate, or remain about the same?

Political scientists fielded questions like this:

> Do you expect that after the next election in the U.S., the current incumbent/party [i.e., Democrats or Republicans] will lose

control, will retain control with reduced popular support, or will retain control with greater popular support?

As predictions go, these were pretty basic—nothing more strenuous than multiple-choice and fill-in-the-blank questions. Tetlock was trying to create such clear questions that experts would have nowhere to hide if they were wrong. So he began collecting predictions, on a small scale, in the mid-1980s, but when he found out how rich and interesting the data was, his enthusiasm for the project surged. By 2003, he had accumulated 82,361 predictions. Two years later, he published his brilliant analysis in a book called *Expert Political Judgment: How Good Is It? How Can We Know?*

How'd the experts do? They underperformed, to say the least. Even the best forecasters did worse than what Tetlock calls a "crude extrapolation algorithm," a simple computation that takes the base rates and assumes that the trends from the past few years will continue (e.g., predicting that an economy that has grown at an average of 2.8% over the past three years will continue to grow at 2.8%). (If you recall the advice from the past chapter—to trust experts about base rates but not predictions—then Tetlock's finding won't come as a surprise.)

Tetlock delivers the bad news: "Surveying these scores across regions, time periods, and outcome variables . . . *it is impossible to find any domain* in which humans clearly outperformed crude extrapolation algorithms." In other words, if you gave a teenager some base-rate information and a calculator, she could handily outpredict the experts.

Extra education didn't boost accuracy. Tetlock found that PhDs did no better than those without a PhD. Nor did experience: Experts with two decades of experience did no better than newbies. One trait did prove predictive, though: media attention. Specifically, experts who made more media appearances tended to be *worse* predictors. (Anyone who has spent even a single hour watching cable news can readily attest to this.) These are bracing findings. Experts with impeccable credentials underperform a dumb algorithm that merely assumes that what happened last year will happen again this year.

Sadly, pundits aren't the only experts who have prognostication problems. Previous research has shown that psychologists, doctors, engineers, lawyers, and car mechanics are also poor at making predictions. One academic paper that surveys this research has a subtitle that says it all: "How can experts know so much and predict so badly?"

Does this mean that expertise is worthless? No. At one point Tetlock gave a group of Berkeley psychology majors a page of basic factual information about the politics and economies of various countries and asked them to make a similar set of predictions. They did much worse. For instance, when the students proclaimed themselves 100% certain that something would happen, they were wrong 45% of the time. When the experts were completely certain, they were wrong "only" 23% of the time. (Which is still not so great. Imagine if a home pregnancy test had that kind of "certainty.")

So if you're scoring at home, what the data shows is that applied base rates are better than expert predictions, which are better than novice predictions. (And bringing up the rear are all the people who retreated into the woods in the days leading up to the year 2000, predicting the fall of civilization.)

Tetlock's research demands a bit of humility from us when it comes to our predictive abilities. Whenever possible, we should get out of the business of prediction altogether. If you are a software executive, for instance, there's no reason to think it will be easier for you to predict the evolution of a chaotic technology market than it was for political scientists to predict the presidential-election results of a stable Western democracy.

Ooching provides an alternative—a way of discovering reality rather than predicting it.

· · ·

SARAS SARASVATHY, A PROFESSOR at the University of Virginia's Darden School of Business, has found that entrepreneurs are the polar opposite of pundits. One similarity among many entrepreneurs, she said, was an aversion to prediction. "If you give entrepreneurs data that has to do with the future, they just dismiss it," she told *Inc.* magazine. Entrepreneurs don't seem to believe that forecasting is worth the bother: One survey found that 60% of *Inc.* 500 CEOs had not even written business plans before launching their companies.

To study the way entrepreneurs think, Sarasvathy conducted in-depth interviews with 45 founders of companies that ranged in size from $200 million to $6.5 billion. In the interviews, she presented the founders with a case study about a hypothetical start-up and asked how they would make certain critical decisions.

One of the questions was "What kind of market research would you conduct if you were in the entrepreneur's shoes?" In response, one of Sarasvathy's entrepreneurs, trying to be cooperative, began to speculate gamely on the research that he might undertake. Then, in the middle of his answer, he abruptly stopped and reversed course. "I wouldn't do all this research, actually," he said. "I'd just go sell it. I don't believe in market research. Somebody once told me that the only thing you need is a customer. Instead of asking all the questions, I'd try and make some sales."

That's exactly what happened in the late 1990s, in the thick of the dot-com era, when Bill Gross had an idea he wanted to test. Gross, the founder of a start-up incubator called idealab!, got excited about selling cars directly to consumers online. As he envisioned it, customers could search quickly for the exact car they wanted and have it delivered right to their door, thus dodging the car-salesman experience.

He knew, conceptually, that the idea could work, but it was still risky. He could offer a discounted price online, because he wouldn't have to maintain an expensive car lot filled with inventory, but even a discounted car is still a huge purchase to conduct online. Would people really spend $20,000 on a car they'd never test-driven—or even *seen* in person?

To shed some light on the matter, he designed an ooch. He hired a CEO for 90 days and gave him a mission: Sell one car. Andy Zimmerman, the COO of idealab! at the time, recalls what happened:

In the brainstorming session there was a lot of resistance because some thought it was unlikely that people would buy a big-ticket item like that through the Web. At that time no one was selling cars through the Web. So rather than continue debating it, we put up a Web site with a couple of pages that looked like it would allow you to order a car. But actually the message went to a clerk, who looked up the price in the Kelley Blue Book and sent it back to the user. The next morning Bill discovered we had sold three cars. We had to quickly shut down the site because we were offering a heavy discount on the cars.

Rather than continuing to debate, the team ooched and resolved the uncertainty. The ooch led to the founding of CarsDirect.com, which within three years of its founding was the largest auto dealer in the nation.

Sarasvathy, the professor, found that this preference for testing, rather than planning, was one of the most striking differences between entrepreneurs and corporate executives. She said that most corporate executives favor prediction; their belief seems to be, "To the extent that we can predict the future, we can control it." In contrast, though, entrepreneurs favor active testing: "To the extent that we can control the future, we do not need to predict it."

This entrepreneurial reasoning is beginning to penetrate large organizations. Scott Cook, the founder of Intuit, has become so convinced of the virtues of ooching that he now endorses what he calls "leadership by experiment." Leaders, Cook believes, should stop trying to have all the answers and make all the decisions. In a 2011 speech he said, "When the bosses make the decisions, decisions are made by politics, persuasion, and PowerPoint." None of those three *P*'s, Cook notes, ensures that good ideas will triumph. By making decisions through experimentation, the best idea can prove itself.

As an example, Cook cited some tense discussions with a team in India that had been working on a new product for Indian farmers. The idea was that farmers would pay a small subscription fee to receive, via their cell phones, information about the current prices being paid for various crops at different markets. That way, they could take their harvest to the market offering the highest price. Cook and some of his leadership team scoffed at the idea. "I thought it was harebrained," he said. But they agreed to let the team in India test a crude prototype of their idea.

To Cook's surprise, the pilot was a hit, and 13 experiments later, the India team had designed a sophisticated product that was paying dividends for farmers, boosting their income by an average of 20%. For many that extra money was enough to allow them to send their kids to school. By 2012, 325,000 farmers were using the system. That number would have been zero if Scott Cook and other Intuit execs hadn't given the idea a chance to prove itself.

IF YOU CAN OOCH in the corporate world, can you also ooch at home? Gabe Gabrielson thinks so. A real estate broker and dad who lives in San Jose, Gabrielson has a nine-year-old son named Colin. Like many nine-year-olds, Colin frequently finds himself in disagreement with parental policies. In the spring of 2011, for example, he protested Gabe's policy that he get fully dressed before coming down to breakfast. Gabe didn't particularly care what Colin wore at the breakfast table, but he worried that if Colin didn't dress first, he'd wind up late for school. "But I'm more comfortable in my PJs!" Colin argued.

After a few debates that left both of them feeling frustrated, Gabe decided to change strategy. Taking a page out of Scott Cook's playbook, he announced, "Okay, Colin, we'll try it your way for three days. But if you're late to school any of those days, then we go back to the old system."

Colin, amazed by the change in response, aced the trial run. He wore his PJs *and* stayed punctual. As a result, the new practice stuck, and both sides are happier with the outcome. For Gabe, there's less arguing, and for Colin, there's the satisfaction of a successful protest.

Now it's time for a caveat. While we've celebrated the advantages of ooching so far, it's important to point out that ooching is not a decision-making wonder drug. As we've seen, it can be very effective in helping us Reality-Test Our Assumptions, but ooching has one big flaw: It's lousy for situations that require commitment.

Imagine if Colin had been playing baseball and, tired of going to baseball practice after school, wanted to experiment with quitting the team—just missing a few practices to see how it felt. For most parents, that would feel like a breach of obligation: *You committed to play for this team, so you need to see it through.* Or what if the military let people ooch into boot camp, so they could evaluate whether it was good for them? We'd probably have an army of five people.

Ooching is best for situations where we genuinely need more information. It's not intended to enable emotional tiptoeing, in which we ease timidly into decisions that we know are right but might cause us a little pain. Consider two men, Marshall and Jason, who both quit college after two years and now, in their mid-twenties, find that they're getting nowhere in their careers. Marshall knows for sure that he needs a degree to advance in his career, but he puts it off. He doesn't like school very much, so it's always easy to find a reason to delay. For him, ooching—by, say, taking one class per semester—would be a cop-out, a way of stalling. It would also be likely to end poorly. At that pace of course work, he'd need many years to complete his degree, and with each passing year, it would be easier and easier to quit altogether.

Jason, meanwhile, has always been fascinated by marine biology, but he is wise enough to know that he doesn't fully understand what it entails. He *should* ooch. He should shadow a marine biologist for a few hours a week—does the work appeal to him?—and also audit a class or two at a local university to see if he can handle the course work. If, after he ooches, he becomes convinced that marine biology is a good fit, then he should stop ooching and leap headfirst!

Ooching, in short, should be used as a way to speed up the collection of trustworthy information, not as a way to slow down a decision that deserves our full commitment.

3.

In the spring of 1999, Dan Heath interviewed a guy named Rob Crum, who was applying for a job as a graphic designer at Thinkwell, the textbook-publishing firm Dan cofounded. Here's how he remembers the interview process:

> Crum was a young man with close-cropped hair, glasses, and clothes that were awfully hip for an interview. He had earrings and a big nose ring that was shaped roughly like the ones you see on bulls. During the interview, he answered questions haltingly, as if deciding how much he should share, and some of his comments seemed a little sarcastic. I didn't click with him. Over a few weeks, about 10 candidates interviewed for two designer positions, and Rob was toward the bottom of my list.
>
> As a separate part of the interview process, the candidates were asked to complete a work sample—a timed test, conducted in our office, that simulated the kind of work they'd be doing for us (e.g., creating a clean-looking graph for a calculus textbook or illustrating the concept of Bernoulli's principle). A colleague coded these samples with numbers, rather than names, so that we could score them without knowing which candidate had submitted them. When my cofounder and I compared our scores, we were excited to discover that we'd ranked the same sample as number one. Then we asked our colleague whose sample it was. It was Rob Crum's.

We debated for a long time whether to hire Rob. I was skeptical; he didn't seem like he was a "culture fit." (Wasn't that crucial?) My first impression had not been very positive. (Aren't you supposed to trust your instincts?) In the end, though, I agreed to trust the sample and hire him.

Thank goodness I caved. From the beginning, Rob was one of our best people and, after two promotions, he became the art director, overseeing a department of about a dozen artists. He was a gifted designer with a knack for clean and simple visuals, and beyond that, he was a hardworking and conscientious manager. Most embarrassing for me, my first impressions of him had been dead wrong. Ridiculously wrong. Rob turned out to be kind, humble, and sincere. He became a good friend as well as a colleague.

I cringe at how much I struggled with the decision to hire Rob and how much weight I gave to my own flawed first impressions. In retrospect, I wonder why I bothered to interview him at all. I was trying to size him up—to peer into his soul and assess him as a potential colleague. I was trying to predict how good an employee he'd be. But I didn't need to *predict* that! The work sample told me everything I needed to know.

By way of comparison, imagine if the U.S. Olympic track coach used two tests in selecting the men who'd run on the 4x100 relay team. Test 1: Get the man on the track to see how fast he runs. And test 2: Meet him in a conference room and see if he answers questions like a fast runner would.

Note that in most of Corporate America, our hiring process looks more like test 2 than test 1. Let's all slap our foreheads in unison.

Research has found that interviews are less predictive of job performance than work samples, job-knowledge tests, and peer ratings of past job performance. Even a simple intelligence test is substantially more predictive than an interview.

In one study, reported by the psychologist Robyn Dawes, a unique situation emerged that allowed the value of interviews to be assessed. In 1979, the University of Texas Medical School system interviewed the top 800 applicants and scored them on a seven-point scale. These ratings played a key role in the admissions decision, in addition to the students' grades and the quality of their undergraduate schools. UT admitted only students who ranked higher than 350 (out of 800) on the interview.

Then, unexpectedly, the Texas legislature required the medical school to accept 50 more students. Unfortunately, by the time the school was told to admit more students, the only ones still available were the dregs of the interviewees. So the school admitted 50 of these bottom dwellers, who'd ranked between 700 and 800.

Fortunately, no one at the medical school was aware who were the 700s and who were the 100s, so fate had created a perfectly designed horse race between the good interviewees and the lousy ones. The performance difference? Nada. Both groups graduated and received honors at the same rate.

Well, sure, you scoff, the dregs might do fine in the course work, but a good interviewer picks up on social skills! So once the dregs started working in a real hospital, where relationships are critical, it would become easy to sort the socially skilled from the socially skewed.

Nope, didn't happen. Both groups performed equally well in the first year of residency. The interviews seemed to correlate with nothing other than, well, the ability to interview.

With so little proof that interviews work, why do we rely on them so much? Because we all think we're good at interviewing. We are Barbara Walters or Mike Wallace. We leave the interview confident that we've taken the measure of the person. The psychologist Richard Nisbett calls this the "interview illusion": our certainty that we're learning more in an interview than we really are. He points out that, in grad-school admissions, interviews are often taken as seriously as GPA. The absurdity, he says, is that "you and I, looking at a folder or interviewing someone for a half hour, are supposed to be able to form a better impression than one based on three-and-a-half years of the cumulative evaluation of 20 to 40 different professors."

HopeLab, the nonprofit mentioned earlier that uses technology to improve kids' health, has tried to evolve away from interviews. "Often our best interviewees turn out to be our worst performers," said Steve Cole of HopeLab. In response, HopeLab has begun to give potential employees a three-week consulting contract.

Cole said, "It's unbelievably effective. No more fear. How are we going to make our hiring decisions? We make our decisions based on the empirical performance of the employee in our community, on the kinds of jobs that we do. The job market totally prevents you from getting this kind of useful information. So collect your own personal performance data in your own personal context. In some ways it really doesn't matter how well they did in their last job."

Next time you've got a job opening to fill, consider Steve Cole's advice. What's the best way you could give your potential hires a trial run?

TO OOCH IS TO ask, Why *predict* something we can *test*? Why *guess* when we can *know*? Those questions bring us to the end of this section, in which we've been studying strategies for fighting the confirmation bias. The basic problem we face, in analyzing our options, is this: We will usually have an inkling of the one that we want to be the winner, and even the faintest inkling will propel us to gather supportive information—and sometimes *nothing but* supportive information. We cook the books to support our gut instincts.

To avoid that trap, we've got to Reality-Test Our Assumptions. We've seen three strategies for doing that. First, we've got to be diligent about *the way we collect information*, asking disconfirming questions and considering the opposite. Second, we've got to go looking for *the right kinds of information*: zooming out to find base rates, which summarize the experiences of others, and zooming in to get a more nuanced impression of reality. And finally, the ultimate reality-testing is to ooch: to take our options for a spin before we commit.

Where does this leave us? Armed with better information to make a good choice. In making that choice, which is where we're headed next, we face an unlikely obstacle. If you've ever carefully plotted out a budget, using your best information and analysis, and then promptly ditched it when you came across the perfect pair of shoes—or if you've impulsively bought stocks or fearfully dodged a critical relationship conversation—then you've already encountered the person who is often the foremost enemy of a wise decision: *you*.

Next up: what to do about *you*.

CHAPTER SEVEN IN ONE PAGE
Ooch

1. Ooching = running small experiments to test our theories. Rather than jumping in headfirst, we dip a toe in.

   - *John Hanks at NI ooched with wireless sensors in the Costa Rican jungle.*
   - *Physical therapy students volunteer for at least a hundred hours before they enroll.*
   - *Legal secretary Peggy made a conscious decision to ooch away from her obsessive editing habits.*

2. Ooching is particularly useful because we're terrible at predicting the future.

   - *Tetlock's research showed that experts' predictions are worse than simple extrapolations from base rates.*

3. Entrepreneurs ooch naturally. Rather than create business forecasts, they go out and try things.

   - *CarsDirect.com asked: Can we sell one car over the Internet?*
   - *Researcher Sarasvathy on attitudes of successful entrepreneurs: "To the extent that we can control the future, we do not need to predict it."*
   - *Intuit's Scott Cook believes in "leadership by experiment," not by "politics, persuasion, and PowerPoint." The successful India mobile-phone service would have failed a debate.*

4. Caveat: Ooching is counterproductive for situations that require commitment.

   - *The mid-twenties guy who wonders about marine biology should ooch. The guy who knows he needs a degree—but dreads going back—should not.*

5. Common hiring error: We try to *predict* success via interviews. We should ooch instead.

   - *Dan Heath wrongly agonized about whether to hire an obviously qualified artist.*
   - *Studies show that interviews are less diagnostic than work samples, peer ratings, etc. Can you nix the interview and offer a short-term consulting contract?*

6. Why would we ever *predict* when we can *know*?

Widen Your Options

Reality-Test Your Assumptions

Attain Distance Before Deciding

Prepare to Be Wrong

8

Overcome Short-Term Emotion

1.

In 2000, the journalist Chandler Phillips, who'd ghost-written two books about cars, inquired about a writing job at Edmunds.com, a Web site filled with car reviews and sales data (similar to the Kelley Blue Book). To his surprise, the Edmunds.com editors actually pitched *him* on a story idea. One asked him, "How would you feel about an undercover assignment?"

They proposed that Phillips get himself hired as a car salesman, work for three months, and then write about the experience. He'd learn what the auto-sales business looked like from the inside, what kinds of sleazy tricks the salesmen used, and how consumers could survive the sales pressure and walk away with a good deal.

Intrigued by the concept, Phillips accepted the assignment. Soon afterward, he landed himself a job at a car dealership in Los Angeles that was notorious for high-pressure, high-volume sales. His account of the job appears in a piece called "Confessions of a Car Salesman," which has become one of the classic insider accounts of the industry. In the story, Phillips recalls the first time he greeted some customers on the lot:

> As I reached the couple I gave them a cheerful, "Good afternoon!" They turned and, in an instant, I saw the fear on their faces. Fear of me! . . . What were they afraid of? The short answer is, they were afraid they would buy a car. The long answer is that they were afraid they would fall in love with one of these cars, lose their sense of reason and pay too much for it. They were afraid they would be cheated, ripped-off, pressured, hoodwinked, swindled, jacked around, suckered or fleeced. And, as they saw me approaching, all these fears showed on their faces as they blurted out, "We're only looking!"

Phillips quickly learned that the art of car sales was getting customers to stop thinking and start feeling. A fellow salesman advised Phillips that, when he was walking the lot with a customer, he should watch carefully which car drew her attention and then cajole her to sit in the driver's seat. *See how good that feels?* Then, not taking no for an answer, he should go grab the keys and insist she test-drive it. The salesman assured Phillips, "My friend, the feel of the wheel will seal the deal."

Once the customer expressed an interest in buying a car, the manipulation continued. The salesmen would make a show of calling upstairs to see if the car she wanted was still available—adding a false urgency to the process—then announcing the "great news" that, in fact, it was! (Grocery-store managers should try this strategy, rushing up to customers and shouting with delight that the Honey Nut Cheerios in their shopping carts *are still available for purchase!*)

In one of Phillips's first attempted sales, he was working with a couple who were interested in a minivan. Following protocol, he brought in Michael, the assistant sales manager, to meet them. "I noticed that he always began by praising the car the customer was considering, as if they had made a wise decision. He would say something like: 'So you're interested in the minivan. Did you know that's our best-selling vehicle here? Everyone loves it. It can hold seven people, but it drives like a car. You can't go wrong with it. And the prices here are the best in the area.' Later, I would learn how this was called 'raising the customer's excitement level.' If they were excited about the car, they wouldn't be rational when it came to making a deal."

When price negotiations began, the car salesmen played the "good guys," bravely fighting with their managers for a better deal. The key principle was to keep pushing for a deal *that day*, while the customers' emotions were still fresh. "Car salespeople are good at making us feel obligated to buy from them," said Phillips.

IT WAS PRECISELY THE fear of being overcome by emotion that led Andrew Hallam, a Canadian high-school English teacher, to invent his own car-buying process. Hallam was no ordinary teacher. On his meager salary, he scraped and invested his way to becoming a debt-free millionaire in his thirties. In his book, *Millionaire Teacher*, he shared his secrets. Many of them involved truly pioneering ways of being cheap/frugal (half empty/half full). Tired of paying for gas to get to work, he started riding his bike for the *70-mile round-trip*. In the winters, he'd live rent free by house-sitting for couples who'd gone south for the winter. He never turned on the heat—not even when his dad visited—preferring to walk around the house wearing many layers of shirts and sweaters.

So, in 2002, when he was ready to buy a car, Hallam refused to let himself be hoodwinked by car salesmen. He had a healthy fear of their sales prowess. "Imagine wandering onto a car lot. . . . A sharply dressed salesperson will soon be courting you through a variety of makes and models. They could have the very best of intentions, but if you're anything like me, your pulse will race a bit faster as you're shadowed, and the pressure of being shadowed by a slick talker might throw you off. After all, you're on their turf. A minnow like me needs an effective strategy against big, hungry, experienced fish."

His strategy was simple: First, he decided exactly what he wanted in a used car: namely, a Japanese car with a stick shift, original paint, fewer than 80,000 miles, and a walk-out price of less than $3,000. (He didn't want a new paint job because he worried that it might hide rust spots or damage from accidents.) He didn't care about the age or model of the car.

Committed to stick with his criteria, he started calling up car dealerships within a 20-mile radius. Many tried "tempting him into their lairs," encouraging him to visit for a test-drive or a great deal that was *just outside* his budget range. Some scoffed at his budget and tried to talk him upward. "I did have to hold my ground with aggressive sales staff," said Hallam. "But it was a lot easier to do over the telephone than it would have been in person."

Eventually, one dealership called him back. An elderly couple had traded in an older Toyota Tercel with only 30,000 miles on it, and it hadn't yet been cleaned or inspected. They offered to sell it for $3,000, and Hallam accepted. He'd beaten the high-pressure sales game by avoiding it altogether.

HALLAM'S STRATEGY IS A good inspiration for what we're seeking in this section: ways to Attain Distance Before Deciding. So far, we've spent some time thinking about how to generate more options for ourselves by Widening Our Options and how to assess those options by Reality-Testing Our Assumptions. And now it's time to choose.

In theory, this should be the climax of the book, the part where we come to a fork in the road and make the right choice. Actually, we believe this section may be the least important of the four. For one thing, many decisions don't really have a "choice" stage. Often in the course of exploring our options, we find that one of them is so obviously right that we don't deliberate much about it.

Also, you can usually break the logjam on a tough decision by unearthing some new options or some new information. So if you're facing a dilemma and you feel stuck, our first advice is to loop backward in the

WRAP process, using some of the tools we've already encountered: Run the Vanishing Options Test. Find someone who has solved your problem. Look for a way to ooch.

Occasionally, though, we'll encounter a truly tough choice, and that's when we've got to attain distance. It's easy to lose perspective when we're facing a thorny dilemma. Blinded by the particulars of the situation, we'll waffle and agonize, changing our mind from day to day.

Perhaps our worst enemy in resolving these conflicts is short-term emotion, which can be an unreliable adviser. When people share the worst decisions they've made in life, they are often recalling choices made in the grip of visceral emotion: anger, lust, anxiety, greed. Our lives would be very different if we had a dozen "undo" buttons to use in the aftermath of these choices.

But we are not slaves to our emotions. Visceral emotion fades. That's why the folk wisdom advises that when we've got an important decision to make, we should sleep on it. It's sound advice, and we should take it to heart. For many decisions, though, sleep isn't enough. We need strategy.

The millionaire teacher Hallam understood that if he got tempted into the lair of the car salesmen, he might get so enthused that he'd make a foolish purchase. So he plotted a way to avoid it. He added distance before deciding. In his case, the distance was literal—staying far away from the car lots. In general, the distance we need will be emotional. We need to downplay short-term emotion in favor of long-term values and passions.

There's a tool we can use to accomplish this emotion sorting, one invented by Suzy Welch, a business writer for publications such as *Bloomberg Businessweek* and *O* magazine. It's called 10/10/10, and Welch describes it in a book of the same name. To use 10/10/10, we think about our decisions on three different time frames: How will we feel about it 10 minutes from now? How about 10 months from now? How about 10 years from now?

The three time frames provide an elegant way of forcing us to get some distance on our decisions. Consider a conversation we had with a woman named Annie, who was agonizing about her relationship with Karl.* They'd been dating for nine months, and Annie said, "He is a wonderful person and in most ways exactly what I am looking for in a lifelong mate."

She worried, though, that they weren't moving forward in their relationship. Annie, at 36, wanted to have kids and didn't feel she had an unlimited amount of time to cultivate her relationship with Karl, who was 45. After nine months, she still hadn't met Karl's adopted daughter (from his first marriage), and neither person had told the other, "I love you."

Karl's divorce had been horrendous, leaving him gun-shy about another serious relationship. After the divorce, he'd resolved to keep his daughter separate from his dating life. Annie empathized with him, but it hurt her to have a critical part of his life ruled off-limits to her.

When we talked to Annie, she was about to take her first extended vacation with Karl, a road trip up Highway 1 from Los Angeles to Portland. She wondered whether she should "take the next step" during the trip. She knew that Karl was slow to make decisions. ("He's been talking about getting a smartphone for like three years.") Should she be the first to say, "I love you"?

We asked Annie to try the 10/10/10 framework. *Imagine that you resolve right now to tell him, this weekend, that you love him. How would you feel about that decision 10 minutes from now?* "I think I'd be nervous but proud of myself for taking the risk and putting myself out there."

How would you feel about it 10 months from now? "I don't think I'll regret this. I don't. I mean, obviously, I really would like this to work. I think he's great. Nothing ventured, nothing gained, right?"

How about 10 years from now? Annie said that, regardless of how he'd reacted, it probably wouldn't matter very much after a decade. By then they'd either be happily together or she would be in a happy relationship with someone else.

So notice that, according to 10/10/10, this is a pretty easy decision:

---

*Names are disguised because of the personal nature of the story.

Annie should take the initiative. She'd be proud of herself for doing it, and she doesn't think she'd regret it, even if the relationship ultimately didn't work out. But without consciously doing the 10/10/10 analysis, it didn't feel like an easy decision. Those short-term emotions—nervousness, fear, and the dread of a negative response—were a distraction and a deterrent.

We followed up with Annie a few months later to see what had happened on the road trip, and she e-mailed the following:

> I did say "I love you" first. I am definitely trying to change the situation and feel less in limbo about things. . . . Karl hasn't yet said he loves me too, but he's making progress overall (in terms of getting closer to me, being vulnerable, etc.), and I do believe that he loves me and just needs a bit more time to get over his fear of saying it back. . . .
>
> I'm glad that I took the risk and won't regret it even if things don't ultimately work out with Karl. I'd say it's about 80/20 odds right now that Karl and I will stay together past the end of this summer.

10/10/10 helps to level the emotional playing field. What we're feeling now is intense and sharp, while the future feels fuzzier. That discrepancy gives the present too much power, because our present emotions are always in the spotlight. 10/10/10 forces us to shift our spotlights, asking us to imagine a moment 10 months into the future with the same "freshness" that we feel in the present.

That shift can help us to keep our short-term emotions in perspective. It's not that we should ignore our short-term emotions; often they are telling us something useful about what we want in a situation. But we should not let them be the boss of us.

Of course, we don't check our emotions at the door of the office; the same emotion rebalancing is necessary at work. If you've been avoiding a difficult conversation with a coworker, then you're letting short-term emotion rule you. If you commit to have the conversation, then 10 minutes from now you'll probably be anxious, but 10 months from now, won't you be glad you did it? Relieved? Proud?

If you've been chasing a hotshot job candidate, 10 minutes after you decide to extend an offer, you might feel nothing but excitement; 10 months from now, though, will you regret the pay package you're offering her if it makes other employees feel less appreciated? And 10 years from now, will today's hotshot have been flexible enough to change with your business?

To be clear, short-term emotion isn't always the enemy. (In the face of an injustice, it may be appropriate to act on outrage.) Conducting a 10/10/10 analysis doesn't presuppose that the long-term perspective is the right one. It simply ensures that short-term emotion isn't the *only voice at the table.*

2.

The strange words appeared anew every day, printed in capital letters in the corner of the blackboard, right underneath a warning to the cleaning crew to "Please save." The university students who attended the class were mystified by the words, which appeared to be in a foreign language: **SARICIK. RAJECKI. KADIRGA. NANSOMA. ZAJONC.**

On some days, only one of the words appeared; on other days, there would be two or three. "Zajonc," in particular, seemed to appear a lot more than the others. The professor never acknowledged the words. Students were mystified; one later said of the words, "They haunt my dreams."

After the words had been appearing on the blackboard for nine straight weeks, the students received a survey with a list of 14 foreign words on it, and 5 of the 14 words were the ones from the blackboard. They were asked to assess how much they *liked* each word. Rick Crandall, the researcher who designed this study, found that the most-liked words were the ones the students had seen the most. Familiarity doesn't breed contempt, then, but more like contentment.

For decades, psychologists have been studying this phenomenon, called the "mere exposure" principle, which says that people develop a preference for things that are more familiar (i.e., *merely* being *exposed* to something makes us view it more positively).

One of the pioneers in the field was Robert Zajonc (whose name now feels strangely likable . . .). When Zajonc exposed people to various stimuli—nonsense words, Chinese-type characters, photographs of faces—he found that the more they saw the stimuli, the more positive they felt about them.

In a fascinating application of this principle, psychologists studied people's reactions to their own faces. To introduce the study, let's talk about you for a moment. This may sound odd, but you're actually not very familiar with your own face. The face you know well is the one you see in the mirror, which of course is the reverse image from what your loved ones see. Knowing this, some clever researchers developed two different photographs of their subjects' faces: One photo corresponded to their images as seen by everyone else in the world, and the other to their mirror images as seen by them.

As predicted by the mere-exposure principle, the subjects preferred the mirror-image photo, and their loved ones preferred the real-image photo. We like our mirror face better than our real face, because it's more familiar!

The face-flipping finding is harmless enough, though weird and surprising. But what's more troubling is that the mere-exposure principle also extends to our perception of truth. In one experiment, participants were presented with unfamiliar statements, such as "The zipper was invented in Norway," and told explicitly that the statements might or might not be true. When the participants were exposed to a particular statement three times during the experiment, rather than once, they rated it as more truthful. Repetition sparked trust.

This is a sobering thought about our decisions in society and in organizations. All of us, in our work, will naturally absorb a lot of institutional "truth," and chances are that much of it is well proven and trustworthy, but some of it will only *feel true* because it is familiar. As a result, when we make decisions, we might think we're choosing based on evidence, but sometimes that evidence may be ZAJONC—nonsense ideas we've come to like because we've seen them so much.

This mere-exposure principle, then, represents a subtler form of short-term emotion. It's not as vivid as emotions like fear or lust or embarrassment, but it tugs at us nonetheless, and usually it's tugging us *backward*, like a parent grabbing the back of a child's shirt to stop her from running off. A preference for familiar things is necessarily a preference for the status quo.

Compounding this preference for the status quo is another bias called loss aversion, which says that we find losses more painful than gains are pleasant. Imagine that we offer you the chance to play a game. We'll flip a coin; if it turns up heads, you'll win $100, and if it lands on tails, you owe us $50. Would you play? Most people wouldn't, because they are loss averse: Losing $50 is so painful that even a potential gain twice as large doesn't seem sufficient to compensate. Indeed, researchers have found again and again that people act as though losses are from two to four times more painful than gains are pleasurable.

Loss aversion shows up in many different contexts. Consumers who buy expensive electronics often buy warranty coverage that is outrageously overpriced—they might pay $80 for an insurance policy that has an actuarial value of $8. ("Purchase protection" insurance is the most lucrative part of the consumer-electronics business.) They're making a bad economic decision because they fear loss. When they imagine the horror of dropping their fancy new TV on the way home and being forced to buy a new one, that vision is visceral enough to make them overpay.

Research suggests that we set ourselves up for loss aversion almost instantly. In a brilliant series of studies, researchers walked into university classrooms and gave a gift at random to roughly half of the students: a coffee mug with the university's logo. The students who weren't given a mug were asked, "How much would you pay for one of those?" On average, they said $2.87.

But the surprise came from the students who'd received the mugs. Asked at what price they'd sell the mugs, they reported that they couldn't part with them for less than $7.12.

Five minutes earlier, all the students in the class would presumably have valued the mugs at $2.87. Yet the students who received mugs grew attached to them in the span of a few minutes! The perceived pain of giving up their new gift made it unthinkable for them to sell at $2.87.

If loss aversion can kick in quickly for a trivial object like a coffee mug, think about its consequences for a more important decision, like that of someone who is contemplating giving up her seniority (or benefits or social network) to take a new job in another industry. Or someone who must give up a comfortable lifestyle to go back to school.

These studies suggest that organizational decisions will be subject to a powerful emotional distortion. When an organization's leader proposes a change in direction, people will be feeling two things: *Ack, that feels unfamiliar.* (And thus more uncomfortable.) Also: *Ack, we're going to lose what we have today.* When you put these two forces together—the mere-exposure principle and loss aversion—what you get is a powerful bias for the *way things work today.*

THIS STATUS-QUO BIAS MIGHT be most evident in big, bureaucratic institutions. As a stereotype, imagine a middle manager at your state's DMV mumbling, "We've always done it this way." But the status-quo bias is far more prevalent than that. PayPal is one of the most successful (and least DMV-like) companies of the Internet era, yet even its young, innovative founders almost fell prey to the status-quo bias.

In 1998, at age 23, a recent college graduate named Max Levchin cofounded PayPal. At that time, the company had nothing to do with online payments. Rather, it made security software for handheld devices. In college, Levchin had grown fascinated with software and cryptography, and purely as a hobby, he had created some security software for PalmPilots, making it available for free download. After thousands of people downloaded the software, it occurred to him that he might have a business on his hands.

Levchin's freeware had solved an incredibly complex problem. Implementing cryptographic algorithms on a PalmPilot, with its hamster-league 16 MHz processor, was kind of like restocking a large warehouse using men on unicycles—conceptually possible, certainly, but difficult to do elegantly (much less quickly).

Levchin and his cofounder, Peter Thiel, brainstormed about ways to turn Levchin's innovations into a commercial product, and eventually they hit upon the idea of developing software that allowed people to store money on their PalmPilots and exchange it wirelessly. Financial transactions clearly needed the kind of security that Levchin's code provided. When Thiel and Levchin began to talk up their idea, their peers in Silicon Valley loved it. Levchin said, in an interview with Jessica Livingston in her book *Founders at Work*, "The geek crowd was like, 'Wow. This is the future. We want to go to the future. Take us there.' So we got all this attention and were able to raise funding on that story."

In fact, the funding event itself became a story. On the day their first venture-capital deal was due to close, the PayPal team met its investors at a restaurant called Buck's, and the $4.5 million investment was transferred, live, from one PalmPilot to another. Millions of dollars were sailing around the restaurant on infrared beams. The future had come to Buck's. (Levchin had coded around the clock for five straight days to allow the "beaming at Buck's" to take place. After the successful transfer of funds, he fell asleep at the table and woke up hours later next to his partially eaten omelet. Everyone else had left, figuring he could use the rest.)

PayPal's application for PalmPilots became popular, attracting about

300 users a day. To boost interest, Levchin's team built a Web site that showcased a demo version of the handheld product. By early 2000, the team had started to notice something strange: A lot of people were using the Web demo to handle transactions, rather than bothering with the handheld product. In fact, the usage of the Web version was growing faster than that of the handheld version, which Levchin described as "inexplicable, because the handheld device one was cool and the website was just a demo." He added:

> Then all these people from a site called eBay were contacting us and saying, "Can I put your logo in my auction?" And we were like, "Why?" So we told them, "No. Don't do it." So for a while, we were fighting, tooth and nail, crazy eBay people: "Go away, we don't want you."

Eventually, the PayPal team had an "epiphany" and realized that they were crazy to fight off a horde of potential customers. They spent a year developing and refining the Web product, and by the end of 2000, they had given up on the PalmPilot product entirely. It had peaked at 12,000 users. On the Web, meanwhile, their customer base was well over a million strong.

"It was an emotional but completely obvious business decision," said Levchin.

"COMPLETELY OBVIOUS" WOULD SEEM to be the operable phrase here. A choice between 12,000 customers and 1.2 million customers is no choice at all. But if you put yourself in Levchin's shoes, in the context of what we've seen in this chapter, you can understand why this would be a harder choice than it looks.

Think of how you'd feel: Your company was founded on the strength of some amazing cryptographic acrobatics you'd performed, and yet people seem to naively prefer the crude Web demo. It's like an accomplished sculptor who finds that all he can sell is $15 pet rocks.* On top of that, you're experiencing the mere-exposure effect—the comfort of working with the handheld technology you've mastered, not to mention the comfort of dealing with the sophisticated users of handheld devices (who have been asking you, for months, to take them to the future). Your enthusiastic customers on the Web, by contrast, are unfamiliar to you, a bunch of people who sell owl macramé art to one another on eBay. Wouldn't you feel some misgivings about throwing in your lot with them?

Meanwhile, you've got loss aversion kicking in: *We can't give in now! We'll be sacrificing our lead in the handheld market! What if two years from now, the whole world runs on PalmPilots? We'll feel like idiots having sacrificed our strength.* Shouldn't you stick with your original gut instinct that handheld devices are the wave of the future? Shouldn't you be true to your vision?

If you can imagine how these emotions would complicate Levchin's decision, even as he faced a total no-brainer of a choice, then you can surely understand how the same kinds of emotions might tip you to make the wrong call in a more ambiguous situation.

So how can you avoid letting these subtle emotions get the best of you? Get some distance. There are some surprisingly simple ways to do that. Recall the story from the first chapter about Andy Grove at Intel, who agonized about how to handle the company's struggling memory business. The mere-exposure principle pushed him to keep the memory business, since it was so familiar, having endured since Intel's earliest days. Loss aversion, too, weighed in favor of the memory business. How could Intel give up the competitive position it had fought so hard to achieve?

Yet with one question—"What would our successors do?"—Grove managed to add some distance to the decision. By imagining what a clear-eyed replacement CEO would do, Grove sidestepped short-term

---

*Later, of course, PayPal's online "pet rock" became fiendishly complicated as well—particularly PayPal's fraud-detection systems.

emotion and saw the bigger picture. He knew, in an instant, that they should abandon memories in order to focus on the thriving microprocessor business.

It's odd that such a simple question would have such a huge effect. Why does "distance" help so much? A relatively new area of research in psychology, called construal-level theory, shows that with more distance we can see more clearly the most important dimensions of the issue we're facing. In a study by Laura Kray and Richard Gonzalez, students were asked to consider a choice between two jobs:*

> **Job A** represents a career you're well prepared for. You took a lot of courses on the subject in college, though your interest in it was mainly due to pressure from your parents and friends. Your early years in the career would be grueling, but in the long run, it practically guarantees a high-paying job and prestige.

> **Job B** represents a nontraditional career that you've always been interested in. Your expected earnings will be much more modest, but you think the work will be more fulfilling. It will give you profound freedom to discover yourself and to benefit humanity.

> Which job would you choose?

When students were asked to choose for themselves, 66% chose Job B. Later, however, when those same students were asked to advise their best friends about which job to take, 83% recommended Job B. Somehow the choice was clearer when students thought about their best friends than when they thought about themselves. Distance yielded clarity.

Psychologists have come to understand why this happens. In essence, when we're giving advice, we find it easier to focus on the most important factors. So when we are advising a friend, we think, *Job B is going to make her happier and more satisfied over the long term.* It seems relatively

---

*This is a *Cliffs Notes* version of their longer descriptions.

simple. But when we think about ourselves, we let complexity intrude. *Wait, wouldn't it disappoint Dad if I gave up the prestige of Job A? Could I really live with myself if that moron Brian Moloney ended up making more money than me?*

The researchers have found, in essence, that our advice to others tends to hinge on the single most important factor, while our own thinking flits among many variables. When we think of our friends, we see the forest. When we think of ourselves, we get stuck in the trees.*

There's another advantage of the advice we give others. We tend to be wise about counseling people to overlook short-term emotions. For instance, consider a male undergraduate who is facing a dilemma like this one:

> You are thinking of calling a girl from your psychology class whom you like, but you've only talked with her once. You're afraid that she won't remember who you are when you call.
>
> You decide to . . .
>
> (A) Wait until you talk to her more before calling.
>
> (B) Call her.

If you poll a group of guys about this dilemma, their responses are pretty hilarious. Most say they'd wait before calling, but when they're asked what they'd counsel a friend to do in the same situation, they say, *Go for it!*

---

*In these studies, psychologists are not arguing that the forest perspective is the right one. They are simply demonstrating the phenomenon without adding a value judgment. But we want to go a step further and argue that the forest perspective really is the right one, because when people fail to prioritize the most important factor in the decision, their decision gets muddled. When we revel in complexity, we may cycle through our options constantly, changing our minds from day to day. But that kind of mental circling is risky, because it means that our choice may be determined by where we are on the merry-go-round when we're forced to make a final call.

And come on, isn't the right advice in this situation to go for it? Think about it using 10/10/10. On the 10-minute scale, if you decide to call the girl, you might dread every minute leading up to it, and if she seemed perplexed by your call, you might well be embarrassed. But in 10 months, you might have a friend or a girlfriend, or else you will have long since forgotten the whole thing. In 10 years, there's a small chance you're with your soul mate and no chance whatsoever that you're still burning with shame.

All in all, it becomes clear this is a risk worth taking, and it's easier to recognize that truth for other people than for ourselves.

The advice we give others, then, has two big advantages: It naturally prioritizes the most important factors in the decision, and it downplays short-term emotions. That's why, in helping us to break a decision log-jam, the single most effective question may be:

What would I tell my best friend to do in this situation?

It sounds simple, but next time you're stuck on a decision, try it out. You'll be surprised how effectively that question can clarify things. The two of us have talked to many people about thorny personal or professional decisions they were facing, and often they seemed flummoxed about the right thing to do. Then we'd ask them the "best friend" question, and almost always—often within a matter of seconds!—they'd come up with a clear answer. Usually, they were a bit surprised by their own clarity. When we'd ask, "Do you think maybe you should take your own advice?" they'd admit, "Yes, I guess I should."

THE BIAS TO OVERWEIGHT short-term emotions can have paradoxical effects. Sometimes it makes us erratic and too quick to act, as when we react aggressively to a driver who cuts us off on the road. More commonly, though, short-term emotion has the opposite effect, making us slow and timid, reluctant to take action. We see too much complexity and it stymies us. We worry about what we must sacrifice to try something new. We distrust the unfamiliar. Together, these feelings make individuals and organizations biased toward the status quo.

As we've seen throughout the book, though, a bias isn't destiny. We can distance ourselves from these emotions by using some quick mental shifts—the time shifting of 10/10/10 or the perspective shifting of "What would I tell my best friend to do?" Those shifts let us see the outlines of the situation more clearly, and they help ensure that, in times when decisions are difficult, we'll be able to make choices that are wiser and bolder.

CHAPTER EIGHT IN ONE PAGE
Overcome Short-Term Emotion

1. Fleeting emotions tempt us to make decisions that are bad in the long term.

    - *Car salesmen are trained to prey on customers' emotions to close a deal quickly.*

2. To overcome distracting short-term emotions, we need to attain some distance.

    - *Millionaire teacher Andrew Hallam avoided car lots so he could stick to his criteria.*

3. 10/10/10 provides distance by forcing us to consider future emotions as much as present ones.

    - *A 10/10/10 analysis tipped Annie toward saying "I love you" first to Karl.*

4. Our decisions are often altered by two subtle short-term emotions: (1) mere exposure: we like what's familiar to us; and (2) loss aversion: losses are more painful than gains are pleasant.

    - *How many of our organizational truths are ideas that we like merely because they've been repeated a lot?*
    - *Students given a mug won't sell it for less than $7.12, even though five minutes earlier they wouldn't have paid more than $2.87!*

5. Loss aversion + mere exposure = status-quo bias.

    - *PayPal: Ditching the PalmPilot product was a no-brainer—but it didn't feel that way.*

6. We can attain distance by looking at our situation from an observer's perspective.

    - *Andy Grove asked, "What would our successors do?"*
    - *Adding distance highlights what is most important; it allows us to see the forest, not the trees.*

7. Perhaps the most powerful question for resolving personal decisions is "What would I tell my best friend to do in this situation?"

9

Honor Your Core Priorities

1.

In October 2010, 26-year-old Kim Ramirez received a call from a former coworker, and it quickly became clear that he was trying to recruit her to the tech start-up he'd joined. At the time, Ramirez lived in Chicago, working in sales for one of the leading Internet companies, and she wasn't looking for other work. Her friend persisted, offering to set up a lunch for her with the founder of the start-up. Figuring she had nothing to lose, she agreed.

Soon afterward, she met the founder, and she left the meeting captivated. His vision was exciting, and the start-up's small size appealed to her. She found herself agreeing to come visit the company's headquarters in Boston.

The opportunity intrigued her. The position being offered to her, account executive in Chicago, represented a big step up in responsibility from her current job. But she also knew she had a lot to lose. In her current role she had lots of flexibility, which made it easier to spend time with her husband, Josh. (They'd married just a few months earlier, in the summer of 2010.) For the first time in their relationship, their work schedules were in sync; neither one of them traveled every week or worked crazy hours.

In mid-December, she made her visit to Boston. She met with the other account executives and asked about their lifestyle: *How often do you travel? How many hours per week do you work?* She quizzed them about their experience selling the start-up's product: *When people don't buy the product, what are the usual reasons? When customers don't renew their purchases, why is it?* (Notice that she's pushing for disconfirming information.)

She found their answers a bit salesy—they were trying to recruit her, after all—but she liked everyone she met. They paraded her around the office like a visiting celebrity, and she was swept up in the enthusiasm and energy and ambition of the team. "I came away on a very big high," she said.

At the end of her visit, the founder made her a formal job offer, and both the compensation and the role were a substantial step up from her current job. (Not to mention the lottery-ticket excitement of owning start-up stock options.)

After the meeting, she called Josh from the airport in Boston and raved, "This is such an amazing opportunity! I need a new challenge, and I think this is it."

RETURNING FROM THE VISIT, she sent her boss a note about the job offer, feeling she owed him that. He called her immediately, telling her how much her work was valued. A few minutes after that, her boss's boss called, saying she wanted a bit of time to put together a counteroffer. It was just before the Christmas holidays, so Ramirez knew it would likely be a week or two before she'd hear back.

Suddenly, Ramirez was in an enviable situation, with two companies vying for her help, but the choice made her anxious. As the rush of the Boston visit had faded, she'd begun to have doubts. The team had tried to reassure her about the workload, but her intuition was clear: *It's a start-up. You're going to have to work crazy hours. Is it worth it?*

The more she thought about the choice, the less certain she was. During the holidays, she said, "I felt nauseous pretty much every day. . . . I felt like I couldn't get my head straight. I didn't know what I wanted to do."

She started calling her best friends, asking them for advice: *What should I do?* One friend, Gina, was supportive of the start-up opportunity but cautioned Ramirez not to discount the flexibility of her current job. "You've seemed really happy," she said.

Ramirez continued to agonize about the decision until, eventually, she realized why she was stuck: It wasn't just a job decision; it was a values decision. Growing up, she'd always viewed herself as an "ambitious career woman," and from that perspective, the start-up role was a no-brainer. It offered more responsibility and more growth. She'd be able to put her stamp on the place. On the other hand, as she'd gained experience in her career, she'd come to value balance in her life: time with Josh, time with friends, time with family.

For the first time, she was being forced to make a concrete choice between the two visions of herself. She said, "You can just go along for a very long time without calling into question anything like that: What did I value more?"

As she waited for a counteroffer from her current company, the leaders of the start-up were e-mailing and calling her, asking about her decision. She felt awful putting them on hold. Then came the turning point.

One day in late December, she went for a run at her gym. Five miles into the run, it suddenly hit her. A question. *What do I work for? What's the purpose of it?* The thought hit her like a lightning bolt. "I almost fell off the treadmill," she said.

The thoughts came tumbling out: *I work to make enough money to be secure, to travel with Josh, to take a photo class if I want, or to take my sister out for dinner. But if I don't have enough time to do these things that I love, it won't matter that I have more money or responsibility.*

It became crystal clear to her: She needed to stick with her current job. "I felt at peace about it," she said.

A week later, her company came back with a counteroffer that gave her even more peace: She was offered a compensation package almost as good as the start-up's, as well as an assurance that she'd be promoted within a year. On paper, the start-up's offer was still better, but her mind was made up. She politely declined its offer.

Looking back, she marvels that if she hadn't taken the time to let the excitement of the Boston visit fade, she probably would have accepted the job, at unknown cost to her relationships and sense of balance. She reflected on the emotion in the moment: *You know how after you ride a roller coaster, they try to sell you a photo of you shrieking during the ride? You might impulsively buy the photo because you're flush with adrenaline.*

"But the next day," she said, "do you really want that picture? Not really. No one looks good on a roller coaster."

IN MAKING HER DECISION, Kim Ramirez had to distance herself from short-term emotion. She felt euphoric after the Boston visit—"This is such an amazing opportunity!"—but she was wise enough to give herself time to reflect.

Even after she let her feelings settle, though, she was still confused, and this is where we move beyond the principles from the last chapter. What made Ramirez's decision difficult wasn't the distraction of short-term emotion; it was the need to pick between two great options. Ultimately, Ramirez recognized that she couldn't make a decision about the job offer without first considering her preferences in life.

But the phrase "considering her preferences in life," while accurate, is a pretty colorless description of what she experienced. She wasn't rationally cataloging her preferences in the clearheaded way you might compile a weekly to-do list. She agonized. She felt nauseous. Her decision was *loaded with emotion*—it's just that it wasn't visceral emotion, the kind that fades when you "sleep on it."

And this is a critical point: The goal of the WRAP process is not to neutralize emotion. Quite the contrary. When you strip away all the rational mechanics of decision making—the generation of options, the weighing of information—what's left at the core is emotion. *What drives you? What kind of person do you aspire to be? What do you believe is best for your family in the long run?* (Business leaders ask: *What kind of organization do you aspire to run? What's best for your team in the long run?*)

Those are emotional questions—speaking to passions and values and beliefs—and when you answer them, there's no "rational machine" underneath that is generating your perspective. It's just who you are and what you want. The buck stops with emotion.

And because different people will have different answers to those questions, the WRAP process can't tell you the right answer to your dilemma. Two people making the same decision might make polar-opposite choices—and they might both be wise to do so! In the end, for instance, Kim Ramirez decided that she valued the "in balance" vision of herself more than the "ambitious, hard-charging" vision of herself. But another woman might have drawn the opposite conclusion.

All we can aspire to do with the WRAP process is help you make decisions that are good for *you*. In the last chapter, we saw that part of what's "good for you" is distancing yourself from short-term emotions, because they'll often distract you from your long-term aspirations.

Now we'll turn our attention to dilemmas like Ramirez's, in which you find yourself torn between two options, both of which have long-term appeal. An agonizing decision like hers is often a sign of a conflict among "core priorities." We're using the word "core" to capture the sense of long-term emotion we've been discussing; these are priorities that transcend the week or the quarter. For individuals that means long-term goals and aspirations, and for organizations it means the values and capabilities that ensure the long-term health of the enterprise.

How can you ensure that your decisions reflect your core priorities? And, going a step beyond that, how can you actually take the offensive against the less-important tasks that threaten to distract you from them?

2.

In the late 1990s, the nonprofit Interplast struggled with this painful process of prioritization, with two camps on the leadership team divided over the proper mission of the organization. Interplast was founded in 1969 by Donald Laub, a plastic surgeon at Stanford University Medical Center. Laub had been moved by his encounter with Antonio, a 13-year-old boy from Mexico with a cleft lip, a birth defect that divides the upper lip in the middle and interferes with a child's ability to eat and speak. Children with cleft lips are often shunned by their communities. In some parts of the world, a cleft lip is considered a curse or a bad omen.

Separated from his parents and siblings, Antonio was being raised by his grandmother, who didn't allow him to attend school. The tragedy of a case like Antonio's is that the procedure to repair a cleft lip is simple and reliable in the developed world. One doctor has said that "a good surgeon can do a cleft lip in 35 minutes to an hour and get a great result. You can do it with a few instruments which you could carry right in your pocket."

After Laub repaired Antonio's cleft lip at Stanford, Antonio returned to a normal life in Mexico and performed well in school, which made Laub wonder, *How many other kids like Antonio are there in the world, and why can't we help them?* He began to schedule a regular trip down to Mexicali, Mexico, to perform other cleft-lip surgeries.

Over the next two decades, the work expanded beyond Mexico as Interplast attracted more volunteer surgeons and nurses. In fact, by the mid-1990s, Interplast's volunteers were performing several thousand surgeries every year in locations across Latin America and Asia. What had started with one boy had become a global mission.

Interplast's success attracted other ventures, such as Operation Smile and Operation Rainbow, to do similar work. Suddenly Interplast found itself competing for donations and volunteers. Faced with this new competition, as well as the ongoing pressure to grow, Laub became convinced that Interplast needed to bring in a new executive team. So in 1996 he replaced himself, with Susan Hayes joining as president and CEO and David Dingman as chief medical officer.

During her first few years, Hayes found herself navigating a few thorny issues. One sounded simple on the surface: Should surgeons be allowed to bring their family members on trips? Traditionally, this had been a common practice, and it was easy to understand why a surgeon, traveling around the world to do volunteer work, might want to bring her partner or children. The presence of the families had caused problems, though. Sometimes the surgeons would bring their kids into the operating room, an intrusion that would never be permitted in the United States, or else they'd leave their kids in the waiting areas to be babysat by local medical personnel.

Another seemingly small issue was whether medical residents should be allowed to join the trips. A longtime board member and volunteer, Dr. Richard Jobe, said, "It's a tremendously valuable experience for young surgeons, pediatricians, and anesthesiologists to go and experience this." But the presence of the residents sometimes caused problems at the local sites. Local doctors who were eager to learn the procedures often found themselves in line behind the residents, who got most of the surgeon's attention.

These two issues were incredibly contentious on the board. Hayes recalled one board meeting where "we went for six hours talking, arguing, debating, no small amount of rancor in the room, about family members on trips. And the next day, the board met, and we went for another six hours."

As we saw with Kim Ramirez, an agonizing decision is often a sign of a priorities conflict. These "small" issues actually reflected a showdown over two core priorities. In fact, the tension was built right into the organization's mission statement: Interplast resolved "to provide free reconstructive surgery for people in developing nations" and also to "assist host country medical colleagues toward medical independence." In other words, Interplast wanted to perform surgeries *and* to ensure that it no longer needed to perform surgeries.

The new management team, led by Hayes and Dingman, believed that training local personnel was the more critical priority. Interplast should "work itself out of a job," said Hayes, noting that many more kids could be helped by training local surgeons who, over the course of their careers, could perform thousands of operations on needy children. Chief medical officer Dingman agreed, saying, "You create no infrastructure by going with your good equipment and then jumping on a plane and coming home."

Their emphasis on training clashed with Interplast's traditional focus on pleasing its volunteer surgeons, who were the lifeblood of the organization. These surgeons had grown attached to the work; many had returned to the same communities year after year. They had built relationships there. The work had been important for their families too. In one case, a surgeon's son, who had accompanied his father on a mission, was inspired to become a plastic surgeon himself so that he could volunteer for Interplast.

Compared with the concrete heroism of the surgeons—restoring faces in faraway operating rooms—the idea of training local personnel seemed somewhat abstract and uninspiring to some within Interplast. If surgeons were willing to give up their scarce vacation time to volunteer, then shouldn't they have the ability to bring their families along? To some board members, it seemed petty and shortsighted to prohibit it.

The values issue came to a head in the midst of another board meeting where the arguments had resurfaced. One of the newer board members turned to one of the long-serving surgeons and said, "You know, the difference between you and me is you believe the customer is the volunteer surgeon and I believe the customer is the patient."

It was a penetrating comment. Whom did Interplast serve, ultimately? Successful surgeons volunteering their time, or children with cleft lips? After more discussion, a majority of the board members agreed to put a stake in the ground: When there is a conflict, we'll prioritize the welfare of our patients over our surgeons.

"It changed everything," said Hayes. "Because then, when you got into a policy debate with some board or volunteers or the volunteer committees or whatever, you could always go back to our intent. Our intent is to build an organization where our customer is the patient, nobody else." Tough decisions were often resolved by asking, *What's best for the patient here?*

That question pushed Interplast further in the direction of supporting local surgeons. The demand for cleft-lip surgeries was practically infinite; the organization could not attract enough volunteer surgeons to fill the need. By training dozens of local surgeons around the world, though, they could make a permanent difference. Surgeries would be performed every day, rather than a few select weeks per year.

Today, Interplast, which has since been renamed ReSurge International, conducts 80% of its surgeries using local doctors. One Kathmandu-based doctor named Shankar Man Rai, mentored by Interplast, performs 1,000 surgeries annually. Another local partner, Dr. Goran Jovic, runs the only plastic-surgery center in Zambia. ReSurge International supports 11 permanent centers in nine countries, including Bangladesh, Peru, and Ghana.

And every one of those surgeries changes a life. As Hayes said about the struggles of children with cleft lips, "Even if the culture more or less accepts the child, they're not permitted to go to school, because the other children will make fun of them and the other children will be scared of them. And they basically live at home, they don't have any friends, they don't have any economic future, because no one will hire them. . . . So, they lead quiet lives of isolation without a future."

In 90 minutes, she said, "we can simply reverse that future, and reverse that experience."

• • •

ONCE THE LEADERS OF Interplast realized that the patient, rather than the surgeon, was their top priority, they did something important: They *enshrined* that priority, making it known to everyone in the organization, so that it could influence dozens or even hundreds of future decisions. It helped employees navigate decisions between two good options. (*Is allowing medical residents on trips best for the patient? No, because they distract the visiting physicians from training time with local doctors, who will be there all the time for new patients.*)

Of course, this navigational role is supposed to be the whole point of organizational mission statements and values. Unfortunately, the top executives of most organizations have chosen to retreat behind vague endorsements of values like "diversity," "trust," "integrity," and so on (thus taking a bold stand against the haters of integrity!). Only in the most extreme cases are these values sufficient to tip a decision. Certainly no one at Interplast could have resolved the family-member debate by asking which option showed more "integrity."

That's why it's so important to enshrine core priorities, not just cheerlead for generic values. Even the cash-register guy at Hot Dog on a Stick will routinely encounter conflicts among priorities. If a customer drops a corn dog, should he offer a free replacement? (Is his top duty to ensure that the customer is satisfied or that the owner is profitable?) Without clear priorities to draw on, the decision will be made idiosyncratically, depending on the employee's mood at the moment. While we can probably tolerate some randomness when it comes to fumbled hot dogs, alignment is critical in many other situations.

That's why some managers, such as Wayne Roberts, have grown diligent about offering guidelines to inform decisions. Roberts joined Dell in 2000 to lead its push into services. Traditionally, Dell had been a hardware company, selling desktop computers and servers, but its customers frequently needed consulting—say, on the best way to upgrade the PC infrastructure of a whole sales force. Previously, Dell had handled those situations by putting together ad hoc teams of sales engineers. Now Dell was ready to build a serious consulting team, and Roberts was brought in to make it happen.

To start, Roberts pulled together a team of 20 at Dell's headquarters in Round Rock, Texas. Because they were in the same location, it was easy to communicate and make decisions. Soon it grew tougher, as Roberts began to hire consultants in the field. Within 18 months, he was leading a team of over 100 Dell consultants. At any given time, they might be spread across up to 50 customer sites.

As a result, decisions were being made constantly that Roberts couldn't participate in. In many cases, consultants would work at a customer's facility with no direct access to a Dell manager. Sometimes they worked at night to avoid disrupting the customer's employees, which meant that they couldn't call anyone for help either. Roberts said, "I didn't want them to have to consult headquarters all the time. I wanted them to use their judgment."

This is one of the classic tensions of management: You want to encourage people to use their judgment, but you also need your team members' judgments to be correct and consistent. So Roberts began to study his team's most common predicaments, in order to understand what kind of guidance to provide. He found that his consultants struggled with dilemmas like these: Should they agree informally to a small change in scope or wait for headquarters to approve it? Could they approve a $1,000 purchase on their own, or should they seek permission?

Roberts craved a list of simple principles that could serve as guardrails for handling those dilemmas. He sought, as he put it, "guardrails that are wide enough to empower but narrow enough to guide." So he formulated a list of guiding principles that we will call Wayne's Rules.

One of the rules was "Have a bias for action: Do first, apologize later." Consulting projects never go like clockwork; there are always unanticipated changes. In the middle of a project, the customer might request a change that would cost Dell more time and money. That kind of request would tend to make a consultant nervous, because she doesn't want to be blamed if, as a result, the project makes less profit.

The "bias for action" rule was intended to calm those nerves. Roberts knew that most of his team's projects were only one to three weeks long; if his consultants spent a day or two debating about a change, those deliberations would throw off the schedule and potentially delay the start of a project for the next customer. Better to make the change quickly than debate about it. "We're not looking to haggle over $2,000 with legal or procurement," said Roberts. After all, the team's consulting projects were often attached to hardware orders worth hundreds of thousands of dollars.

Another one of Wayne's Rules was: "Be easy to do business with." When the group started, customers' requests for changes had to be documented in a "change order," then submitted for approval to corporate headquarters. With the Dell consultants working nocturnally, this often led to 48-hour delays as customer requests wound their way from the consultant (night) to headquarters (day), back to the consultant (night), and on to the customer (day). Clearly, this was a poor example of "being easy to do business with." Roberts's group worked to push most change-order decisions to the frontline consultant.

Wayne's Rules enshrined the priorities for his group. They ensured that different people would make similar decisions in similar circumstances and do so quickly.

When we identify and enshrine our priorities, our decisions are more consistent and less agonizing.

3.

Maybe this advice sounds too commonsensical: *Define and enshrine your core priorities.* It is not exactly a radical stance. But there are two reasons why it's uncommon to find people who have actually acted on this seemingly basic advice.

First, people rarely establish their priorities until they're forced to. Kim Ramirez didn't decide hers until she confronted a job choice. Interplast had never resolved the tension in its mission statement until two values came directly into opposition. Furthermore, it's easy to imagine how other organizational leaders, facing Interplast-style values conflicts, might escape without pinning down their priorities. A more egotistical CEO might have simply said, *Here's what I've decided*, settling the issue by fiat without articulating anything about priorities. Or a more wishy-washy CEO might have resolved the issue politically, supporting whichever faction she needed to curry favor with that quarter. In short, while priorities are vital for making good decisions, they are also totally voluntary. You will never be required to articulate yours.

Second, establishing priorities is not the same thing as binding yourself to them. In one series of interviews led by William F. Pounds of MIT, managers were asked to share the important problems they were facing in their organizations. Most managers mentioned five to eight problems. Later in the interview, they were asked to describe their activities from the previous week. Pounds shared the punch line that "no manager reported any activity which could be directly associated with the problems he had described." They'd done no work on their core priorities! Urgencies had crowded out priorities.

Parents experience this too: Quality time with your kids gets pushed out by last-minute errands and meal preparations. The problem is that urgencies—the most vivid and immediate circumstances—will always hog our spotlight.

Our calendars are the ultimate scoreboard for our priorities. If forensic analysts confiscated your calendar and e-mail records and Web browsing history for the past six months, what would they conclude are your core priorities? (We worry that ours would include drinking coffee, playing Angry Birds, and carefully deleting junk e-mail on an hourly basis.)

To spend more time on our core priorities (which, surely, is our goal!) necessarily means spending less time on other things. That's why Jim Collins, the author of *Good to Great*, suggests that we create a "stop-doing list." What sparked the idea was a challenge from one of his advisers to consider what he would do if he received two life-changing phone calls. In the first call, he'd learn that he'd inherited $20 million, no strings attached. The second call would inform him that, due to a rare and incurable disease, he had only 10 years left to live.

The adviser asked Collins, "What would you do differently, and, in particular, what would you stop doing?" Since that time, Collins said, he has prepared a "stop-doing" list every year.

It's tempting but naive to pretend that we can make time for everything by multitasking or by working more efficiently. But face it, there's not that much slack in your schedule. An hour spent on one thing is an hour not spent on another. So if you've made a resolution to spend more time with your kids, or to take a college class, or to exercise more, then part of that resolution must be to decide what you're going to stop doing. Make it concrete: Look back over your schedule for the past week and ask yourself, *What, specifically, would I have given up to carve out the extra three or four or five hours that I'll need?*

In organizations, especially, the "stop-doing" list may require some up-front work—10 hours spent now to forestall 30 hours spent later. This approach became a specialty of Captain D. Michael Abrashoff when he took over command of the USS *Benfold*, a guided-missile destroyer commissioned in 1996 for duty in the United States' Pacific Fleet.

As recounted in his book *It's Your Ship*, one of Captain Abrashoff's first moves was to interview every one of the 310 crew members on the ship. He learned their personal histories and their motivations for joining the navy, and he sought their opinions about the *Benfold*: *What do you like most? Least? What would you change if you could?*

Drawing from those conversations, Captain Abrashoff sorted all the jobs performed on the *Benfold* into two lists: List A contained the mission-critical tasks, and List B contained the things that were important but not core, "the dreary, repetitive stuff, such as chipping and painting." After compiling the two lists, Captain Abrashoff declared war on List B.

Perhaps the most dreaded task on List B was painting the ship, so Captain Abrashoff and his sailors hunted for ways to minimize the need for repainting. One sailor suggested replacing the ship's ferrous-metal bolts—which streaked rust down the side of the ship, ruining the paint job—with stainless-steel bolts and nuts.

Captain Abrashoff loved the idea, but his crew quickly hit a roadblock: The navy supply system didn't stock stainless-steel bolts. So, with the admiral's permission, they cleaned out the bolt supplies of many Home Depot and Ace Hardware outlets across San Diego. Once the bolts were installed—a laborious process—the crew was able to wait a full year before the next paint job. (The navy has since adopted the stainless-steel fasteners for every ship.)

Next, his sailors turned their attention to certain metal pieces on the upper parts of the ship, which tended to corrode, requiring scraping and sanding. They discovered a promising new process that might protect the metal from corrosion—it involved baking the metal and then flame-spraying it with a paint that inhibited rust. The process was already used within the navy, but unfortunately, none of the navy's facilities could handle even a fraction of what the *Benfold* crew required.

So again the crew improvised, tracking down a steel-finishing firm in San Diego that could do the whole job for $25,000. It was guaranteed to last for years.

"The sailors never touched a paintbrush again," said Captain Abrashoff. "With more time to learn their jobs, they began boosting readiness indicators all over the ship."

Pruning the List B activities allowed the crew to spend more time enacting battle simulations and learning a wider range of skills. These investments in the crew's capabilities led to an unexpected triumph. At one point, the *Benfold* crew was scheduled for a standard six-month training exercise required by the navy. The sailors were so far ahead of the curve that they passed the final graduation challenge to the training exercise in the first week! In the process, they earned a higher score than any other ship, including those that ended up completing all six months.

The navy higher-ups couldn't bring themselves to call off the exercise completely for the *Benfold* crew, but they did reduce it from six months to two months, allowing the *Benfold* crew to train between port visits to Cabo San Lucas, San Francisco, and Victoria.

Later, the *Benfold* and its crew became a linchpin in U.S. efforts during the Persian Gulf War, tackling some of the toughest assignments and winning praise for their performance.

EVERY DAY, ALL OF us struggle to stay off List B and get back to List A. It's not easy. Remember that MIT study showing that, over the course of a week, managers spent *no time whatsoever* on their core priorities? Peter Bregman, a productivity guru and blogger for the *Harvard Business Review*, recommends a simple trick for dodging this fate. He advises us to set a timer that goes off once every hour, and when it beeps, we should ask ourselves, "Am I doing what I most need to be doing right now?"

He calls this a "productive interruption," one that reminds us of our priorities and aspirations. It spurs us to get back to List A.

What we've seen in this section is that, if we want our choices to honor our priorities, we need to Attain Distance Before Deciding. With some distance, we can quiet short-term emotions and look past the familiarity of the status quo. With some distance, we can surface the priorities conflicts that underlie tough choices. With some distance, we can spot and stamp out lesser priorities that interfere with greater ones.

Attaining distance can be painful, as with the interminable discussions held by the leaders at Interplast. But getting distance doesn't *require* delay or suffering. Sometimes it happens almost instantly. Thanks to a guardrail—*Do first, apologize later*—we know what the right choice is. Thanks to a simple question—*What would I tell my best friend to do in this situation?*—we see the big picture. Thanks to a $10 wristwatch that beeps on the hour, we are more mindful of the priorities we've set for ourselves.

What comes next is the aftermath. We've made a tough decision, and now we must see how it unfolds. Of course, we aren't mere spectators. We can't control the future, but with some forethought, we can shape it. (If you've ever childproofed a room, you get the idea.)

After we've made a decision, we must challenge ourselves to consider two questions: *How can we prepare ourselves for both good and bad outcomes? And how would we know if it were time to reconsider our decision?*

In other words, we must *Prepare to Be Wrong.*

CHAPTER NINE IN ONE PAGE
Honor Your Core Priorities

1. Quieting short-term emotion won't always make a decision easy.

   - *Even when Kim Ramirez's initial excitement faded, she still agonized for weeks.*

2. Agonizing decisions are often a sign of a conflict among your core priorities.

   - *Core priorities: long-term emotional values, goals, aspirations. What kind of person do you want to be? What kind of organization do you want to build?*
   - *The goal is* not *to eliminate emotion. It's to honor the emotions that count.*

3. By identifying and enshrining your core priorities, you make it easier to resolve present and future dilemmas.

   - *At Interplast, recurring, nagging debates were settled when executives determined that the patient was the ultimate "customer."*
   - *"Wayne's Rules" allowed Dell's field consultants to make decisions correctly and consistently.*

4. Establishing your core priorities is, unfortunately, not the same as binding yourself to them.

   - *MIT study: Managers had done no work on their core priorities in the previous week!*

5. To carve out space to pursue our core priorities, we must go on the offense against lesser priorities.

   - *On the USS* Benfold, *the crew actively fought the List B items like repainting (e.g., by using stainless-steel bolts that wouldn't leave rust stains).*
   - *Jim Collins's "stop-doing list": What will you give up so that you have more time to spend on your priorities?*
   - *Bregman's hourly beep: Am I doing what I most need to be doing right now?*

Widen Your Options

Reality-Test Your Assumptions

Attain Distance Before Deciding

Prepare to Be Wrong

10

Bookend the Future

1.

One of Byron Penstock's most prized possessions is a photo of him with his hero, investor Warren Buffett. Penstock can quote Buffett's shareholder letters from decades ago, and when he talks about the value investing approach to stocks, he lights up. You get the feeling that if he had a wallet-sized photo of his portfolio, he'd show it to you.

Penstock didn't always want to be an investor. In his early twenties, he was a minor-league hockey player—a goalie—for the Baltimore Bandits. Later he went into corporate law, a profession he quickly grew to despise. But when he discovered investing, he fell hard. After attending Harvard Business School, he landed his first investing job at RS Investments, a mutual-fund company based in San Francisco. Determined to succeed, Penstock would show up at the office at 3:00 a.m. to get a head start on the day.

In late 2009, Penstock was keeping an eye on the stock of Coinstar, a company with two primary lines of business. The company's original business was its line of Coinstar machines, usually found in grocery stores, which counted customers' coins and gave them a voucher that could be exchanged for bills (while keeping a small percentage of the haul). This coin-counting business was successful and stable, and Coinstar already dominated the market to such an extent that future growth was expected to be slow.

Coinstar's second line of business was Redbox, a line of DVD-renting kiosks. The company's early experiments with Redbox had yielded mixed results, but at one point the executives tried pricing the DVD rentals at $1 per movie per night. Sales exploded. At first, executives weren't sure they could make money at such a low price, but the volume of rentals spiked so dramatically that it compensated for the lower margin. Coinstar suddenly had a fast-growth business on its hands. On the strength of the Redbox business, Coinstar's revenues more than doubled between 2007 and 2008, from $307 million to $762 million. The Redbox kiosks multiplied rapidly, with 13,700 units installed by the end of 2008.

In December 2008, Redbox encountered some trouble. Universal Studios announced that it would no longer sell its DVDs to Redbox. The studio executives were concerned that Redbox threatened Universal's lucrative DVD sales: Why should customers pay $18 to own a DVD when they could watch it anytime for $1?

About nine months later, two more of the biggest Hollywood studios—Warner Bros. and 20th Century Fox—cut off Redbox. Investors started to freak out: How could you run a DVD business without DVDs? As the uncertainty sank in, Coinstar stock plunged by about 25% in a month.

But Penstock knew the panic was overblown. The previous year he had felt blindsided by Universal's announcement, so he'd begun to investigate the relationship between the studios and Redbox. One thing that surprised him was that, after Universal cut off Redbox, the kiosks were still carrying Universal movies such as *Forgetting Sarah Marshall* and *Frost/Nixon*. How was Redbox getting the DVDs?

Some calls to Redbox cleared up the mystery. The drivers who restocked the Redbox kiosks had added a new stop on their routes: Walmart. They were buying Universal's new releases over the counter at Walmart and then loading them into Redbox's machines!

This guerrilla approach seemed absurd at first, but Penstock's research suggested it wasn't crazy. There were no legal issues prohibiting Redbox from buying DVDs over the counter and then renting them.* In fact, Redbox sometimes saved money by buying the DVDs from Walmart, because the new-release DVDs were discounted so heavily.

So when 20th Century Fox and Warner Bros. cut off Redbox, Penstock knew it was a nuisance rather than a catastrophe. Investors were overreacting, he thought. He began to create some financial models to see whether he could make money on the stock.

Penstock uses a method he calls "bookending," which involves estimating two different scenarios: a dire scenario (the lower bookend), where things go badly for a company, and a rosy scenario (the upper bookend), where the company gets a lot of breaks.† For example, suppose Penstock ran the numbers and predicted that, depending on what happened in the global oil markets, the bookends for ExxonMobil stock would be $50 per share and $100 per share:

If the current price for the stock was $90, then he'd never make that investment. It would be too close to the upper bookend, offering a small

---

*Contrary to the threatening-sounding warnings at the beginning of some DVDs, the "first sale" legal doctrine preserves the rights of a buyer to rent, sell, or lend their purchase to others.

†"Dire" and "rosy" scenarios are not intended to be the most extreme outcomes imaginable (e.g., bankruptcy versus an accidental discovery of a universal weight-loss pill), just very negative and very positive outcomes with real-world assumptions.

upside and a huge downside. Even a price right in the middle—$75 per share—would be too risky for Penstock.

"I'm looking for businesses that have a wide range of potential outcomes but a stock price that's to the far left of the range," he said.

Penstock guessed that Coinstar fit the favorable pattern, so he began to analyze the company's bookends. To set the lower bookend, he considered a truly draconian scenario in which executives abandoned the Redbox business altogether, selling all the kiosks and DVDs to a competitor for their replacement value. By Penstock's estimates, that scenario would justify a share price of roughly $21. Then, turning his attention to the upper bookend, Penstock computed that, if the Redbox team had some good fortune, the share price could climb to $62 within two years.

Meanwhile, after the Fox and Warner announcements, the actual stock price had begun to creep downward toward $30 per share. Now Penstock became convinced he had a great investment on his hands: The stock price was moving toward his lower bookend.

And in his eyes, the lower bookend was absurd! In his liquidation scenario, he had assumed that Redbox was just selling its machines, that its locations were worth *nothing*, when in fact Redbox had locked up the best locations in the market, including Walmart and most grocery-store chains. The rights to those locations would be of immense strategic value to competitors, worth much more than the machines. Redbox's customer relationships and its brand were also "free" in the bleak scenario.

Using this analysis, Penstock convinced his colleagues at RS Investments to place a big bet on Coinstar. When the stock hit $28, they began to buy shares. According to his analysis, their downside was $7 and their upside was $34:

In November and December 2009, Penstock's firm bought almost 1.4 million shares at an average price of $26.70.

In the months that followed, he monitored the stock anxiously, and the price began to tick up. Investors grew increasingly confident that Coinstar wasn't in serious danger. The stock price cracked $30 and continued to climb. By the fall of 2010, the stock price was bouncing around in the forties. Penstock was elated; his firm had made more than $25 million on his analysis.

As the price rose, though, he grew less confident in the investment. The price was inching steadily toward the upper bookend he had created.

By mid-October, Penstock had concluded that the stock was no longer a good bet, and he recommended that the firm sell its holdings, and it did, at an average price of $46.54. The firm had scored a return of about 75% in 10 months.

Penstock's strategy of bookending is atypical of investors. Many investors, he said, try to make a precise prediction of what a stock is "really worth." It's sometimes called a "target price," and if the target price is higher than the current price, investors decide they should buy. Penstock rejects this kind of thinking. His belief is that computing a precise target stock price reflects a false confidence about the future.

He said, "It's my job as an investor to think about the future, but the future is uncertain, so my investments can't hinge on knowing the future. I look for situations where the bookends suggest that I can invest wisely without knowing exactly what the future holds."

He calls this "low-IQ investing."

OUR PURPOSE IN OFFERING this example is not to encourage you to run Penstock's game plan as you invest your retirement dollars. Investing in individual stocks is a losing proposition for most people. For one thing, you're competing against full-time professionals like Penstock who are waking up at 3:00 a.m. to work on their analyses—and even so, 96% of them manage to underperform a simple index fund. (See the endnotes if you want our full soapbox rant on why your retirement dollars are better off in index funds than in individual stocks or mutual funds.)

We offer the example because we *do* want to recommend Penstock's approach to life decisions. His humility about his predictive abilities is critical to making a good decision. What if we, like Penstock, could make wise choices without knowing exactly what the future holds?

To do this we have to Prepare to Be Wrong about our predictions of the future—that's the *P* in the WRAP model. We need to stretch our sense of what the future might bring, considering many possibilities, both good and bad, which is exactly the discipline reflected in Penstock's bookending philosophy.

Penstock developed his procedure intuitively, but there's research evidence that backs up his approach. In one study, researchers Jack Soll and Joshua Klayman asked participants to make a series of guesses. As one example, they were asked to estimate the average box-office receipts of movies in the 1990s that featured Angelina Jolie. They specified a range that was 80% sure to contain the true value (e.g., *I'm 80% certain that the average Angelina Jolie film grossed between $30 million and $100 million*). At 80% confidence, the participants should have been surprised only

20% of the time, but it turned out they were overconfident: The actual box-office average fell outside of their ranges 61% of the time.

What's interesting is that people's estimates grew much more accurate when they were asked to explicitly consider the high and low ends of the range.* The researchers suggested that by considering each bookend separately, people tap different pools of knowledge. So if you think about why Jolie's average films might be low grossing, you might remember some of the low-budget indie films she made in the mid-1990s, when she was a relatively unknown actress. Or if you're thinking about why her average film might gross more than $100 million, you might recall *Lara Croft: Tomb Raider*, which was such a big hit that it might inflate the average.

The actual answer is that Jolie's average box office in the 1990s was only $13 million. (*Lara Croft: Tomb Raider*, with a box office of $131 million, didn't appear until 2001.) Overall, the researchers found that when people did not consider the bookends, they produced ranges that were only 45% as wide as they should have been (when compared to a statistically optimal model). When they were asked to consider the bookends, their guesses improved to 70% of optimal, and when they also added their best guess in the middle (which tapped a third pool of knowledge), their ranges improved to 96% of the optimal size, only 4% away from perfection.

When we think about the extremes, we stretch our sense of what's possible, and that expanded range better reflects reality. Penstock and other investors use that expanded range to make smart bets on stocks. But the rest of us aren't *betting* on the outcome—we're living it. So we need to be prepared to deal with any outcome between the two bookends we've charted.

To prepare for the lower bookend, we need the equivalent of insurance. If you buy a new car, you'll increase the amount of collision insur-

---

*The researchers asked questions such as "What's a high value for Angelina Jolie's average box office that you think has only a 10% chance of being exceeded?" and "What's a lower boundary so low that there's only a 10% chance of the real number falling below it?"

ance you buy, so that if you wreck your car, you can replace it. (Have you thought about how to "insure" your organization against a wreck of a new hire?) For the upper bookend, we need a plan for dealing with un-expected success. Think of a boutique designer who finds out that Oprah will be endorsing her product soon. Will she be ready to handle the huge spike in demand? When we bookend the future, we anticipate and plan for the best outcomes as well as the worst.

In the absence of bookending, our spotlights will lock on to our "best guess" of how the future will unfold, like investors trying to esti-mate the "true" target stock price of a company:

Even if we have a pretty good guess about the future, the research on overconfidence suggests that we'll be wrong more often than we think. The future isn't a point; it's a range:

How can we learn to sweep a broader landscape with our spot-lights—to attend to the bookend of possibilities ahead? Psychologists have actually created some simple tools for exactly this purpose. Try the following thought experiment:

How likely is it that an Asian American will be elected president of the United States in November 2020? Jot down some reasons why this might happen.

That scenario was adapted from the work of decision researchers J. Edward Russo and Paul J. H. Schoemaker. Now try the second part of the thought experiment, which is similar but has a twist. Pay attention to how it "feels" to think about this one:

It is November 2020 and something historic has just happened: The United States has just elected its first Asian American president. Think about all the reasons why this might have happened.

Russo and Schoemaker have found that when people adopt the second style of thinking—using "prospective hindsight" to work backward from a certain future—they are better at generating explanations for why the event might happen. You may have experienced this yourself. The second scenario feels a bit more concrete, offering firmer cognitive footholds.

In the original study of prospective hindsight, researchers presented participants with a description of an employee who'd just started a new job, including a quick sketch of the relevant company and industry. Half the participants were asked to generate plausible reasons why the employee *might* quit six months from now. On average, they generated 3.5 reasons each.

The other half were told to use the hindsight approach: *Imagine that it's six months from now and the employee has just quit. Why did he quit?* In this group, participants generated 4.4 reasons apiece, about 25% more than the other group, and their reasons tended to be more specific and relevant to the scenario presented. Prospective hindsight seems to spur more insights because it forces us to fill in the blanks between today and a certain future event (as opposed to the slipperier process of speculating about an event that may or may not happen).

The psychologist Gary Klein, inspired by this research, devised a method for testing decisions that he calls the "premortem." A postmortem analysis begins after a death and asks, "What caused it?" A premortem, by contrast, imagines the future "death" of a project and asks,

"What killed it?" A team running a premortem analysis starts by assuming a bleak future: *Okay, it's 12 months from now, and our project was a total fiasco. It blew up in our faces. Why did it fail?*

Everyone on the team takes a few minutes to write down every conceivable reason for the project's failure. Then the team leader goes around the table, asking each person to share a single reason, until all the ideas have been shared. Once all the threats have been surfaced, the project team can Prepare to Be Wrong by adapting its plans to forestall as many of the negative scenarios as possible. The premortem is, in essence, a way of charting out the lower bookend of future possibilities and plotting ways to avoid ending up there.

2.

A variation of this premortem strategy was used by the 100,000 Homes Campaign, an effort to house 100,000 chronically homeless individuals. The campaign, with its unprecedented scale, was orchestrated by a small organization of a few dozen people called Community Solutions. Its leader was Becky Kanis, a woman who combined the passion of an activist with the discipline of a soldier—she was a West Point graduate who'd spent nine years as an army officer.

In planning the campaign, Kanis and her colleagues sought advice from experts like Christina Gunther-Murphy, an executive who had worked on a similar campaign in health care to save 100,000 lives by changing medical practices. (*Find someone who has solved your problem.*) Gunther-Murphy introduced them to a technique called "failure mode and effect analysis" (FMEA), a precursor to the premortem that has been used for decades in the military and government.

In an FMEA, team members identify what could go wrong at every step of their plans, and for each potential failure they ask two questions: "How likely is it?" and "How severe would the consequences be?" After assigning a score from 1 to 10 for each variable, they multiply the two numbers to get a total. The highest totals—the most severe potential failures—get the most attention.*

At a spring 2010 meeting of the 100,000 Homes team, an FMEA revealed a number of possible stumbling blocks. One of them was particularly troubling: *What if our approach violates laws about fair housing?*

A staffer named Beth Sandor described a tricky situation in Los Angeles: A developer had refused to give preference to a homeless person for an open subsidized-housing slot in the building he owned. He had a waiting list for the unit, and he argued that letting the homeless man skip to the top of the line would be an illegal act of favoritism that would put his federal subsidies at risk.

Sandor's response was that the homeless person deserved housing soonest because he was in danger of dying if he wasn't sheltered quickly. (The 100,000 Homes staffers prioritized the most vulnerable homeless people for housing.) She argued, "Look, everyone on your waiting list has *an address.* If they've had an address for the five years they've spent on the list, then they can't be the neediest people."

After Sandor shared her experience at the meeting, others piped up with similar stories. When they conducted the FMEA, the housing issue scored as one of the highest potential threats. If landlords wouldn't move quickly to place the homeless, the campaign would be in trouble. The group brainstormed about how to prevent the problem.

One woman on the team knew a lawyer who was a nationally recognized expert on fair-housing law, and the team agreed to seek his opinion. He warned them that he'd need to research the matter and that he couldn't guarantee that his opinion would support them. Nonetheless, the team agreed to proceed, reasoning that if the law was against them, it was something they needed to know sooner rather than later.

A few months later, the attorney came back with a strong legal brief

---

*Note that this is how the Community Solutions team implements FMEA. Other flavors of FMEA include a third question, "How likely is it that we'll be unable to detect the failure if it happens?" and multiply the three variables together.

demonstrating that the team's work did not violate the fair-housing laws.

Since then, the brief has essentially eliminated the issue. "Now the issue never comes up anymore," said Sandor. "It allowed us to move on."

Thanks to its premortem, the team was able to surface and eliminate a threat to the campaign. And that allowed them to spend less time worrying about legal issues and more time finding shelter for the most vulnerable people in the country.

One of those people was Myron, a veteran who was living on the streets of Phoenix. Myron and his brother Howard had been homeless for about 30 years. Then, on a brutally hot night in July 2009, Howard died in his brother's arms. Myron cradled him on a park bench, crying, until help arrived.

"He didn't care about anything after his brother passed," said Mattie Lord, the project lead at Project H3, a local affiliate of the 100,000 Homes Campaign. Lord and her colleagues met Myron when they were surveying the homeless population of Phoenix. They rated Myron one of the 15 most vulnerable people on the streets of Phoenix. Lord said, "We are going to house this man, come hell or high water."

Other local agencies scoffed at the idea that Myron could get off the streets. He was disagreeable, cantankerous, and depressed. He had an alcohol problem. He hated bureaucrats. But within three months, Lord and her team had located an apartment for him. When they handed him the keys, Myron couldn't believe it. It would be his first home in over three decades.

Move-in day was emotional. The campaign workers cooked Myron his favorite meal, spaghetti, and as a housewarming gift, they gave him a framed picture of him with his brother. It brought Myron to tears. He immediately took it to the bedroom and placed it beside his bed.

Having his own home transformed Myron. He no longer had to focus all his energies on survival. He reconnected with his family, going to visit his sister, whom he hadn't seen in many years. "People who knew Myron before are in disbelief," said Lord. "He is happy."

Myron grew very sick in the winter of 2010, and he was relocated to the state veterans' home. He has since recovered, though he is still frail. Lord describes him as a "social butterfly" who knows everything about people's kids and relatives. He still talks to his family every week.

Lord takes special pride in Myron's new life. "He was the case everybody said, 'It can't be done.' We proved them wrong."

Across the country, people like Myron are being given keys to new homes—and new lives. By the summer of 2012, communities participating in the 100,000 Homes Campaign had placed 20,000 homeless people in homes.

Months prior, when they'd housed the ten thousandth homeless person, the team held a celebration, and Kanis, the West Point graduate who leads the campaign, actually had the number tattooed on her arm. But she deliberately put the comma in the wrong place: 100,00.

She told her team, "I want to show you my full faith and confidence that together we will help 100,000 people move off the streets for good!" And when they succeed, Kanis said, she'll add that final *0* to her tattoo: 100,000.

THE FMEA AND ITS sister technique, the premortem, stop people from focusing on a single, usually optimistic, guess about how the world will unfold and instead compel them to pay attention to the uncertainty surrounding the guess. The effort it takes to explore the full spectrum of possibilities and to prepare for the worst possible scenarios acts powerfully to counteract overconfidence.

Our judgment can be wrong in multiple ways. We might err by failing to consider the problems we could encounter, and that's why we need premortems. However, we might also err by failing to prepare for unexpectedly *good* outcomes. When we bookend the future, it's important to consider the upside as well as the downside.

That's why, in addition to running a premortem, we need to run a "preparade." A preparade asks us to consider success: *Let's say it's a year from now and our decision has been a wild success. It's so great that there's going to be a parade in our honor. Given that future, how do we ensure that we're ready for it?*

In 1977, a small entrepreneurial company called Minnetonka found itself with a potential blockbuster on its hands. Minnetonka was known for niche novelty items such as bubble baths, scented candles, and flavored lip balm, but a new product was showing extraordinary potential. It was called Softsoap: a liquid soap dispensed from a plastic hand pump, intended to be used for hand washing at home.

At the time, most people used bars of soap to wash their hands, and the bar soap market was dominated by mature brands such as Dial, Ivory, and Zest. The companies behind them battled fiercely for every percentage point of market share. Yet Minnetonka's pilot testing, conducted in small markets under the radar of the bar soap manufacturers, found that Softsoap rapidly captured 4% to 9% market share within a short time.

Having ooched successfully with these pilot tests in multiple markets, Minnetonka's executives were ready to leap. It was time for a national product rollout.

Were they ready? The company's prior products—the lip balms and bubble baths—never had the market-shifting potential of Softsoap. The executives began to discuss how they could prepare for the huge success they thought might be possible.

The supply chain was a critical consideration. If consumers responded nationally with the same enthusiasm they'd shown in the local tests, then Minnetonka would need to make *millions* of bottles of Softsoap. Unfortunately, there were only two suppliers of the kind of plastic pumps that could be used to dispense the liquid soap. What if they couldn't get enough pumps to satisfy the consumer demand?

To prepare for a world that might unfold in this favorable way, Minnetonka's executives took a bold step. They signed options contracts with *both* suppliers, for a total of up to 100 million units. They'd effectively locked up the world's entire supply of plastic pumps for a period of 18 to 24 months.

By conducting a preparade, the company's executives ensured that Minnetonka would have *the ability to handle success*. The clever plastic-pump contracts kept the big bar soap manufacturers out of the market for two years, and by the time they eventually entered the market, Softsoap had created a dominant position for itself that would last for decades.

PREMORTEMS AND PREPARADES ARE most effective at tackling problems and opportunities that can be reasonably foreseen. There's another technique that is useful in guarding against the unknown. It's surprisingly simple, in fact: Just *assume* that you're being overconfident and give yourself a healthy margin of error.

Many engineers, for example, have learned to build a "safety factor" into their projects. Safety factors emerged from engineers' healthy paranoia about defects, since their computations can have life-and-death consequences: How much concrete is needed to support a dam? How strong do the materials in an airplane wing need to be?

Engineers can compute the appropriate numbers using highly sophisticated tools, but these numbers have a false certainty about them. One of the variables could change in a completely unexpected way. Suppose, as a far-fetched example, that a commercial airplane pilot plowed through a flock of Canadian geese, disabling his two engines and necessitating an emergency landing on a river. That impact would put huge, unexpected strain on the airplane wings. (This "far-fetched" example really happened, of course. In 2009, pilot Chesley "Sully" Sullenberger landed the plane safely in the Hudson River. Amazingly, no lives were lost, thanks to his skill and, also, the engineers' safety factors!)

In a more everyday example, engineers might compute, in designing a ladder, that it needed to be able to support 400 pounds, but then they'd multiply that number by a safety factor of, say, six. As a result, the ladder would be built to withstand 2,400 pounds; that way, if eight huge men (of questionable judgment) someday decide to climb the ladder together, it will hold. No one will get hurt and no one will get sued.

The safety factor varies by domain. For the space shuttle's ground equipment, it's four. For an elevator cable, it's eleven. (So next time you're in a crowded elevator, doing an anxious computation of group weight, just relax.)

What's remarkable here is the odd mixture of scientific precision and crude guesstimation. In computing the required strength of an elevator cable, engineers use incredibly sophisticated algorithms and tools. Then, having found the best answer that science has to offer, they take that answer and multiply it by the semiarbitrary number of eleven. It's like an exercise that a third grader would do in a math workbook.

But this crude approach saves lives, and it exhibits an admirable humility: *We engineers know that we'll be prone to overconfidence, and it's not possible to render ourselves immune to it, so why not just correct for it?*

The same principle works in less risky contexts as well. Software companies have evolved their own safety factors to pad their project deadlines. Developers at Microsoft, confident in their programming prowess, will often grossly underestimate the amount of time required to reach a goal. So the leaders of the software projects, aware of the developers' overconfidence, have learned to tack on a "buffer" factor equal to, say, 30% of the schedule. For more complex projects, such as an operating system, the buffer might reach 50%. (Though given past OS delays, that buffer factor might need its own buffer factor.)

3.

Notice that these corrections for overconfidence have in common a kind of ego-checking, balloon-bursting effect. We run a premortem, which forces us to ask, "Our precious project has flopped. Why?" Or we add buffer time to a schedule because we've learned to distrust our own optimism. This ego checking is good for us; it helps to stack the deck in our favor.

Often, though, we instinctively do the opposite. When it comes to hiring a worker, for instance, the process is all about positivity and ego inflation. The worker presents a glowing portrait of her talents, and the employer presents a rosy portrait of the job. It's like dating; the dirty laundry isn't aired until much later. Because of this false sunniness, it can be difficult for both parties, employer and candidate alike, to get an accurate picture of the choice they're making: "Can I tolerate this job?" "Can we tolerate this employee?"

The cost of a mismatch is high. For entry-level jobs—call-center representatives, food-service workers, and so on—it's not uncommon for annual turnover to be as high as 130%. This means that if a call center has 100 jobs, then the HR team would need to hire 130 people every single year to keep the positions filled. That constant rotation causes enormous waste for companies, who must recruit and train workers who end up leaving in a few weeks. Not to mention the unnecessary misery for employees, who find themselves in environments they can't abide.

In response to this problem, some companies are experimenting with a new approach to hiring—a balloon-bursting approach. Consider a Web site that was created in 2011 to allow people to apply for a call-center position. It exposes applicants to a set of cautions and warnings: "You will interact with frustrated and demanding customers every day. You will be expected to provide superb customer service and be friendly under stressful conditions."

After reading some sobering information about compensation— "You will receive pay only for the time you spend taking customer calls!"—applicants are required to listen to an audio clip labeled "Sample Challenging Call," taken from an actual call:

CALL-CENTER REP: My name is Jose. May I have your first and last name, please?

CUSTOMER: Yes, this is [name censored].

JOSE: Thank you. How may I help you today, please?

CUSTOMER: Yeah, we've had this problem before. This is a complaint about billing and about overbilling and about data-usage charges. If you would, could you bring up my bill summary?

JOSE: Okay, yes, sir.

CUSTOMER: You'll see that under usage charges, it says "Data: $1.10." You all have charged us for data before, a couple of times, and we've called each time and said that we *don't use data* on our phones. We've actually even had data *disabled* on our phones! And I know for a fact that you sneak these charges in . . . because people don't call about $1.10, because it's just $1.10. And you sneak this into people's bills and everybody pays it. But this is criminal! It's awful! [voice getting angrier] I want this $1.10 removed from my bill, and I NEVER WANT TO BE CHARGED FOR DATA USAGE AGAIN!

After listening to the irate customer, applicants are asked: "Are you sure you will be able to tolerate on a daily basis assisting customers who are rude, frustrated, or confused?"

On subsequent pages, applicants are warned about the difficult IT system; the stringent "on-time" policy; the requirement to work overtime and holidays; the discomfort of sharing a desk with people who work other shifts (which means they won't be able to hang photos or otherwise humanize their work space); and the need to find a reliable way to get to work other than public transportation, since they will frequently work after the city buses have shut down.

Relative to any normal hiring process, this is a serious buzz kill. It's like a guy kicking off a first date by declaring, "I should tell you up front that I'm broke and depressed; my belly roll strongly suggests a future as a diabetic; and, like an infant, my moods tend to vary directly with my digestion. Shall we head out to dinner?"

The call center's "warts and all" hiring approach is called a "realistic job preview." Max Simkoff, the CEO of Evolv, the company that built the realistic job preview described above, said that many hiring professionals don't understand the power of setting expectations. In a typical call center, Simkoff said, "there are seats that turn over three or four times a year. So then the call-center people immediately react: 'We're hiring the wrong people. We need to revisit our competency model.' And we say, 'No, you're actually not doing a good job of explaining the job situation to the people that you hire.'"

Realistic job previews have been proven, by a large research literature, to reduce turnover. Simkoff shared one of Evolv's own case studies concerning a call center that had been hiring roughly 5,400 people per year. After implementing realistic job previews, new hires dropped by more than 10% over the next 12 months: 572 fewer hires, with a cumulative savings of about $1.6 million.

The idea has been tried with a host of professions, including grocery baggers, customs inspectors, nurses, army and navy recruits, life-insurance agents, bank tellers, and hotel desk clerks. Analyzing 40 different studies of realistic job previews, researcher Jean Phillips found that, as in the case of the call center, the practice consistently reduces turnover. But the reason why may be different from what you'd guess.

You might assume that realistic job previews succeed by scaring away people who couldn't have handled the job. That's true to some extent, but it's a relatively small factor. In fact, in some of the studies Phillips reviewed, people exposed to the job preview were no more likely to drop out of the recruitment process than other recruits who didn't get the full, unvarnished truth.

Instead, the success of realistic job previews seems to be driven by what Phillips calls a "vaccination" effect. By exposing people to a "small dose of organizational reality" before they start work, you vaccinate them against shock and disappointment. So at the call center, when a new customer-service rep finds herself on a call with an angry guy, she isn't taken aback. She was expecting it.

This explains an otherwise puzzling fact: Realistic job previews have been shown to reduce turnover *even when they are given after the employee is hired.* The previews are not just helping the "wrong" people opt out of the hiring process; they're helping all people cope better when they confront the inevitable difficulties of the role. In fact, realistic job previews not only reduce turnover but also increase job satisfaction.*

As a manager, you could use a realistic job preview to help "vaccinate" the new hires at your organization. You might also use one yourself to prepare for decisions you've made. If you've got a product launch looming in three months, for example, wouldn't it be worth getting a "job preview" of the launch period from someone who's handled a similar project? Or, in another domain, what would happen to college dropout rates if all freshmen got a "realistic job preview" from senior students describing their toughest moments in college?

REALISTIC JOB PREVIEWS TRIGGER our coping mechanisms, but they also spark us to think about how we'll react. In other words, we don't just think about tough situations; we think about how we'll respond when we encounter them.

A similar "mental simulation" approach is used by counselors specializing in cognitive behavioral therapy (CBT). CBT emphasizes the value of mentally rehearsing how to respond in difficult interpersonal situations.

In the book *Thoughts and Feelings: Taking Control of Your Moods and Your Life*, therapists Matthew McKay, Martha Davis, and Patrick Fanning recount the case of Sandra, who wanted to ask her boss for a raise but was very nervous about it. Sandra wrote out a script that represented

---

*Parenthetically, this is why the realistic job preview fits in the "Prepare to Be Wrong" part of the WRAP process: because it's not primarily a tool designed to help people decide which option to pick. As mentioned before, Phillips found that applicants only rarely changed their decision and withdrew after being exposed to the preview. Their decision had been made: *I want this job.* But what the realistic job preview does, via the vaccination effect, is improve the odds that the person's decision will succeed, that they'll stay in the job and be happy with it.

the way she wanted to behave—and also anticipated how she would respond if the situation took a wrong turn.

In the initial part of her mental script, she imagines herself approaching her boss and asking for 15 minutes of his time to discuss a raise. He gets a little evasive, but she tells herself to "be persistent" and eventually pins him down on a meeting time.

Later, when the time comes, she pictures herself walking into his office and sinking into the blue chair where guests are always asked to sit. She imagines having to turn the conversation from casual small talk to her request: a 10% raise. She explains that she's been stuck at the same salary level for a long time, despite her track record of good performance.

Now we pick up on her imagined script in her own words:

- He looks displeased and replies that the department isn't doing well and we all have to learn to live with less.

- I think, "I deserve this. Don't give up."

- I point out that it would be more cost-effective to give me a raise than to train a new employee to take over my responsibilities.

- He continues to be negative.

- I take a deep breath and remind myself to be strong and calm, and that I deserve the raise.

- I say that if I can't get the raise I deserve, I'll start looking for a new job.

- He offers a 5% raise.

- I stick to my demand and remind myself and him that I'm competent and experienced.

- He eventually agrees after seeing that I won't be budged.

- I thank him, make sure to ask when the raise goes into effect, and walk out of his office feeling elated.

Note that Sandra is preparing for various ways the interaction could go wrong. She imagines her boss looking "displeased" with her request.

When he invokes social pressure—"we all have to learn to live with less"—she rallies herself to keep pressing her argument, noting that it is "more cost-effective to give me a raise than to train a new employee."

She practiced this scene four times in her imagination and then asked her husband to role-play the "tough boss." Finally, after all of these preparations, she was ready.

The next time she encountered her boss in the staff lounge, she asked for a meeting. He accepted. She made her pitch, and the boss, as expected, was a tough negotiator.

Nevertheless, she left with an 8% raise.

What Sandra had done, in essence, was give herself a "realistic job preview" of what it would be like to ask for a raise. Her decision was made; she knew she needed to ask for a raise. Given the decision, how could she best improve her odds? She found that anticipating the future, including its potential unpleasantness, helped her prepare. That's a strategy we can all emulate.

OVERCONFIDENCE ABOUT THE FUTURE disrupts our decisions. It makes us lackadaisical about preparing for problems. It tempts us to ignore early signs of failure. It leaves us unprepared for pleasant surprises.

Fighting overconfidence means we've got to treat the future as a spectrum, not a point. Byron Penstock didn't try to predict a target price for the Redbox business; instead, he created a bookend of possibilities. His "low-IQ" investment strategy helped him make a bold investment choice.

To bookend the future means that we must sweep our spotlights from side to side, charting out the full territory of possibilities. Then we can stack the deck in our favor by preparing for both bad situations (via a premortem) and good (via a preparade). The 100,000 Homes team staved off a critical legal problem by running a premortem; Minnetonka set itself up for success with Softsoap by locking down the world's supply of plastic pumps.

Even when we can't minimize bad outcomes, we still do ourselves a favor by considering them. Realistic job previews inoculate people against disappointment and increase their satisfaction, even in the midst of a difficult job. It's easier to cope with setbacks when we're mentally prepared for them.

Stacking the deck makes us more likely to succeed, but even with the best forethought and planning, sometimes things don't go well. We've all seen people make a bad initial decision and then double down on their choice, throwing good money after bad. How do we know when it's time to reassess a choice we've made? What could we learn that would make us retreat from a choice we've made? Conversely, what would make us redouble our efforts?

What we need is a tool for snapping us awake at just the right moment, ensuring that we don't miss a chance to cut our losses—or to maximize our opportunities.

What we need, in short, is a tripwire.

CHAPTER TEN IN ONE PAGE
Bookend the Future

1. The future is not a "point"—a single scenario that we must predict. It is a range. We should bookend the future, considering a range of outcomes from very bad to very good.

    *   *Investor Penstock bet on Coinstar when his bookend analysis showed much more upside than downside.*
    *   *Our predictions grow more accurate when we stretch our bookends outward.*

2. To prepare for the lower bookend, we need a premortem. "It's a year from now. Our decision has failed utterly. Why?"

    *   *The 100,000 Homes Campaign avoided a legal threat by using a premortem-style analysis.*

3. To be ready for the upper bookend, we need a preparade. "It's a year from now. We're heroes. Will we be ready for success?"

    *   *The producer of Softsoap, hoping for a huge national launch, locked down the supply of plastic pumps for 18 to 24 months.*

4. To prepare for what can't be foreseen, we can use a "safety factor."

    *   *Elevator cables are made 11 times stronger than needed; software schedules include a "buffer factor."*

5. Anticipating problems helps us cope with them.

    *   *The "realistic job preview": Revealing a job's warts up front "vaccinates" people against dissatisfaction.*
    *   *Sandra rehearsed how she would ask her boss for a raise and what she'd say and do at various problem moments.*

6. By bookending—anticipating and preparing for both adversity and success—we stack the deck in favor of our decisions.

11

Set a Tripwire

1.

Zappos, the online shoe store, has earned a reputation for exceptional customer service, and stories circulate about the company's most outlandish service feats. In one case, a customer had traveled to Vegas, where Zappos is headquartered, only to realize that she'd forgotten her favorite shoes. So she called Zappos, hoping to buy a second pair, but the customer-service rep found that the shoes were out of stock. Unfazed, the rep hopped in his car, drove to a competitor's store, purchased the shoes, and dropped them off at the customer's hotel.

In another situation, a customer had been given a refund for a pair of shoes, but she hadn't yet mailed back the shoes to Zappos. So a rep called her to check on the shipment, and the customer apologized but explained that her mom had just died. She said she'd take the shoes to UPS as soon as she could. A few minutes later, she got an e-mail saying that the rep had arranged a home pickup by UPS so she wouldn't have to worry about making the trip. The next day, a florist delivered a big basket of white lilies and roses.

Zappos's culture is fun and intense. For some people it's heaven, and for others it's just too much. As a result, in hiring new employees, the company pays a lot of attention to "fit." Consider the experience of Jon Wolske, who interviewed in 2007 for a customer-service job. He was 30 years old and had spent the previous few years working in the production of live Vegas shows. Exhausted by the grind of show business, he was ready for a change.

Having worked previously at a call center, he was not eager to return to the corporate world, but he thought, "I'm 30 years old, I'm on call at all hours, and I have no insurance. If I break my leg, I'm in trouble." He'd heard that Zappos was hiring, so he applied. When he got a call to come in and interview, he strapped on his power tie and headed out to the company's headquarters on the outskirts of Vegas.

He was led into a corporate conference room that had been redecorated to look like a beach cabana. He took his seat in a beach chair and glanced up at the ceiling, which was painted sky blue. His interviewers, wearing jeans, asked him strange questions: *Do you feel lucky in life? On a 10-point scale, how weird are you?* (He gave himself a 7 or 8.)

Eventually he asked if he could take off his tie, which was evidently the right move, because he was offered a position in the next customer-service class. His fellow trainees in the four-week program included a wide range of people, even the incoming head of IT. (Everyone at Zappos, no matter what role, begins their job with customer-service training.)

By the end of the first day, everyone in the class had spent two hours side by side with experienced customer-service reps, listening to how they handled customer calls. Wolske found that he had a lot to learn about shoes. "Before Zappos, my shoe IQ was really, really bad," he said. "For a long time I didn't even know wide-width shoes existed. I was 26 before I realized I had a wide foot."

The second week of the training class held a surprise. The group's primary trainer left the room and another person came in to address them, saying, "You've seen what we have to offer and who we are. . . . If we hire you, believing you're a fit for the culture, but you don't like it here, then it's not going to be a great place for you to grow. We don't want you to just stick around and feel like you're stuck because you've got a job. So today we want to make you an offer."

The trainees, intrigued, listened to the offer: "If at any time you feel this is not the right place—that you're not going to excel and grow here—then pull a trainer aside and say, 'I want to take the offer.' And we'll pay you $1,000 to leave."

That's right, Zappos offers its new employees $1,000 to quit. (In fact, by late 2011, the amount had increased to $4,000.) Wolske went home and told his wife, "You're never going to believe this . . ."

The offer prodded him to think carefully about his commitment to the firm. Did he really want to spend his time providing the maniacal customer service that Zappos expected? Was the loud, chaotic environment too much to handle every day? Was he sufficiently weird to appreciate the quirks of the culture? And was he sure enough about his answers to turn down $1,000 in cash? "If I say no to this offer," he thought, "then I am buying in."

He rejected the offer and has worked at Zappos ever since.

In fact, only 2% of Zappos's trainees take the money and leave. Often they are the same people the trainers already had doubts about.

The offer manages to make everyone involved a little happier: Departing employees leave happy because of the check. Zappos's execs are happy because they avoid the far more expensive prospect of managing people who aren't a good fit. Even the employees who turn down the offer are happier. They've put a stake in the ground—"I'd rather be here than take the money"—in a way that feels good.

Why is this offer, an artificial choice inserted into the training regimen, so effective at separating good hires from bad ones?

• • •

BARRY KIRSCHNER, A SALES manager for Showtime Networks in Cincinnati, said YouTube has provided him with a few "aha moments" in life. One of the most enlightening, in a day-to-day sort of way, was a 56-second video on how to peel a banana. "Since a young age," he said, "I have always peeled a banana from the stem. But often you mush the banana as you try to force your fingers into the peel." The YouTube video he saw, which has been viewed over 3.3 million times, shows that you can peel a banana more easily from the bottom. No mushing required. (It also eliminates the temptation, when the stem doesn't break easily, to bite it and experience the banana-skin taste backlash.)

When we act on autopilot, our behavior goes unexamined. When's the last time you thought carefully about the way you peel a banana or take a shower? We gain a lot from this ability to selectively tune out parts of our experience—when we can take a shower on autopilot, it frees up our minds to consider other things. (Like whether you could make a living from offering fruit-peeling tips on YouTube.)

The problem, of course, is that sometimes these autopilot behaviors deserve more scrutiny. Most of us have been mashing bananas since childhood. And while that's no big tragedy, what if there were better ways to deal with more important activities: Handling our e-mail inbox? Or responding to customer requests? Or carrying on a good conversation with our family at dinner?

It's hard to interrupt these autopilot cycles because, well, that's the whole point of autopilot. We don't think about what we're doing. We drift along in life, floating on the wake of past choices, and it's easy to forget that we have the ability to change direction.

A woman from Alabama dreams of visiting Italy. One year she has the chance to go but postpones the trip because of responsibilities at work. Time slips by, and she thinks often of Italy, but years turn into decades, and eventually her health deteriorates to the point where she can't make the trip. When, exactly, did she "choose" not to visit Italy? Was it every day? Or never? She surely never expected that her first decision, to postpone the trip, would become a permanent one.

One solution to this is to bundle our decisions with "tripwires," signals that would snap us awake at exactly the right moment, compelling us to reconsider a decision or to make a new one. Think of the way that the low-fuel warning in your car lights up, grabbing your attention. (If only the woman from Alabama had an Italy warning that lit up before she lost her health.) The goal of a tripwire is to jolt us out of our unconscious routines and make us aware that we have a choice to make.

For David Lee Roth, a brown M&M in the bowl backstage at the band's concerts acted as a tripwire, warning him to pay careful attention to the staging. Zappos uses a tripwire with its new hires. Its $1,000 offer takes the quiet, nagging doubts experienced by some employees—*I'm not sure if this is the right job for me*—and crystallizes them into a moment of decision. The Zappos trainer explicitly warns them about autopilot: "We don't want you to just 'stick around.' . . ."

Inside organizations, though, it can be hard to change course, because an infrastructure gets built up around past decisions. A decision to launch a new product, for instance, creates a budget and a staff and a set of processes, all of which will tend to deter a change in direction.

Because of this inertia—the deep footprints of past decisions—it can be hard for leaders to change even when they know they must. The company Eastman Kodak makes a fascinating example of this, because twice it succeeded, against the odds, at making critical transformations, only to fall short on the third.

THE FOUNDER OF EASTMAN Kodak, George Eastman, was a bank clerk in Rochester, and in the late 1870s, he planned a sunny vacation to Santo Domingo. Hoping to take photos on his vacation, he bought the requisite tools—camera, film, chemicals, developing equipment— but was frustrated with how messy and bulky the gear was. He was so frustrated, in fact, that he canceled his vacation and resolved to create a better solution himself.

At the time, cameras used wet chemicals on glass plates to capture images, but Eastman pursued a dry process, which he'd heard had been used successfully in England. In 1881, after three years of tinkering, he obtained a patent on a dry-plate process and founded Eastman Dry Plate (later renamed Eastman Kodak, which we will abbreviate as Kodak). Surely he would have been shocked to learn that his company would still exist over 130 years later (though, sadly, in January 2012, the company declared bankruptcy, due substantially to the story that follows).

The company's extraordinary longevity was due, at least in part, to its leaders' knack for reinventing their core technology. The first reinvention came shortly after the founding of the company. Eastman came to realize that glass plates, even dry ones, would never be suitable for amateurs. They were too big and fragile and expensive.

So he invented a roll of film made of paper, which later evolved into the celluloid film still available today. Professional photographers scoffed at the poor quality of the paper-based images, but the camera was an immediate hit with the public. It made photography convenient. By 1898, Eastman had rolled out the first "Brownie" camera, which cost only one dollar, with rolls of film available for 15 cents. Within four years, the company sold 80% to 90% of the world's celluloid film.

Kodak's second reinvention came early in the twentieth century, with the advent of color film. As with the first generation of paper film, the image quality of the color prints was poor at first, but Eastman could see that color film would be the future. He invested heavily in the company's R&D efforts, and in the 1920s, after repeated failures, Kodak released a high-quality color film. After the color revolution, the market for film stabilized for decades, with Kodak holding steady as a market leader.

By the 1960s, the stage had been set for a third revolution: digital photography. During some of the first flights into space, NASA used digital technology to send images back to Earth, and in 1972, Texas Instruments filed a patent on a filmless electronic camera. Less than a decade later, Sony Corporation introduced the world's first commercial electronic camera, the Mavica.

Kodak's leaders monitored all of these developments and encouraged experimentation with digital technology in the company labs. But they never seemed to admit to themselves that the future was digital. Even when pushed by their partners and suppliers, they were slow to move. Often this reluctance emerged from a kind of scientific pride: *Film is simply superior to digital.* It was hard for them to imagine that the public would abandon a superior technology for an inferior one. (An ironic attitude, of course, for the company that had offended photo snobs with its Brownie camera.)

In 1981, a team inside Kodak assessed the threat that would be posed by digital technology during the decade to follow. The report concluded that during the 1980s:

- The quality of prints from electronic images will not be generally acceptable to consumers as replacement for prints based on the science of photography [i.e., film].

- The consumer's desire to handle, display, and distribute prints cannot be replaced by electronic display devices.

- Electronic systems (camera and viewing input device for TV) will not be low enough in price to have widespread appeal.

There's a whiff of confirmation bias in these conclusions. They seem to say, "We're doing just fine, aren't we?" To be fair, though, the report's predictions were dead-on accurate; all of them proved correct during the 1980s and, in fact, well into the 1990s.

During that period, though, the groundwork was being laid for a permanent transformation of the industry. Once the public embraced cell phones and the Internet—crucial enabling technologies—the move to digital technology was irreversible. By 2002, sales of digital cameras had eclipsed those of traditional cameras. By 2011, a generation of students was enrolling in college who had likely never developed a roll of film.

• • •

THIS WAS A WAVE that Kodak had seen coming for decades, yet the company was capsized. After reaching a peak market capitalization of $31 billion in 1997, Kodak began to decline, slowly at first but with a nasty plunge starting in 2007. By mid-2011, the company's market cap had sunk below $2 billion, and in January 2012 it filed for bankruptcy.

What happened? The story of the decline is complex, featuring a succession of highly touted but ultimately unsuccessful CEOs, as well as a series of deals that attempted to put a digital veneer on the company's traditional film business. One of those attempts was the Advantix Preview camera, which featured a cutting-edge digital display on the back. Sounds promising, right? Except that the display existed only so that you could *preview* the pictures you'd take on film and subsequently get developed at the local Fotomat. Which is a bit like selling a tiny, pocket-sized phone that must be plugged into the wall to make a call.

During this long period, when Kodak's goose was being slow-cooked, the company's executives missed opportunity after opportunity to reverse course. The alarm bells, signaling that the film business was in trouble, were omnipresent, yet they were never insistent enough to overcome the seductive voice that kept telling Kodak execs, *The film business is still lucrative. . . . Let's just wait and see what happens.*

It's the same voice we've all encountered in different forms. *My boyfriend still doesn't treat me the way I want him to, but maybe he will change. . . . I'll just wait and see what happens.* Or, *I know our sales aren't going as well as we'd predicted, but before we reconsider our strategy . . . let's just wait and see what happens.*

Kodak's executives were trapped in autopilot; they were coasting with the momentum of past choices. They needed a tripwire to snap them to attention and force a choice.

What kind of tripwire could Kodak's executives have used? The answer is right in their own 1981 report. Notice how easy it is to turn a hopeful prediction into an early-warning alarm system. For instance:

The quality of prints from electronic images will not be generally acceptable to consumers as replacement for prints based on the science of photography [i.e., film].

WE WILL ACT WHEN:
More than 10% of the public express satisfaction with digital images.

The consumer's desire to handle, display, and distribute prints cannot be replaced by electronic display devices.

WE WILL ACT WHEN:
Some kind of electronic viewing system is acquired by more than 5% of the public.

Electronic systems (camera and viewing input device for TV) will not be low enough in price to have widespread appeal.

Because day-to-day change is gradual, even imperceptible, it's hard to know when to jump. Tripwires tell you when to jump. Setting tripwires would not have guaranteed that Kodak's leaders made the right decisions. Sometimes even a clear alarm is willfully ignored. (We've probably all ignored a fire alarm, trusting that it is false.) But tripwires at least ensure that we are *aware* it's time to make a decision, that we don't miss our chance to choose because we've been lulled into autopilot.

2.

Chances are you know someone who has been stuck on autopilot too long. Sometimes autopilot causes people to neglect opportunities; maybe you have a friend who has talked about writing a novel for years but never seems to make any progress. Other times, autopilot leads people to persist at efforts that seem doomed, like a couple whose relationship makes them both miserable, or a relative with a naive dream of making a living as a landscape painter, or an executive who refuses to recognize that her pet project has failed. At some point, the virtue of being persistent turns into the vice of denying reality. When that transformation happens, how can you snap someone out of it?

One option is to set a deadline, the most familiar form of a tripwire. Some deadlines are natural, such as the deadline for filing stories at a daily newspaper—the printing press has to roll at a certain time, whether the story is ready or not. But it's easy to forget that most of the deadlines we encounter in life are simply made up. They are artificially created tripwires to force an action or a decision.

Some deadlines are backed by the force of law, such as the IRS's April 15 deadline for submitting taxes, and it's no shock that these deadlines are effective. What's stranger is the effectiveness of made-up deadlines in getting us to do what would have been good for us anyway.

The psychologists Amos Tversky and Eldar Shafir offered college students a five-dollar reward for filling out a survey. When given a five-day deadline, 66% of the students completed the survey and claimed their rewards. When given no deadline, only 25% ever collected their money.

The same phenomenon has been noted with substantially higher stakes. In Great Britain, the Economic and Social Research Council, which gives grants to university researchers in areas such as global economics, security, and education, decided to eliminate submission deadlines and accept proposals on a rolling basis. Research professors should have been relieved. Instead of having to submit proposals on a couple of fixed dates, usually smack dab in the midst of teaching commitments, they were now being given the flexibility to submit a proposal whenever they had time to do so.

Proposal submissions promptly declined by 15% to 20%.

This is not rational behavior: If students like the idea of getting five dollars for a survey, and if researchers need grant money, then they shouldn't need a deadline to follow through. Yet while irrational, this behavior probably makes sense to all of us. Deadlines focus our mental spotlight on a choice. They grab us by the collar and say, *If you're gonna do this, you have to do it now.*

In this light, consider the tradition of the annual performance review for employees. People (including us) have poked fun at the idea of giving feedback to employees only once a year. (What parents would swallow their feedback day after day, storing it up for one December day when they'd sit their kids down and let it rip?)

While once-a-year feedback is inadequate, though, it's superior to never-a-year feedback. Absent the deadline, that would probably be the norm. The annual review, then, is really a kind of desperate tripwire, ensuring that something critical happens at least once a year.

If you have a relative or colleague who is pursuing a bad path on autopilot, or if you think they're being overconfident about their chances of success, work with them to set up tripwires—and hold them accountable to what they predicted. "Six months ago, you thought you'd have a recording contract by now."

These will not be easy conversations to have. No one likes to be reminded of failure. Nor is there any certainty that they will change course; overconfidence is a powerful force. The optimistic entrepreneur will always believe that sales will skyrocket next year, and the aspiring singer will feel that she could be "discovered" at any moment. But certainly you have a better chance of reining in foolish decisions when those decisions are *considered* than when they are left unexamined.

ANOTHER STRATEGY, BEYOND DATES and measurements, is to use a "partition" as a tripwire. Imagine that you're eating lunch in a sub shop, and you've bought a small bag of chips to go with your meal. When you finish the bag, you might still crave more chips, but to get them you'd have to make an active decision: to walk up to the counter and buy another bag. Almost certainly, you wouldn't do that. However, what if the sub shop had provided chips in a refillable bowl, like a Mexican restaurant that brings out tortilla chips? It's easy to imagine that you might have eaten two or three small bags' worth of chips in one sitting.

In the terminology of the researchers Dilip Soman and Amar Cheema, the small bag acts as a "partition." It breaks up a resource (chips) by dividing it into discrete portions. Soman and Cheema have found that partitioning is an effective way to make us more thoughtful about what we consume, because it forces us to make a conscious decision about whether to continue.

In one study, participants volunteered to help with a "cookie-tasting study." (Tough gig.) Every participant received 24 cookies in a box that was easily resealable to keep the cookies fresh. But inside half the boxes was a minor difference: Each cookie was individually wrapped in foil.

That minor difference had a major effect. The people who got the unwrapped cookies finished them, on average, in 6 days. Meanwhile, those who got the individually wrapped cookies took 24 days! The foil wrapper was acting as a partition, forcing people to contemplate whether they wanted to keep going. (Which suggests that we might be able to help casino-addicted retirees by wrapping slot machines in foil.)

Actually, that slot-machine comment isn't entirely a joke. In another study, participants gambled less when their funds were spread across 10 envelopes, rather than crammed into a single envelope. Soman also found that day laborers, paid in cash, dramatically increased their savings rates when they divided their wages across several envelopes. This kind of partition effect probably explains why credit cards encourage excessive spending—they permit us to spend without partitions, like eating from a bag of chips the size of your couch.

Some venture-capital investors use a variety of this partitioning logic. Rather than investing a huge chunk of money up front, the investors might choose to dole it out over time, across a series of rounds. Each round would initiate a new conversation: Do we have the right plan? Are customers happy with what we are producing? The partitions compel the entrepreneurs to be intentional about their behavior.*

What we're seeing with these partitioning examples is an additional advantage of tripwires. Initially, we highlighted the useful way that trip-wires can snap us out of autopilot. But partitions are doing something different: They're setting boundaries.

Boundaries are necessary because of people's tendency to escalate their commitment to their choices. For a simple example, think of a kid playing an arcade game. She's been on a zombie-killing mission, but she made a mistake and her character died, and now she must burn a few more credits to keep playing. It feels so hard to walk away at that point. She might have invested several dollars and 20 minutes to get where she was. If she walks away, she "loses" everything. Isn't it worth a few more credits to keep going?

This is a conscious decision, not an "autopilot" choice. But there's still a trap involved, because if she doesn't interrupt the cycle at some point, she'll burn through all her arcade money having never played an-other game. (And that is not a recipe for happiness.)

Imagine, instead, if that same girl had walked into the arcade with three different swipe cards (or piles of quarters, if you have an old-school arcade), and she mentally allocated one swipe card to the zombie game. That's a tripwire. Its role is to disrupt the cycle of steady escalation. Once she burns through the first swipe card, she'll feel some self-generated pressure to quit. And if she decides to break into the second card, it will "hurt" a bit, because she'll know that she's blowing through her mental budget.

---

*Note that partitioning is better suited to self-control-type issues, like saving money or resisting cookies. When you start thinking about how to implement the principle in an office environment, it can get a little weird. For example, imagine that you wanted your coworkers to be more thoughtful about their use of the color printer, so you created a "partition" that required them to click a button after every 10 pages printed. That kind of thing could lead to bloodshed very quickly.

This same budgeting dynamic is present in much more important decisions, of course. Think of romantic relationships or business investments. (*We've committed so much already; isn't it worth just a little more?*) If you're dating someone who has commitment issues, could you set a three-month tripwire to see whether you're making any progress? Or if a project at work has stalled out, could you set a $50,000 budget limit on the funds you'll use to jump-start it?

With the right tripwire, we can ensure that we don't throw good money (or time) after bad.

ALL THIS WORRYING ABOUT traps and contingencies may make tripwires sound overly cautious—the bicycle helmet of decision making. But actually we want to argue the opposite, that tripwires *encourage* risk taking by letting us carve out a "safe space" for experimentation.

Say your husband wants to start a business creating topiary sculptures for clients. You think the idea is bonkers, but you admire his passion, so it seems cruel to veto it. Instead, set a tripwire. *Okay, dear, let's give the topiary-sculpture business a shot, but can we agree that we won't invest more than $10,000 of our savings in it?* Alternatively, you might say: *Go for it, but if you don't have a paying customer within three months, let's talk seriously about Plan B.*

Tripwires like those can cap your risk, and they can also create a kind of psychic comfort, because they allow you and your spouse to stay on autopilot until the trigger is reached. That is, if you're only two months in, or if you've only burned $4,300 of the budget, then you can relax. No reason to worry or fight or agonize about it. You're on track, and you can trust the tripwire to tell you when to pay attention again. Similarly, if Kodak's executives had set tripwires, they could have relaxed and stayed focused on the film business right up until the moment when one of their conditions was tripped.

In short, tripwires allow us the certainty of committing to a course of action, even a risky one, while minimizing the costs of overconfidence.

3.

A variation of the tripwire idea was used, to lifesaving effect, by Lucile Packard Children's Hospital (LPCH), part of Stanford University's hospital system. LPCH is the treatment center of last resort for children in the San Francisco Bay area. "The cases in our general-care wards are like the patients in other hospitals' intensive care units," said Kit Leong, a quality manager at LPCH.

At a conference on quality in medicine, Leong became convinced that some deaths at LPCH were preventable. The conference was sponsored by the Institute for Healthcare Improvement (IHI), which had launched a "100,000 Lives" campaign to stop patient deaths due to medical error and ineffective practices.* The IHI observed that many patient emergencies could be prevented if early signs of trouble were addressed quickly, and to enable that quick response, it urged hospitals to create "rapid-response teams" (sometimes called RRTs). In a typical situation, a nurse who noticed something odd about a patient's vitals could summon a rapid-response team, a diverse team of medical professionals who would convene quickly at the patient's bedside to analyze the situation.

The idea appealed to Leong because she knew that, while adults tend to decline gradually and predictably, kids often crater suddenly. As an experienced cardiovascular ICU nurse, Karla Earnest, said, "They hold on and hold on for a long time, then *boom*, they hit a wall where they can't hold on anymore." Often, by the time a nurse "called a code"— sounding an emergency signal that the kid's life was at stake—it was too late to save them.

The advantage of rapid-response teams, Leong knew, was that they encouraged action before it was too late, before it was necessary to call a code. She convinced her colleagues to give the idea a try.

In the training sessions, the instructor passed out cards listing six tripwires that warranted calling in the RRT. Five of the tripwires involved

---

*We mentioned this campaign briefly in the last chapter. An expert from the IHI was helping the 100,000 Homes team with its campaign.

objective measures such as acute changes in heart rate, blood pressure, or oxygen saturation. The sixth tripwire, at the top of the card, was the most important: *Call the rapid-response team if you are worried about a patient.*

Some of the ICU staffers were skeptical about that provision, worrying that it turned over too much control to frontline nurses. What if nurses overused rapid-response teams, distracting doctors from their work in the ICU? Despite the skepticism, the hospital moved forward with a pilot of the rapid-response program.

Over the next 18 months, RRTs were summoned about twice a week, and the most common reason was the one at the top of the card: A nurse was worried about a patient. Karla Earnest, the ICU nurse, said that it was critical that nurses' worries were legitimized as a tripwire. Earnest said, "As a bedside nurse, it doesn't force you to be able to articulate, 'I'm seeing this change in respiratory rate or that change in heart rate.' . . . You can just ask for help: *Come look at this kid, he doesn't look good.*"

When the doctors and nurses realized they were catching problems earlier than before, their confidence in the program grew. While "calling a code" had always been pretty rare—it only happened 2–3 times per 1,000 patients—it was clear that, thanks to rapid-response teams, the incidents were growing even rarer. Leong and Earnest said that during the first few weeks of the rollout, they kept hearing, "Why didn't we think of this a long time ago?"

A 2007 article in the *Journal of the American Medical Association* summarized the results of the project over the first 18 months. Due to rapid-response teams, the number of code calls outside the ICU had fallen by 71%. Problems were being detected and headed off earlier. That early action saved lives: Hospital mortality dropped by 18%. The 143 rapid-response team calls made over the 18-month period saved an estimated 33 lives.

The fears that critical personnel would be drawn away from the ICU were misguided. In fact, the RRT actually freed up resources. "You're spending 20 minutes turning around a kid in an RRT situation," said Leong, "versus an hour or more in a code situation."

Thirty-three kids went home safely to their parents as the result of a simple set of tripwires.

EARLIER IN THE CHAPTER, the tripwires we encountered were well defined: A $1,000 offer at Zappos. A deadline for completing a survey. A budget limit for your spouse's topiary-sculpture business.

Notice that the children's-hospital situation is a little different. The most important tripwire requires nurses to call for help when they are worried about a patient. It's a little fuzzy, a little subjective. As a result, the rapid-response team members can't predict when they'll hit that tripwire or how many times they'll trip it. These tripwires aren't tripped by clear-cut measures like budgets or dates or partitions; they're tripped by pattern recognition.

This is an important distinction, because in many organizations, pattern matching is the skill that leaders desperately want their employees to have. They want their employees to be alert for threats and opportunities in the environment. They would like employees to recognize the pattern when they see it pop up and to feel that they have permission to act when it does. That was a powerful feature of the rapid-response-team protocol—any time nurses spotted a kid who didn't quite look right, the protocol made it socially acceptable for them to raise their voices and say, *I think we've got a problem.*

Of course, the same idea is applicable to opportunities as well as threats. Organizational leaders need people to be sensitive to changes in the environment and to be brave enough to speak up. *Here's something new. Here's a great opportunity for us.*

Peter Drucker challenged executives to capitalize on "unexpected success." He wrote:

> When a new venture does succeed, more often than not it is in a market other than the one it was originally intended to serve, with products or services not quite those with which it had set out,

bought in large part by customers it did not even think of when it started, and used for a host of purposes besides the ones for which the products were first designed. If a new venture does not anticipate this, organizing itself to take advantage of the unexpected and unseen markets . . . then it will succeed only in creating an opportunity for a competitor.

One great story of "unexpected success" is Rogaine, the drug that helps bald men regrow some of their hair, which was discovered by accident. Rogaine's active ingredient, minoxidil, is also the chief ingredient in a drug called Loniten, which was taken by many patients to lower their blood pressure. Loniten had a surprising side effect, though: Patients started sprouting new hair on their arms, back, and legs. (As you can imagine, this was not a popular side effect.) The scientists at Upjohn were clever enough to recognize the opportunity buried in the problem, and they reformulated the drug into the antibalding elixir that we know as Rogaine today.

The discovery of Viagra was a similar story. Initially, the drug had been tested as a treatment for chest pain (angina), and for that purpose it was a failure. Then patients started reporting a curious side effect. (Imagine those awkward conversations: "Doc, my chest still hurts . . . but, um, I've been noticing an effect somewhere else . . .")

One journalist concluded from these stories and others like them that "the pharmaceutical industry is driven as much by luck as by design." But that's not quite right, because luck didn't make Rogaine. It took discipline to spot and monetize the opportunities represented by these flukes. (Let's be honest, it was not self-evident that unwanted back hair heralded a billion-dollar opportunity.)

This is the same kind of pattern-matching tripwire that allowed the rapid-response teams to succeed. While the nurses were sensitized to signs of trouble, the pharma scientists were sensitized to signs of opportunity.

Could you define a similar tripwire for your team members? Could you sensitize them to the kinds of opportunities that Drucker called "unexpected success"? A small-business owner might coach her employees, "If you see people using our product in a way we haven't anticipated, let's talk about it." A high-school department chair might say, "If you try out a new assignment that really seems to get students motivated, let's discuss it in our next meeting."

By coaching people to recognize patterns of threat or opportunity, you can take advantage of a phenomenon we've all experienced, the "seeing it everywhere" effect: You learn a new concept or word and suddenly you start to notice it everywhere. The Web site *1000 Awesome Things* identifies this phenomenon as Awesome Thing #523. Dozens of commenters have shared their experiences with the phenomenon:

» This is such a very, very true awesome thing. . . . "Haberdashery" was one of the most recent words I learned. Who knew it was even a real word? My prof mentioned that Harry Truman used to be a haberdasher and next thing you know, my grandma uses it, I spot it on little shop signs, it's on the wall at East Side Mario's. . . . Small world!

» I remember as a little kid coming across the world "feasible." Next day at chess club, one of the books we used to give us tips on the game used that word again . . . and again . . . and again. My game didn't really improve that much but my vocabulary did. Awesome, indeed.

» "Justin Bieber" is what I learned and now can't avoid. I'm pretty sure it's made me dumber, though. And, I've started to contemplate suicide.

By labeling a tripwire, you can make it easier to recognize, just as it's easier to spot the word "haberdashery" when you've just learned it. Pilots, for example, are taught to pay careful attention to what are called "leemers": the vague feeling that something isn't right, even if it's not clear why. Having a label for those feelings legitimizes them and makes pilots less likely to dismiss them. The flash of recognition—*Oh, this is a leemer*—

causes a quick shift from autopilot to manual control, from unconscious to conscious behavior.

That quick switch is what we need so often in life—a reminder that our current trajectory need not be permanent. Tripwires provide a sudden recognition that precedes our actions:

I have a choice.

CHAPTER ELEVEN IN ONE PAGE
Set a Tripwire

1. In life, we naturally slip into autopilot, leaving past decisions unquestioned.
   - *E.g., we've all been peeling bananas from the top. Nothing ever compelled us to reconsider it.*

2. A tripwire can snap us awake and make us realize we have a choice.
   - *Zappos's $1,000 offer created a conscious fork in the road for new hires.*
   - *David Lee Roth's brown M&Ms signaled that he needed to inspect the production.*

3. Tripwires can be especially useful when change is gradual.
   - *Digital images killed Kodak; its executives could have used tripwires to spark a bolder response.*

4. For people stuck on autopilot, consider deadlines or partitions.
   - *"Six months ago, you thought you'd have a recording contract by now."*
   - *Partitions: Day laborers saved more when their pay was put in 10 envelopes versus 1.*

5. We tend to escalate our investment in poor decisions; partitions can help rein that in.
   - *E.g., "We won't allocate more than $50,000 to jump-start this failing project."*

6. Tripwires can actually create a safe space for risk taking. They: (1) cap risk; and (2) quiet your mind until the trigger is hit.

7. Many powerful tripwires are triggered by patterns rather than dates/metrics/budgets.
   - *Unexpected problems: A children's hospital told nurses to call the rapid-response team if they were worried about a patient.*
   - *Peter Drucker: Be ready for "unexpected success."*
   - *Rogaine scientists were savvy enough to spot the opportunity in back-hair growth.*

8. Tripwires can provide a precious realization: *We have a choice to make.*

12

Trusting the Process

1.

Most of our day-to-day decisions—which route to take to work, which sandwich to buy for lunch—are pretty effortless. But the tough calls can take a toll. For most of us who work in organizations, those tough calls are likely to be group decisions.

Throughout the book, we've discussed ways of nudging, prodding, and inspiring groups to make better decisions: Seeking out *one more option.* Finding someone else who's solved our problem. Asking, "What would have to be true for you to be right?" Ooching as a way to dampen politics. Making big decisions based on core priorities. Running premortems and preparades. Laying down tripwires. Using these techniques will improve the results of your group decisions.

We should also address the *aftermath* of decisions, because most decisions come with at least a bit of "collateral damage" for those whose ideas weren't accepted—anger, hurt feelings, or loss of confidence in the new direction. How can you ensure that a decision is seen as fair?

The WRAP process, if used routinely, will contribute to that sense of fairness, because it allows people to understand how the decision is being made, and it gives them comfort that decisions will be made in a consistent manner. Beyond WRAP, there are a few additional ideas to consider as you navigate group decisions.

The most direct (and difficult) way to make a fair decision is to involve as many people as possible and get them all to agree. Remember Paul C. Nutt, the collector of organizational decisions, who found that most organizations considered just one alternative? In one of his later studies, he analyzed how the final choice was made across 376 important decisions at organizations such as General Electric, NASA, and General Motors. He found that only one in seven decisions incorporated an approach he called "bargaining," which is basically the art of compromise—ensuring that when multiple parties disagree, they horse-trade until they find a solution that most people can live with. Though bargaining wasn't used very often, when used it *always* improved the success of the decision, and Nutt described the improvement as "dramatic."

You can be forgiven if you're having one of two skeptical reactions right now. One reaction: Compromise is sloppy and inelegant. Compromise is like the old joke, "A camel is a horse made by a committee." The iPhone wasn't a committee product. And if you're in an organization like Apple—with clear alignment of values and a growth trajectory that distracts from disagreements—then some kinds of compromise may be unnecessary or even counterproductive. However, Apple is the exception that proves the rule. Imagine the CEO of General Motors expecting major concessions from unions because of the elegance of his design vision. Good luck with that. When you've got multiple powerful parties involved in a decision, compromise is unavoidable.

The point is not that compromise is a necessary evil. Rather, compromise can be valuable in itself, because it demonstrates that *you've made use of diverse opinions*, which is a way of limiting risk. Here's why: Bargainers come to the table with different options, which helps the group dodge a narrow frame. (Indeed, bargainers typically consider at least two complete alternatives in making a decision, as opposed to the one alternative considered in other decisions.) Also, bargainers tend to act as devil's advocates for each other, asking the disconfirming questions that people don't always ask themselves.

If a superintendent hatches an ambitious new plan for her district and pushes it through, against opposition, she's taking a big risk. What if her diagnosis of the district's problems—and her solution—are flat wrong? On the other hand, if she bargains with her staff and teachers, she may come out with a watered-down plan, but it might be watered-down only in the sense that the parts that were least likely to work have been removed.

The second skeptical reaction you might have to bargaining is this: *Yes, involving lots of people in a decision is a wonderful idea, and it'd be fantastic to negotiate to the point where everyone agreed, but c'mon, get a grip: We don't have time to do that!* The business world thrives on quick decisions, and you can't build consensus quickly.

This objection must be conceded. Bargaining is indeed a slower way to make a decision. But that's not the right way to judge its effectiveness, because decisions are a means to an end. Your group might need to pick a software solution for handling customer-support calls, but that decision isn't the end goal. The end goal is to make customers happier, which means not only that you've picked the right solution but *that your staff is using it enthusiastically* in a way that pleases customers. In other words, success requires two stages: first the decision and then the implementation.

That's why the initial slowness of bargaining may be offset by a critical advantage: It speeds up implementation. The superintendent can make a lightning-fast decision if she makes it autocratically, but if her administrators and teachers hate it, then adoption will come to a standstill.

So where do you want to spend your time? Bargaining up front, or fighting foot draggers later? Bargaining yields buy-in.

• • •

THIS ISN'T TO SUGGEST, of course, that by bargaining you can always make everyone happy. Some decisions will leave a subset of people worse off, as the necessary cost of doing something great for many others or for the organization itself.

If those people who lose consider the decision process fair, it can make a huge difference in the way they react. Consider two different small claims court cases:

> **Case 1:** Carlos is suing Mike, a contractor, for shoddy work installing new granite countertops. Carlos testifies that he had to hire another contractor to redo the installation and he is seeking a refund of the $650 in labor that Mike charged him. The judge listens respectfully to both. Eventually, the judge rules for Carlos, explaining that the verdict hinged on a couple of photos that suggested Mike may not have secured the counter adequately.

> **Case 2:** Analisa is suing her house sitter, Jen, for killing her fish. Analisa contends that Jen failed to feed the tropical fish on the precise schedule she had left. By the time Analisa came home, they were bobbing at the top of the tank. Jen contends that she really did honor the obsessive feeding schedule, as far as she can recall. As Analisa begins to share more evidence, the judge cuts her off abruptly and rules for Jen, muttering something about how "it's just impossible to keep fish alive for long."

These two cases were adjudicated quite differently—case 1 sounds like a fair process and case 2 doesn't. Researchers who study court cases like these find a consistent pattern in the aftermath of the verdicts. The winners—Carlos and Jen—are happy with the decisions. No surprise there. (Though Jen is a bit less happy than Carlos because of the judge's flakiness.)

But there is a sharp contrast in how the losers feel about their experiences. Analisa (the fish owner), who lost the unfair case, is absolutely furious about the outcome. *She didn't even get to finish her testimony!*

The biggest surprise, though, concerns Mike, the contractor who lost the countertop case. While he emerges less happy than Carlos (the winner), he's *almost* as happy. In fact, Mike might actually be happier than Jen, who won the unfair case!

Researchers call this sense of fairness "procedural justice"—i.e., the procedures used to make a decision were just—as distinct from "distributive justice," which is concerned with whether the spoils of a decision were divvied up fairly. An extensive body of research confirms that procedural justice is critical in explaining how people feel about a decision. It's not just the outcome that matters; it's the process.

The elements of procedural justice are straightforward: Give people a chance to be heard, to present their case. Listen—really listen—to what people say. Use accurate information to make the decision, and give people a chance to challenge the information if it's incorrect. Apply principles consistently across situations. Avoid bias and self-interest. Explain why the decision was made and be candid about relevant risks or concerns.

Surely there's no genuine debate about whether this is the right way to make a decision. (Anyone want to argue for inconsistent, disrespectful decisions?) True, there may be times when we value our own idea more than a fair process and times when we choose expediency over procedural justice.

But there may also be times when we are *trying* to deliver procedural justice but find that our efforts aren't recognized. Think about the need to listen attentively, for instance. You might listen carefully to one of your colleagues, nodding to signal your attention. In your own head, you really are listening—you're delivering one of the pillars of procedural justice. From your colleague's perspective, though, it's not as clear. You might be listening, or you might be contemplating your rejoinder. You need a way to make the reality visible.

Robert Mnookin faces this issue as a mediator in high-stakes corporate cases. One case he handled involved Sony suing Apple for copyright infringement and Apple countersuing. Given the amount of animosity he has to contend with, it's critical that he be seen as delivering procedural justice. So he doesn't just listen; as he says, "I state back the other side's position better than they could state it. And then they can relax because they feel heard." When you can articulate someone's point of view better than they can, it's de facto proof that you are really listening.

The same goes for defending a decision. If you've made a decision that had some opposition, those opponents need to know that you haven't made the decision blindly or naively. Our first instinct, when challenged, is usually to dig in further and passionately defend our position. Surprisingly, though, sometimes the opposite can be more effective.

Dave Hitz, the founder of NetApp, says he learned that "sometimes the best way to defend a decision is to point out its flaws." In his funny autobiography, *How to Castrate a Bull*, he explains how he handles opposition:

> Let's say you have decided to pursue Plan A. As a manager, it is part of your job to defend and explain that decision to folks who work for you. So when someone marches into your office to explain that Plan A sucks, and that Plan Z would be much better, what do you do? . . . My old instinct was to listen to Plan Z, say what I didn't like about it, and to describe as best as I could why Plan A was better. Of course, the person has already seen these same arguments in the e-mail I sent announcing the decision, but since they didn't agree, they must not have heard me clearly, so I'd better repeat my argument again, right? I can report that this seldom worked very well.
>
> It works much better if I start out by agreeing: "Yep. Plan Z is a reasonable plan. Not only for the reasons you mentioned,

but here are two more advantages. And Plan A—the plan that we chose—not only has the flaws that you mentioned, but here are three more flaws." The effect of this technique is amazing. It seems completely counterintuitive, but even if you don't convince people that your plan is better, hearing you explain your plan's flaws—and their plan's advantages—makes them much more comfortable.

Hitz's logic defies our natural PR instincts. Aren't we supposed to vociferously defend our positions? Won't we spook people if we admit weakness?

No. Hitz has it right. A manager's self-criticism is comforting, rather than anxiety producing, because it signals that she is making a reality-based decision. The manager is saying, in essence, "We're making an informed bet that this decision will work, but we'll be monitoring it closely." (*We've reality-tested, and we have set tripwires.*) On the other hand, if the manager, confronted with criticism, becomes a press secretary for the decision and immediately retreats to her talking points, it's unsettling, because it makes her team worry that even if the decision is a fiasco, she won't change direction.

2.

The procedural-justice research shows that people care deeply about process. We all want to believe that a decision process that affects us is fair, that it is taking into account all the right information. Even if the outcome goes against us, our confidence in the process is critical. By acknowledging flaws in his decisions, Hitz is encouraging his team to put their faith in a process rather than in a single decision. Individual decisions will frequently be wrong, but the right process will be an ally in any situation.

To see how a process can help, even with a deeply personal decision, consider Matt D'Arrigo, a nonprofit leader. D'Arrigo's story begins with a time when his family was battered by heartbreaking news.

In 1991, during the spring semester of his freshman year at Spring Hill College in Mobile, Alabama, D'Arrigo learned that his mother had been diagnosed with stomach cancer. His dad brought the family—D'Arrigo and his four sisters—together to discuss the situation. The doctors were hopeful that his mom's cancer might be manageable, so D'Arrigo returned to school, worried but optimistic.

During the same semester, his older sister Kate started complaining about pain in her shoulder. The pain continued through the summer, when doctors did an MRI and found a tumor. She had lymphoma. During the late summer and early fall, D'Arrigo's mother and sister went through chemotherapy together. "Our whole world was turned upside down," he said.

D'Arrigo decided not to return to school in the fall, choosing to stay with his family in Boston. During that difficult time, what kept him sane was art. He painted, finding it therapeutic—a way of quieting his anxieties. As the year went on, his sister got better and his mother got worse. In early December, doctors found that his mother's cancer had spread again, and a few weeks after Christmas, she passed away.

D'Arrigo, distraught, continued to paint every day. One day, it dawned on him that what art did for him it could do for others. Suddenly he knew: *This is what I'm supposed to do. I'm supposed to help kids through art.*

He never shared this epiphany with anyone. He was self-conscious about it, worrying that people would think it was a "stupid idea." Eventually he went back to his life—he completed school, took a few jobs, and after a few moves landed in San Diego. Almost 10 years after he'd had his epiphany, he found that he couldn't ignore it anymore. He talked to his dad about the idea, and his dad offered him $5,000 in seed money. His sister Kate sent him books about how to start a nonprofit.

He founded ARTS—A Reason To Survive—in 2001, with a mission to comfort sick kids with art. He volunteered to help at the Ronald McDonald House, a place where families stayed while their kids were treated at the children's hospital across the street. Two of the first kids he helped were Riley, a three-year-old boy going through chemotherapy, and his sister Alexis. For a few precious hours, the sessions helped Riley and his family forget his condition. D'Arrigo taught them how to paint with watercolors, how to do simple drawings. They made get-well cards for other kids at the hospital. One day he put on Beach Boys music, and as they bobbed to the music, they painted a big beach-themed mural.

At the end of 2001, Riley died. D'Arrigo drove four hours to be at the boy's funeral, and the family asked him to say a few words. D'Arrigo was devastated by Riley's death, but he knew that he was doing what he was meant to do. "I wanted to be a bright light for kids in a very dark time," he said.

In the early years, ARTS was just him and a crew of volunteer artists. They learned to design art projects that kids could complete in one sitting, because, as D'Arrigo said, "they were either homeless, abused, or in hospitals, and you weren't sure if you'd see them again the next week or not."

Over time, the organization grew, attracting more volunteers and more donations, and ARTS went from serving dozens of kids to serving hundreds. By 2007, D'Arrigo had raised enough money to open the Arts Center—the first time the organization had a permanent space designed specifically to inspire kids. "It was light, bright, and colorful," he said. "As soon as the kids walk through the door, they feel different."

At the Arts Center, you might see a kid from juvenile court working on a project with a kid from a homeless shelter and a kid with Down syndrome. It served as a home away from home for many of them. One girl told D'Arrigo, "School and home is where you have to keep secrets, and the Arts Center is where you can let your secrets out."

In 2011, ARTS celebrated its tenth anniversary, but the celebrations sparked some internal turmoil in D'Arrigo. For the previous year or two, he'd been feeling a bit unsettled. He'd always dreamed that ARTS would spread its work nationally, but so far it had operated only in San Diego.

When he brought up his ideas for growth with some board members, they'd usually counsel him to stay focused on the local work.

He began to think about leaving ARTS, perhaps to start his own consulting practice—he thought maybe he could counsel like-minded nonprofits in other cities. But it was hard to contemplate leaving the organization he'd founded and led for a decade. He agonized about the decision for months: Should he stay or leave?

At a decision-making workshop (led by Chip), D'Arrigo described his dilemma, and he was asked point-blank: "Imagine that 10 years from now, ARTS has been hugely successful in San Diego, serving many more kids than it's serving today. It's a pillar of the local community. But it has no presence anywhere else. Would you be happy?" D'Arrigo shook his head. "No, I wouldn't," he said.

His response shook him up a bit—it made it clear to him that he had to act. He began to consult with peers and funders and a few board members, asking for their advice. One conversation in particular proved pivotal. He met with a woman who was the CEO of a children's social-service agency in San Diego, and he described agonizing over whether to continue expanding ARTS's local work or leave it to pursue the national agenda. She said, "Matt, why can't you do all of that?" She challenged him to come up with a plan that would keep ARTS strong in San Diego while still allowing him to pursue the idea of spreading the program nationally.

He realized she was right; there was no natural barrier to doing both. So he stopped thinking about leaving the organization and started thinking about how to push the ambitions of ARTS. His first move, in the summer of 2011, was to sound out the board about the new direction.

D'Arrigo asked the board members what would make them comfortable with the expanded focus. Their concerns were understandable: They worried about losing focus and spreading the organization's resources too thin.

D'Arrigo felt that these were solvable problems. He gave himself a one-year deadline to begin the new work: *By the June 30, 2012, board meeting, I will have a plan in place and the approval of the board to move forward on the national expansion of the ARTS strategy.* He knew his San Diego team would need more funding and more staff to make the strategic shift possible, so he hired a new development officer who could lead a more aggressive fund-raising campaign. Then he began to beef up his San Diego program staff, freeing himself up to turn his attention nationally.

To test his ideas about expansion, he pursued a partnership with a group called La Maestra Community Health Centers, which served recent immigrants from more than 60 countries. D'Arrigo knew that La Maestra was serving kids who needed what ARTS offered. (Imagine the daughter of immigrants, struggling with a new language and culture, who has a parent battling a medical problem.) D'Arrigo's idea was to train La Maestra's staff on how to lead ARTS's therapeutic programs. If he succeeded, and the staffers could carry forward his work without his ongoing involvement, it would be solid evidence that he could expand ARTS's reach nationally without requiring a giant expansion in staff.

Meanwhile, ARTS's impact in San Diego continued to snowball. ARTS seized a great opportunity to take over a facility in the low-income National City neighborhood. The building was an old library that had been renovated by the local government. Now the people in the community were excited about transforming it into an art center. For ARTS, it was a perfect situation: The building was three times the size of their current center at one quarter of the rent. Within walking distance of the building were a junior high and high school that served kids from impoverished families, as well as several homeless and domestic-violence shelters. There were countless neighborhood kids who needed ARTS.

In March 2012, three months before his self-imposed deadline, D'Arrigo won approval from his board for the new strategic direction. He felt relieved—and hopeful. His enthusiasm was palpable. "I'm re-energized. Excited. I feel my creativity rising again."

AT PRESS TIME, WE don't know whether the new direction for ARTS and D'Arrigo will be successful. And that's okay; it's the way every decision works. We can't know when we make a choice whether it will be successful. Success emerges from the quality of the decisions we make and the quantity of luck we receive. We can't control luck. But we can control the way we make choices.

D'Arrigo made a good choice.

He avoided framing his situation too narrowly. Instead of thinking, "Should I leave the organization to pursue national expansion or stay at ARTS?" he found a way to do both. He embraced "AND not OR."

He reality-tested his assumptions, talking with friends and board members and other nonprofit leaders. One of them gave him a crucial piece of advice that helped him break out of a narrow frame: "Matt, why can't you do all of that?"

He ooched into his ideas, rather than jumping in headfirst. By working with La Maestra, he could experiment with his new ideas about expansion without taking too much risk.

Struggling with a tough choice, he attained some distance on the decision. Confronted with a question about how he'd feel 10 years in the future if his organization didn't grow beyond San Diego, he realized that he craved more reach. His core priorities demanded that he expand his work.

Together with his board, he tried to bookend the future, exploring the reasons why the new direction might fail. That analysis helped them prepare for the worst: Knowing that fund-raising might suffer in San Diego as D'Arrigo's attention turned outward, ARTS hired a bright, aggressive new development officer. Worried that he might get distracted by the day-to-day firefighting that is a part of every growing organization, he beefed up his program staff and, perhaps most important, set a tripwire: I'll have a plan in place by the June 2012 board meeting.

That's what a good decision process looks like.

It's not a spreadsheet that spits out "the answer" when we plug in the numbers. It's not a tallied list of pros and cons. It's a guardrail that guides us in the right direction.

D'Arrigo is not a man who gravitates toward "process." His career has never been driven by decision trees. What his experience demonstrates is that passion and process can work hand in glove. It was a thoughtful process that allowed him to honor his abiding passion—the desire to use art to comfort children in desperate times, the same way that it once comforted him.

3.

Our goal in *Decisive* has been to inspire you to use a better process for making decisions. Not every decision carries the emotional weight of D'Arrigo's decisions. We've encountered a wide range of decisions, some of them exotic, like those involving shark-inspired swimsuits and zip lines in the Costa Rican jungle and diagnostic bowls of M&Ms.

We've also seen plenty of important, and common, life decisions: How do you decide on a job offer? How should you handle a difficult relationship? How do you choose the right college? How do you hire the best people? How can you get a better deal on a car? How can you ensure that you spend time on things that really matter?

The same process can guide them all. We can learn to find just one more option. To check our assumptions against reality. To make tough choices based on our core priorities. To prepare humbly for the times when we'll be wrong.

The process need not take a long time to be effective. Even if you've only got 45 minutes to consider an important decision, you can accomplish a lot: Run the Vanishing Options Test to see if you might be overlooking a great alternative. Call someone who's solved your problem before. Ask yourself, *What would I tell my best friend to do?* (Or, if you're at work, *What would my successor do?*) Gather three friends or colleagues and run a premortem.

In our quest to convince you of the merits of a process, we realize we've been facing an uphill battle: It would be hard to find a less inspiring word in the English language than "process." It's like trying to get people giddy about an algorithm.

What a process provides, though, is more inspiring: *confidence.* Not cocky overconfidence that comes from collecting biased information and ignoring uncertainties, but the real confidence that comes from knowing you've made the best decision that you could. Using a process for decision making doesn't mean that your choices will always be easy, or that they will always turn out brilliantly, but it does mean you can quiet your mind. You can quit asking, "What am I missing?" You can stop the cycle of agonizing.

Just as important, trusting the process can give you the confidence to take risks. A process can be the equivalent of a mountain climber's harness and rope, allowing you the freedom to explore without constant worry. A process, far from being a drag or a constraint, can actually give you the comfort to be bolder.

And bolder is often the right direction. Short-run emotion, as we've seen, makes the status quo seductive. But when researchers ask the elderly what they regret about their lives, they don't often regret something they *did*; they regret things they *didn't* do. They regret not seizing opportunities. They regret hesitating. They regret being indecisive.

Being decisive is itself a choice. Decisiveness is a way of behaving, not an inherited trait. It allows us to make brave and confident choices, not because we know we'll be right but because it's better to try and fail than to delay and regret.

Our decisions will never be perfect, but they can be better. Bolder. Wiser. The right process can steer us toward the right choice.

And the right choice, at the right moment, can make all the difference.

CHAPTER TWELVE IN ONE PAGE
Trusting the Process

1. Decisions made by groups have an additional burden: They must be seen as fair.

2. "Bargaining"—horse-trading until all sides can live with the choice—makes for good decisions that will be seen as fair.
   - *Nutt: Bargaining always improved decision success; the effect was "dramatic."*
   - *Bargaining will take more time up front—but it accelerates implementation.*

3. Procedural justice is critical in determining how people feel about a decision.
   - *Court cases: Losers who perceive procedural justice are almost as happy as winners who don't.*

4. We should make sure people are able to *perceive* that the process is just.
   - *High-stakes mediator Mnookin: "I state back the other side's position better than they could state it."*
   - *Entrepreneur Hitz: "Sometimes the best way to defend a decision is to point out its flaws."*

5. A trustworthy process can help us navigate even the thorniest decisions.
   - *Matt D'Arrigo, the founder of ARTS, found a way to combine the need to serve local kids with his aspirations to make a national impact.*

6. "Process" isn't glamorous. But the confidence it can provide is precious. Trusting a process can permit us to take bigger risks, to make bolder choices. Studies of the elderly show that people regret not what they *did* but what they *didn't* do.

NEXT STEPS

If you've finished *Decisive* and are hungry for more, visit our website: http://www.heathbrothers.com/

Check out the "Resources" section. You can register to get instant access to *free* materials like these:

One-Page Overview. A printable overview of the WRAP framework, perfect for tacking up next to your desk.

The Decisive Workbook. A collection of tips and suggestions for putting into practice the ideas in this book. For example:

- A technique that stops group discussions from getting stuck in a narrow frame
- Advice about how to find the people who have solved your problem

- A question for challenging the "status-quo bias," which deters us from making useful changes
- More thoughts on setting tripwires in your life and work

12 Decision Situations. Some thoughts on applying the WRAP framework to these dilemmas:

- Should I break up with my boyfriend/girlfriend?
- Which TV should I buy?

- What do I do about the coworker I hate?
- And nine others!

The *Decisive* podcasts. Short podcasts, recorded by the authors, that cover the following topics in more depth:

- "Decisive for the Chronically Indecisive"

- "Decisive for Job Decisions"

Decisive Book Club Guide. If you're reading *Decisive* as part of a book club, this guide offers suggested questions and topics for your discussion.

RECOMMENDATIONS FOR
FURTHER READING

Start Here:

Daniel Kahneman (2011). *Thinking, Fast and Slow*. A very complete picture of what we know about the psychology of decision making from the Nobel Prize winner who did much of the trailblazing research. Brilliant, insightful, and fun to read.

J. Edward Russo and Paul J. H. Schoemaker (2002). *Winning Decisions: Getting It Right the First Time*. This is a powerful and easy-to-read book offering an overview of the problems of decision making, along with the authors' solid recommendations for tackling those problems.

For Even More:

Dan Ariely (2008). *Predictably Irrational: The Hidden Forces That Shape Our Decisions*. A popular book about the irrational decisions we make, written with wit by one of the cleverest researchers in the field of decision making.

Richard H. Thaler and Cass R. Sunstein (2008). *Nudge: Improving Decisions About Health, Wealth, and Happiness*. Great book by a behavioral economist and a law professor. Should be required reading for HR leaders, government officials, and anyone else who designs systems that allow other people to make choices.

Michael A. Roberto (2009). *Know What You Don't Know: How Great Leaders Prevent Problems Before They Happen*. This is an insightful book for leaders in government, health care, public safety, and technology who need to prepare for the unexpected.

Paul B. Carroll and Chunka Mui (2008). *Billion Dollar Lessons: What You Can Learn from the Most Inexcusable Business Failures of the Last 25 Years.* The authors, a journalist and a consultant, analyze a series of billion-dollar mistakes in the business world and share advice on how to avoid similar mistakes (on a smaller scale). If you're involved in strategic decisions for your organization, this book will help you avoid major pitfalls.

John Mullins and Randy Komisar (2009). *Getting to Plan B: Breaking Through to a Better Business Model.* Entrepreneurs everywhere will benefit from this framework, created by a Silicon Valley venture capitalist and a business school professor, that explains how to make the critical decisions that determine whether a good idea will develop into a viable business.

Andrew Hallam (2011). *Millionaire Teacher: The Nine Rules of Wealth You Should Have Learned in School.* If you're worried about how to save effectively for retirement, you'll benefit from the insights and advice in this book. Hallam does a great job summarizing the research literature on this topic and giving practical advice based on it.

Aaron T. Beck (1989). *Love Is Never Enough: How Couples Can Overcome Misunderstandings, Resolve Conflicts, and Solve Relationship Problems Through Cognitive Therapy.* Need fresh ideas about making better choices in your relationship? You might get useful ideas from this book, authored by the founder of cognitive behavioral therapy. Though written for married couples, the book's principles can also be applied to other relationships, such as those with coworkers or kids.

CLINICS

In the following three "Clinics," we'll describe a real-world situation and challenge you to think about how to apply the WRAP framework to make a better decision. We hope that you'll find the Clinics a useful synthesis of the book.

Spoiler alert: There are no neat or happy endings to any of the following situations. This is deliberate. A good decision can't be assessed by the outcome, or else every roulette winner in Vegas would be a decision-making genius. Our focus here is on the process—how can these protagonists tip the odds in their favor by using the WRAP approach?

CLINIC 1

Should a Small Company Sue a Bigger Competitor?

SITUATION

(Note: All the facts in this clinic are drawn from a case study in *Inc.* magazine, written by Jennifer Alsever. See endnotes for link.)

Kim Etheredge and her friend Wendi Levy cofounded Mixed Chicks, a brand of hair products for mixed-race women. After eight years of work, they'd built up the annual revenues to $5 million. Then, in February 2011, Kim got a disturbing e-mail. One of the retailers who stocked Mixed Chicks reported that Sally Beauty Supply—a retail giant with $3 billion in revenue—had just started marketing its own line of products for mixed-race women. The name? Mixed Silk. Etheredge couldn't believe it. An hour later, another retailer called with a similar report.

Etheredge and Levy sent out a colleague to buy a sample, and when they saw the Mixed Silk product, they were furious. It was a rip-off of their own product, they felt, with a similar bottle and package—even the same fonts. And it sold for about half the price of their own product.

They were unimpressed by the quality of Mixed Silk, but they worried that customers wouldn't know the difference when they saw the two products side by side. Soon, they heard from more retailers, who reported that customers were buying the cheaper option.

What are their options?

Etheredge and Levy researched what other entrepreneurs had done in similar situations, and they talked with lawyers about their legal options. They could send a cease-and-desist letter, demanding that Sally Beauty Supply stop making Mixed Silk immediately. But that was risky: If the court ruled against them, they'd have to reimburse the giant retailer for lost revenue, which could be substantial. On the other hand, if they filed a lawsuit and won, they could drive Mixed Silk off the shelves permanently and collect damages on top of that.

The legal option was very expensive: experts estimated $250,000 to $500,000 per year in legal costs. The case could drag on for years. Was it worth the time and the distraction?

Then again, what if Mixed Silk and its lower price point ended up crushing Mixed Chicks? How would they feel having not stood up for themselves?

The two founders agonized over the question: Should we sue or not?

How can they make a good decision?

• *Widen Your Options.* The "whether or not to sue" framing is a warning that they may be trapped in a narrow frame. Remember, one question you can ask, to break out of a narrow frame, is the "opportunity cost" question: *What else could we do with the same time and resources?* Imagine the impact if, instead of spending a half million dollars per year on legal fees, Mixed Chicks spent that money on advertising, or used it to hire 10 new salespeople. A retail expert cited by *Inc.*, James T. Noble, took this analysis a step further, suggesting a great alternative: "Rather than sue, Etheredge and Levy could have repositioned their product as the premium offering and ridden the wave of publicity and market growth created by Sally Beauty. . . . In a way, Sally Beauty's entering the market could be the best thing that ever happens to the business." As another alternative, Mixed Chicks could have used the money and time to wage war on the PR front. They have a classic David vs. Goliath story to tell.

• *Reality-Test Your Assumptions.* Etheredge and Levy were wise to seek out other business owners who had faced similar situations. That's a great way for them to reality-check themselves. They should exercise caution when investigating their legal options, being careful to seek out disconfirming evidence. Certainly the lawyers who might represent them—and earn $500,000 per year in legal fees—will not be neutral parties! (And we hope those cost estimates came from the "base rates" of other business owners, not from the predictions of lawyers. It would be a disaster if the lawyers were lowballing and the real costs came to $1 million per year.) To get more accurate legal information, could the founding duo "consider the opposite"? Suppose they sought out the counsel of a corporate lawyer—the kind of person who might represent Sally Beauty Supply—and pay for a few hours of their advice. That counselor could help them zoom out, understanding the base rates of success for lawsuits of this kind. But the lawyer might also help them zoom in, offering them a close-up of *what it's like to be part of a lawsuit like this*. (How does it feel, day-to-day? Does it take over your life? Does it affect your health?)

• *Attain Distance Before Deciding.* As it happens, a month later—in March 2011—Mixed Chicks filed suit. "Kim and I felt the same way," said Levy. "There was no way we could just sit there." This worries us, because it sounds like a decision that may not have been evaluated with a distanced, long-term view of future consequences. The desire to "stick it" to Sally Beauty Supply is completely understandable—we'd feel it too in their shoes—but is it possible they let their anger dictate their choice? We wonder what would have happened if they'd asked, "What would our successors do?" Looking at the situation from another perspective might have helped them get distance. Another way to look at the situation is to ask: What are their core priorities? If they founded the company to serve the hair needs of mixed-race women, does the lawsuit really serve that goal better than any other option? And what are they going to *stop doing* to make room in their lives for the lawsuit? We suspect they didn't have a lot of idle time, as growth entrepreneurs, before the suit began. What "List A" items will suffer as a result of this choice?

- *Prepare to Be Wrong.* Levy and Etheredge should run a "premortem" to identify the biggest risks of filing the lawsuit. The biggest risk in our minds is that the lawsuit bleeds their cash reserves, dragging on for years, and it saps their entrepreneurial motivation, leaving them stressed-out and distracted from the rigors of managing a growing business. This situation, in which there's no clear-cut ending, cries out for a tripwire. Perhaps they could have promised themselves not to spend a dollar over $750,000. Or that they wouldn't let it drag on longer than 18 months. They can't afford to let the lawsuit take over their work, especially when they can anticipate that the day-to-day emotions will be strong and bitter.

Reflections on the process

To us, the biggest risks to avoid in this decision were (1) getting trapped in the narrow frame of "to sue or not to sue" and missing other good options; and (2) making a costly decision because of visceral emotion. At press time, the lawsuit is still ongoing.

―――――――――――― CLINIC 2 ――――――――――

Should a Young Professional Move to the City?

SITUATION

Sophia, a single woman in her late 20s, was born in China but immigrated to the United States, earning her MBA at a top-ranked business school. In 2012, she lived in Fort Wayne, Indiana, where she worked in corporate strategy for a large fashion company. She liked her job and her coworkers, but she also wanted a family. "I can't picture myself being 35 and not being married," she said. After living in Fort Wayne for five years, and enduring a pretty bleak dating experience, she had begun to worry whether she'd ever find the right guy in the area. "There are no single men here. . . . This is a place where people come to buy a house in the suburbs and raise a family," she said. One of Sophia's colleagues actually lived in Chicago and commuted, when necessary, to the Fort Wayne office. She urged Sophia to do the same. With 1.3 million men in the city, Sophia couldn't complain about a lack of options. (Note: Sophia's name and location are disguised—so Fort Wayne single men should not take offense—but all other details are accurate.)

What are her options?

Sophia had been flirting with the idea of moving to Chicago for a year or two—she believed her boss would sign off on the move—but she hadn't gotten serious about it. It seemed like such a hassle: She'd need to sell her home in Fort Wayne, find a place to live in Chicago, and get to know a totally different city. But as the months flew by, with no progress on the dating front, she wondered whether she needed to take the plunge. Should she move or not?

How can she make a good decision?

• *Widen Your Options.* Note the binary choice: Should she move or not? Most of the time that's a sign of narrow framing. But actually, to her credit, Sophia had considered several other options. She considered finding a new job, which might entail a move to a better place for singles, but decided that she valued her current job and colleagues too much. And she was still considering ways to make a more intense effort to meet people in Fort Wayne, perhaps by finding some kind of social group to join.

•   *Reality-Test Your Assumptions.* How could Sophia gather trustworthy information to guide her decision? First she should consult the world's foremost expert on this subject—i.e., her colleague who lives in Chicago and commutes to Fort Wayne! She should be careful to ask her colleague disconfirming questions: *What's the worst part of living remotely? What regrets do you have about living there? How long did it take you to meet new friends to hang out with there?* On a different front, note that this is a situation where it might be hard to ooch: She could certainly spend a week here and there in Chicago, but that might be the worst of both worlds, with all the hassles of commuting but none of the joys of making new friends and starting a new way of life. This feels like a situation where ooching would be "emotional tiptoeing." She either needs to leap—or, for her own peace of mind, stop thinking about leaping.

•   *Attain Distance Before Deciding.* Sophia had been thinking about the move for some time, and the decision ultimately boiled down to whether she was ready to take a risk. Fort Wayne may have been lacking in single men, but it was familiar. It was comfortable. Chicago was exciting to think about, but there were so many unknowns. What if she hated it? What if it was *worse*? (Notice the echoes here of both mere exposure and loss aversion.) One night, at dinner, a colleague asked her: "What would you tell your best friend to do if she were in this situation?" And Sophia said, without hesitation, "Oh, move to Chicago!" She seemed a bit shocked at how easily the answer had popped out. And that same night, she texted her boss, wondering if he was still amenable to the idea of her moving.

- *Prepare to Be Wrong.* Having resolved to move, Sophia should think through her options if Chicago does not work out. One of her best moves would be to keep her house in Fort Wayne for a trial period of, say, 9 or 12 months, renting it out to pay the mortgage. That way, she could easily come right back to her previous life if need be. Sophia should also get a "realistic job preview" from her friend in Chicago: What's the "warts and all" reality that she should prepare herself for? (Note that by asking disconfirming questions of her friend earlier, she already got some of this texture.) Finally, she could also set a personal tripwire: If she didn't manage to have a few interesting dates within her first year in Chicago, she might conclude that the problem is with her lifestyle rather than her location. In that scenario, she might resolve to travel less or make a bigger effort to get involved in social activities through a volunteer organization, church, or professional group. (Or, better yet, why not think "AND not OR" and do both? That is, move to Chicago AND start new social activities?)

Reflections on the process

We have warned repeatedly about a binary decision like "move to Chicago or not," but this one seems legitimate. (She has explored and rejected other options.) So, to us, the critical part of Sophia's decision was the need to attain distance, to let what was important shine through. In her case, the question "What would you tell your best friend to do?" gave her the distance she needed. At press time, she is still planning to move but had not yet moved. (Maybe she needs a tripwire.)

—————————— CLINIC 3 ——————————

Should We Discount Our Software?

SITUATION

You are a sales executive at a software company. Your primary product is a tool that helps clients manage their online customer-service interactions more effectively. To date, you have developed a stronghold among high-tech clients, but the senior leaders at your firm are eager to expand sales to government agencies that deal with a high volume of citizens. Unfortunately, the early efforts to sell to government clients have not been impressive. Despite six months of effort by two full-time salespeople, only a few small accounts have been landed. One of your sales reps, Tom, has repeatedly told you that you need to cut prices for the government customers. But you've been a sales manager for a long time, and you know that salespeople always want to lower prices. So you have some healthy skepticism about whether lowering prices is the right move.

What are your options?

It's your job to do something to improve sales in the government market. But it's not clear what your options are. You could do nothing—sometimes it takes time to cultivate relationships; maybe it will simply take more time for the sales efforts to pay off. Or you could cut prices right away and see if that makes a difference. It's not clear what else you could try. That ambiguity is part of your problem.

How can you make a good decision?

• *Widen Your Options.* It's important not to be framed by Tom's complaints into a narrow decision about "whether or not" to reduce price. Price isn't the only variable that explains why customers buy. What other options do you have? If none comes immediately to mind, do your "laddering." First look internally at your bright spots. You've already closed a few accounts; what can you learn from those successes? Then you can ladder up and see what other software firms are doing in the government market. What seems to work for them? Laddering further up, you might study any product that is sold both to corporations and to government agencies. What are the differences in how the products are configured and sold? Maybe you'd learn, for instance, that government customers expect more hands-on service than do your savvy tech clients. In short, you shouldn't fixate on pricing before you have more data. You need more options and more information.

•   *Reality-Test Your Assumptions.* First, ooch. Give Tom the leeway to offer substantial discounts to one or two customers. See what happens. Why guess when you can know? Simultaneously, try considering the opposite: If the theory is that price is the problem, go looking for evidence that price is *not* the problem. For example, you could ask your other sales rep to charge a *higher* price—but one that includes an extensive service package. A few experiments with higher and lower pricing should tell you a lot. As you run these experiments, gather more information by zooming out and zooming in. To zoom out, you might look for third parties—market research companies, for instance—who could tell you whether software companies typically discount for government clients, and if so, how much. (That would be a flavor of "base rate.") Also, you could zoom in by joining your sales reps for a few customer visits. Meeting your clients personally and hearing their feedback would give you some much-needed texture on the situation.

•   *Attain Distance Before Deciding.* You aren't ready to make a decision here. You need better information and more options first. That said, if Tom turns out to be right, you may have competing core priorities on your hands: Should you slash prices (cutting profits) for the sake of building a base of government clients? Is the core priority market share or profit margin? It's worth sounding out your leaders for their perspective.

• *Prepare to Be Wrong*. Without knowing your decision, it's hard to prepare for the aftermath. But you can almost always set a tripwire. For instance, you could set a limit on the experiments you're trying with your salespeople. You might work with Tom on an appropriate trip-wire—i.e., if he hasn't closed a deal in two months, given the freedom to discount the price as he requested, then you'll both agree to try a different approach.

Reflections on the process

To deliver procedural justice, it's important to make Tom feel heard in this situation (though that's not the same thing as automatically ac-cepting his perspective). Give him a chance to prove his point of view. As the leader of this effort, though, you can't afford to shut down other options while you pursue Tom's theory. You've got to multitrack. Seek-ing out multiple streams of information, and conducting some smart experiments, will help you clarify what your best options are.

OVERCOMING OBSTACLES

Below are a dozen common roadblocks to using the WRAP process effectively, along with some advice for overcoming them. (Note that the advice is written in jargon-ish shorthand—only someone who has read the book will understand what we're talking about.)

1. I'm a good decision maker, but I make decisions more slowly than I'd like and my choices end up being pretty cautious. How can I be quicker/bolder?

Advice: (1) Sounds like you lean toward the prevention mindset, so ask yourself promotion-minded questions such as, "How would I make this decision if I was focused on opening up opportunities for myself?" (2) Try asking yourself, "What would I advise my best friend to do?" Your caution may be the result of short-term fears (such as embarrassment) that aren't that important in the long run. Attaining some mental distance may help you see that. (3) If you're worried what will happen if your choice turns out poorly, consider setting a tripwire (based on a date or a budget) that will make you comfortable that you've limited your losses.

2. We are an understaffed firm in a chaotic market. We don't have time to work through an elaborate process every time we make a decision.

Advice: Here's an Express Version of the WRAP process. (1) Widen: Add one more option to your consideration set. (If you can't think of one easily, look for someone who's solved your problem, via your network of contacts or a simple

Internet search.) (2) Reality-Test: Call one expert who can educate you about the "base rates" in your situation (for example, odds of success or typical timelines). (3) Attain Distance: Resolve tough dilemmas by asking which option best fits your core priorities. (4) Prepare: Bookend the future—spend an hour thinking about what could go wrong and what could go right, and then do something to prepare for both contingencies.

3. My spouse (or my coworker) wants to do something I think is crazy.

Advice: (1) Perhaps they're falling prey to an overly narrow frame, thinking that the crazy idea is the only one that would achieve their goals. Can you propose a couple of other options that would be attractive but less wacko? (2) Can you get them to "go to the *genba*"? That is, can you send them on a mission where they will absorb useful texture and nuance? (For example, a budding jewelry designer might be sent to a crafts fair to count the underwhelming number of sales made by a particular jeweler in a 30-minute period.) (3) Remember the topiary-sculpture business example from the text: You can use tripwires to specify the acceptable risk for a crazy idea.

4. We analyze and analyze, but nothing ever seems to get decided.

Advice: (1) If your slowness is driven by "bargaining," then maybe it's worth the wait. Your team's decision may improve as a result of considering different options and opposing views. (2) Are you analyzing something that would be quicker to test? Reframe your choice as an experiment, a la Intuit. (3) Ask the Andy Grove question: If you were replaced, what would your successors do? (4) If it's fear of risk that's making you slow to decide, do a premortem analysis and figure out ways to cap your potential losses.

5. The problem we have is that everyone is scared to make a decision. Doing anything new is a big career risk because you are putting your neck on the chopping block. It's safer to keep doing what we're doing.

Advice: (1) Try using the Roger Martin question: "What would have to be true for each option to be right?" Answering that question in a group can help *distribute ownership* of the decision. If everyone agrees on the "conditions" that you'll use to make the final choice, then everyone is equally responsible for the decision. (2) Keep your head off the chopping block by ooching before you leap. If an ooch flops, you've only taken a limited risk. (3) Mere exposure makes the status quo seem safe and comfortable, while new ideas seem risky. Try to make the new idea feel safer by finding someone else who has solved your problem. Talk up the fact that the solution already exists—someone else has already taken the risk. (4) Remember Dave Hitz's comment that the "best way to defend a decision is to point out its flaws"? Acknowledge the risks in your idea AND set tripwires that specify the conditions under which you'd reverse yourself. (If you've publicly anticipated and prepared for bad outcomes, it's less likely you'll be scapegoated.)

6. How do I know when I've got enough options?

Advice: (1) Try to "fall in love twice." Keep searching until you've got two really good options. (2) The purpose of multitracking is to let you easily compare and contrast options, which helps you map out the landscape of what's possible. If incremental options aren't helping you get smarter, you've probably done enough. Call off the search for more. (3) Be careful not to collect so many options that you don't have the time or resources to "reality-test" them. (For example, the aspiring home buyer will need to limit her serious options to about 4 to 7 homes rather than 30, just because of logistical reality.) (4) If one of your options doesn't have any advocates, drop it from contention. (Or, if it's a personal decision, discard any option that never seems to cycle to the top of your mental wish list.)

7. We always go through the motions of exploring and analyzing decisions, but then ultimately the boss does what he wants to do.

Advice: (1) Consider the opposite: Maybe the boss is right. He may be considering a wider set of information than you; recall FDR's advisers who were surprised that he knew their tidbit of gossip and something else besides. But if you're still skeptical about your boss's judgment, read on. (2) If your boss will inevitably make the final call based on his "gut," then could you invest in training his gut? For instance, you could try to arrange a "close-up" for him—some kind of real-world visit (to a retail store, a customer site, a patient's home, etc.) that would inform his intuition. (3) In meetings, find ways to remind the group of the organization's core priorities. Surfacing those priorities might make it harder for your boss to go rogue. (4) Give up on today's decision but start thinking about the next round: Try to get your boss on record about some tripwires. For example, what circumstances would convince him to reconsider the decision nine months down the road?

8. I have tried advising my son/daughter using ideas similar to these and they just won't listen. They do what they want to do anyway.

Advice: (1) For kids of a certain age, parents are genetically disqualified as advisers. So find someone more "credible" whom they might trust. Perhaps you could get someone who has lived their choice to give your kid a realistic preview of what's involved. (For example, a teen contemplating skipping college to pursue an acting career in NYC might benefit from hearing—from the mouth of an actual struggling actor—what that lifestyle will be like.) (2) Ask your kid, "If I let you make this choice, what am I going to see that will convince me that you've made the best possible choice?" (Sample answer for the aspiring NYC actor: "Mom, I just know this is going to make me happy and that I can live frugally enough to make it.") Having these overconfident predictions on record will give you leverage when/if the claims prove false. (Or, conversely, they may help you to realize that your kid was right all along!)

9. We have too much information. A blizzard of customer data. To really process all of it would make our decisions take four times as long.

Advice: (1) Maybe you're too zoomed in. Experts make better predictions when they zoom out and look at base rates rather than trying to predict based on the idiosyncrasies of individual cases. (2) You don't need to predict when you can know. Is there a way you can ooch and thereby avoid the cycle of over-thinking? (3) Could you be obsessing about a decision that just isn't worth it? Try doing the 10/10/10 analysis to see whether the outcome truly matters enough to agonize about.

10. The culture here makes no one want to give up on a bad project or bad idea, because that means you have to admit failure. This silly persistence hurts us because it drains resources that could go to new projects. What should I do?

Advice: (1) Remember to toggle between the prevention and promotion mindsets, as did the companies who fared best after recessions. In your situation, the promotion mindset may help people reorient themselves toward seizing new opportunities rather than sticking with failed choices. (2) Try to insert some disconfirming views. Can you have people war-game what competitors or customers will do if the bad project persists? Better to admit failure now than face disaster in the future. (3) Andy Grove faced a similar situation with Intel's memory business, which had begun as a tremendous success but slid slowly into trouble. The question "What would our successors do?" gave him the strength to declare defeat on memories—while doubling down on microprocessors. (4) Set up a tripwire in the form of a resource partition that forces re-evaluation at a specified time. (For example, "We are going to give this legacy project six more months, or $250,000 in additional investment, but if it doesn't turn around by then, we'll rethink it.") That may make it easier and less political to change course.

11. I know what the right thing to do is, but I'm not sure I could ever sell it politically. So should I fight for the right thing or just resign myself to the "sausage factory"?

Advice: (1) Think "AND not OR": Be careful not to frame the issue in black-and-white terms until you've made sure there are no solutions that would allow you to do the right thing AND satisfy your colleagues' issues. (2) Be a devil's advocate. Even if you don't sway the final decision, you might still have an impact on the way the decision is implemented. (3) Appeal to core priorities. If the "right thing" is what's most consistent with your organization's stated values, then the burden should be on your colleagues to dispute those values, instead of arguing with you personally. (4) If the cause is lost, shift to bookending. Find ways to cap the potential harm you envision. In doing so, you'll be protecting the organization—and also marking yourself as the one wise person who saw the harm coming. (5) And don't forget to assume positive intent: Your colleagues may be wrong (or you may be), but chances are all of you want to do what's best.

Introduction

2   **Daniel Kahneman.** The "rarely stumped" quote is from page 97, and the "normal state" quote is from page 85 of Daniel Kahneman (2011), *Thinking, Fast and Slow* (New York: Farrar, Straus & Giroux). In this book, Kahneman brilliantly simplifies the confusing zoo of biases and errors that have been documented by the decision literature and shows how they are systematically produced by "what you see is all there is." To see how this principle produces the biases we cover in *Decisive*, see his analysis of narrow framing (p. 87), overconfidence (pp. 199–201, 209–12, and 259–63), confirmation bias (pp. 80–84), and emotion and indecision (pp. 401–6).

3   **Career choices.** The 40% failure rate is described in Brooke Masters, "Rise of a Headhunter," *Financial Times*, March 30, 2009, http://www.ft.com/cms /s/0/19975256-1af2-11de-8aa3-0000779fd2ac.html#axzz2401DwtbW. Describing the costs of these decisions, Kevin Kelly, the CEO of the prominent executive search firm Heidrick & Struggles, says, "It's expensive in terms of lost revenue. It's expensive in terms of the individual's hiring. It's damaging to morale." The teaching study is National Commission on Teaching and America's Future, "Policy Brief: The High Cost of Teacher Turnover," http://nctaf.org/wp -content/uploads/NCTAFCostofTeacherTurnoverpolicybrief.pdf. The lawyer statistic is from Alex Williams, "The Falling-Down Professions," *New York Times*, January 6, 2008, http://www.nytimes.com/2008/01/06/fashion/06professions .html. (Interestingly, 60% of doctors had considered getting out of medicine because of low morale.)

3   **Business decisions.** The study of 2,207 business decisions is cited in Dan Lovallo and Olivier Sibony (2010), "The Case for Behavioral Strategy," *McKinsey Quarterly* 2: 30–45. A study by KPMG International in 1999 looked at shareholder returns on corporate mergers relative to the performance of other companies in the same industry one year after the announcement of the

merger. Using this commonly cited standard of success, it "found that 83% of mergers failed to unlock value." David Harding and Sam Rovit (2004), *Mastering the Merger* (Boston: Harvard Business School Press). Of mergers, 83% failed to increase shareholder and half actually destroyed it.

3   **On the personal front.** Elderly regrets are discussed in Thomas Gilovich and Victoria Husted Medvec (1995), "The Experience of Regret: What, When, and Why," *Psychological Review* 102: 379–95.

4   **Guts full of questionable advice.** The Ultimate Red Velvet Cheesecake is here: http://abcnews.go.com/Business/diet-disasters-top-calorie-heavy-menu-items/story?id=14114606#.UA2nOLTUPYQ;McDonald'scheeseburgers, http://nutrition.mcdonalds.com/getnutrition/nutritionfacts.pdf; Skittles, http://www.wrigley.com/global/brands/skittles.aspx#panel-3. Liz Taylor's marriage history can be found in her entry in Wikipedia.

5   **Guts can't make up their minds.** Tattoo reversals: http://www.boston.com/lifestyle/fashion/articles/2011/09/02/tattoo_remorse_fuels_reverse_trend_tattoo_removal/ (accessed 9/27/2012). The New Year's resolutions study was by Richard Wiseman of the University of Hertfordshire and is discussed in Alok Jha, "New Year Resolution? Don't Wait Until New Year's Eve," *Guardian*, December 27, 2007, http://www.guardian.co.uk/science/2007/dec/28/sciencenews.research.

5   **Lovallo and Sibony study.** This impressive study is described in Dan Lovallo and Olivier Sibony (2010), "The Case for Behavioral Strategy," *McKinsey Quarterly* 2: 30–45. The Sibony analogy of the courtroom is in Bill Huyett and Tim Keller (2011), "How CFOs Can Keep Strategic Decisions on Track," *McKinsey on Finance* 38: 10–15. The Lovallo quote is from an interview of Dan Lovallo by Chip Heath in April 2012.

7   **Franklin moral algebra.** The full text of this letter is widely available on the Web or in John Towill Rutt (1831), *Life and Correspondence of Joseph Priestley in Two Volumes*, vol. 1 (London: R Hunter). See entry for September 10, 1772, on page 182.

Chapter 1: The Four Villains of Decision Making

9   **Steve Cole, AND not OR.** Cole quotes are from interviews of Cole by Chip Heath in May 2011 and June 2012.

11 **One vendor that was uniquely capable.** Paul Nutt, whom we'll introduce in chapter 2, found in one large study that when organizations asked vendors for one round of solutions and picked the best option (the typical proposal process in most organizations), they ended up choosing an option

that was a long-term success 51% of the time (see table 4, page 83). When they used the input from the initial search to learn about the field and then conducted a second search, their success rate jumped to 100%. Paul C. Nutt (1999), "Surprising but True: Half the Decisions in Organizations Fail," *Academy of Management Executive* 13: 75–90.

11 **Confirmation bias.** The smoker study is Timothy C. Brock (1965), "Commitment to Exposure as a Determinant of Information Receptivity," *Journal of Personality and Social Psychology* 2: 10–19. The Lovallo quote is from an interview of Dan Lovallo by Chip Heath in April 2012.

14 **Memory chips at Intel.** This story is on pages 81–93 of Andy Grove's memoir. Andrew S. Grove (1996), *Only the Paranoid Survive* (New York: Currency Doubleday). The Grove quotes summarizing 1984 and the "new CEO" test are on page 89. The Intel stock calculations were performed on Wolfram-Alpha on April 3, 2012. Barry M. Staw, who has done more than any other researcher to understand the organizational reasons why people irrationally escalate commitment to losing courses of action, predicted that the Grove technique would be effective. He says that one way to distinguish reasonable effort from overcommitment is to "schedule regular times to step back and look at a project from an outsider's perspective. A good question to ask oneself at these times is, 'If I took over this job for the first time today and found this project going on, would I support it or get rid of it?'" See page 5 of Barry M. Staw & Jerry Ross (1987), "Knowing When to Pull the Plug," *Harvard Business Review*, March–April 1987: 1–7.

15 **Decision-making as spreadsheets.** The field of decision analysis is based on this kind of approach. For a smart, accessible version of this style of advice, see John S. Hammond, Ralph L. Keeney, and Howard Raiffa (1999), *Smart Choices: A Practical Guide to Making Better Life Decisions* (Boston: Harvard Business School Press).

16 **Odds of a meltdown.** "Odds of Meltdown 'One in 10,000 Years,' Soviet Official Says," April 29, 1986, search "odds of meltdown" at www.apnewsarchive.com.

16 **Who wants to hear actors talk?** Clifford Pickover, "Traveling Through Time," PBS *Nova* blog, October 12, 1999, http://www.pbs.org/wgbh/nova/time/through2.html.

16 **An electrical toy.** This quote is widely reported, but it is so hubristically wrongheaded that we thought it might be an urban legend. The technology historian David A. Hounshell says that this particular version of the quote may or may not be apocryphal, but he reports multiple examples from letters at the

time of Bell's patent where knowledgeable telegraph scientists and business-people referred to it as a "toy." David A. Hounshell (1975), "Elisha Gray and the Telephone: On the Disadvantages of Being an Expert," *Technology and Culture* 16: 133–61.

16 **Beatles story.** See Josh Sanburn, "Four-Piece Groups with Guitars Are Finished," *Time*, October 21, 2011, http://www.time.com/time/specials/packages /article/0,28804,2097462_2097456_2097466,00.html, and the Beatles Bible, http://www.beatlesbible.com/1962/01/01/recording-decca-audition/. The Lennon quote is from The Beatles (2000), *The Beatles Anthology* (San Francisco: Chronicle Books), p. 67. Dick Rowe later repented of his "guitar groups are finished" decision and, on the advice of George Harrison, signed the Rolling Stones a year later in 1963. According to Wikipedia, Decca Records' "regret at not signing The Beatles" made Decca willing to bend a great deal in the negotiations with the Rolling Stones. The Stones got "three times the typical royalty rate for a new act, full artistic control of recordings, and ownership of the recording masters" (see http://en.wikipedia.org/wiki/The_Rolling_Stones).

18 **Four steps.** There is wide agreement across authors on the basic stages of a decision process, although in practice every decision book slices and labels them a tad differently. Our slicing of the steps probably owes the most to a great book by J. Edward Russo and Paul J. H. Schoemaker (2002), *Winning Decisions: Getting It Right the First Time* (New York: Currency/Doubleday). Chip taught students for years from an earlier version of their model in a book called *Decision Traps* and is eternally grateful to them for making his early years of teaching easier. The award for the decision model that is most likely to inspire a cartoon spin-off goes to the GOFER model (Goals clarification, Options generation, Fact-finding, consideration of Effects, Review and implementation), from Leon Mann, Ros Harmoni, Colin Power, and Gery Beswick (1988), "Effectiveness of the GOFER Course in Decision Making for High School Students," *Journal of Behavioral Decision Making* 1: 159–68.

19 **Joseph Priestley.** The pros-and-cons analysis is based on Priestley's letters, as compiled by John Towill Rutt (1831), *Life and Correspondence of Joseph Priestley in Two Volumes*, vol. 1 (London: R Hunter). See, especially, letters in 1772 to Dr. Price (July 21, August 25, September 27), Reverend W. Turner (August 24), Reverend T. Lindsey (undated), and Reverend Joshua Toulmin (December 15) and the famous moral-algebra letter *from* Dr. Franklin (September 10) on pages 175–87. Our overview of Priestley's career benefited from material on his life and accomplishments by the American Chemical Society, which

awards a Priestley Medal each year for contributions to chemistry (search for "Priestley" at acs.org).

25 **Intuitive decisions.** A few years back, there was a strong move to celebrate intuition in day-to-day and business decisions. See, for example, Malcolm Gladwell's (2007) account in *Blink: The Power of Thinking Without Thinking* (New York: Back Bay Books), or Gary Klein (2003), *The Power of Intuition: How to Use Your Gut Feelings to Make Better Decisions at Work* (New York: Crown Business). Recently, thanks in part to Daniel Kahneman's accessible explanation of intuition in *Thinking Fast and Slow*, there is a growing popular awareness of the limitations of intuition.

What is sometimes lost in the work celebrating intuition is a sense of the relatively limited domain where it can help us make good decisions. A research consensus is now emerging about situations where intuition reliably generates reasonable answers. Robin Hogarth, one of the researchers who have done the most to clarify situations where intuition does and doesn't work, describes learning environments along a continuum from kind to wicked. When we acquire our intuitions in a kind environment, our gut instincts are likely to be good, but intuitions acquired in wicked environments are likely to be bad. Feedback in kind environments is clear, immediate, and unbiased by the act of prediction. Forecasting the weather for tomorrow is a kind environment. Feedback is rapid (next day) and clear (it snows or it doesn't). And the act of making a prediction doesn't bias the outcome—the rain and snow don't care about the forecaster.

In contrast, the learning environment in an emergency room is wicked because of the lack of long-term feedback. Most ER docs and nurses get good short-term feedback (I either help the patient stop bleeding or I don't) but bad long-term feedback, since they don't see what happens to a patient once he or she leaves the emergency room (e.g., did something we did to stop the bleeding cause greater complications down the road?). The learning environment for new-product launches is wicked on all three dimensions. Feedback is unclear (perhaps Pets.com was a bad idea or perhaps it was just ahead of its time), it is delayed (often for months or years), and it is biased by the very act of prediction (classifying a launch as high priority or low has self-fulfilling ramifications for, say, its ad budget or the quality of the personnel on the launch team). Because of the environments they operate in, we will be better off trusting the intuitions of the weatherman than the entrepreneur or brand manager launching a new product. We should trust the ER doc to find an effective short-term solution to a health crisis but not to recommend good long-term actions for a chronic condition. For a brief summary of Hogarth's argument, see Robin Hogarth (2001), *Educating Intuition* (Chicago: University of Chicago Press), pp. 218–19.

Somewhat depressingly, the situations where we should most trust our instincts don't characterize many of the most important decisions that we make in life—which college to go to, whom to marry, which product to launch, which employee to promote. Professor Rick Larrick of Duke University has a compact summary of the kinds of environments that have been reliably found to develop good intuition: He calls them "video game worlds"—they are environments that provide quick, unambiguous, unalterable feedback. Video games, however, allow you to die and come back to life multiple times as you learn. For the kinds of decisions that we cover in this book, life doesn't typically allow many do-overs.

Interestingly, Danny Kahneman and Gary Klein had a long debate, extending over several years, about the value of intuition and ended up converging in their views (and in a direction consistent with Hogarth's account above). Even Klein, a strong proponent of the value of intuition, treats intuitive feelings as just one input to the decision process. When asked by *McKinsey Quarterly* whether executives should trust their gut, he responded, "If you mean, 'My gut feeling is telling me this; therefore I can act on it and I don't have to worry,' we say you should never trust your gut. You need to take your gut feeling as an important data point, but then you have to consciously and deliberatively evaluate it, to see if it makes sense in this context." Kahneman and Klein eventually agreed that intuition was more trustworthy in situations where the learning environment (1) is predictable and (2) provides good feedback. For the Klein quote, see "When Can You Trust Your Gut?" *McKinsey Quarterly* 2010 2: 58–67. For the account of their conversation written for psychologists, see Daniel Kahneman and Gary Klein (2009), "Conditions for Intuitive Expertise: A Failure to Disagree," *American Psychologist* 64: 515–26.

26 **Van Halen, brown M&Ms.** We first wrote a version of the David Lee Roth tale in a *Fast Company* column published in March 2010. All David Lee Roth quotes are from his autobiography: David Lee Roth (1997), *Crazy from the Heat* (New York: Hyperion). The television story is on page 156, and the brown M&M clause is on pages 97–98. Roth says a university in Colorado didn't pay close attention to the weight guidelines in the contract and the Van Halen stage *sank* through its new rubberized basketball flooring, leading to a replacement cost of $80,000. The press reported that Roth had trashed the

dressing room and done $85,000 of damage. "Who am I to get in the way of a good rumor?" says Roth.

28 **Baumeister turns.** Roy F. Baumeister, et al. (1998), "Ego Depletion: Is the Active Self a Limited Resource?" *Journal of Personality and Social Psychology* 4: 1252.

Chapter 2: Avoid a Narrow Frame

33 **Teen decisions.** The "break up or not?" discussion is from http://www .ask.com/answers/177313841/break-up-or-not. The research study is described in Baruch Fischhoff (1996), "The Real World: What Good Is It?" *Organizational Behavior and Human Decision Processes* 65: 232–48. See Fischhoff's summary on page 234 and table 1. (Fischhoff says that 65% of the teens' decisions had no explicit alternatives or one, 30% had two or more real alternatives; a final 5% of cases were decisions that Fischhoff called "seeking or 'designing' options" such as decisions about "what to do about . . ."; we didn't know exactly how to classify the final 5%, so our discussion in the text refers only to the first two categories.) The one category of decisions that violated the "whether or not" tendency to consider only one option was decisions related to clothing. The world's marketers have made it much easier to consider alternatives. Even so, 40% of the teenagers' clothing decisions lacked a second option.

35 **Quaker acquires Snapple.** Most of the background and analysis of this case study is in Paul C. Nutt (2004), "Expanding the Search for Alternatives During Strategic Decision-Making," *Academy of Management Executive* 18: 13–28. He covers the Snapple acquisition on pages 17–18. The "billion dollars too high" assessment is in Barnaby J. Feder, "Quaker to Sell Snapple for $300 Million," *New York Times*, March 28, 1997, http://www.nytimes.com/1997/03/28/business /quaker-to-sell-snapple-for-300-million.html?pagewanted=all&src=pm. On the day that Smithburg announced this largest acquisition in company history, the stock of both companies sank, Quaker's by 10%. See Glenn Collins, "Quaker Oats to Acquire Snapple," *New York Times*, November 3, 1994, http://www.nytimes .com/1994/11/03/business/company-reports-quaker-oats-to-acquire-snapple .html?pagewanted=2. The "arguing the 'no' side of the evaluation" quote is from page 98 of one of our favorite reads on business decision making, Sydney Finkelstein (2003), *Why Smart Executives Fail* (New York: Portfolio). Finkelstein also discusses the problem of the debt incurred by Quaker. The Feder article above notes that shares of Quaker *rose* when it sold off Snapple at a loss, suggesting that investors applauded the belated decision to get out of a bad situation.

36 **A KPMG study.** The Sydney Finkelstein book *Why Smart Executives Fail* devotes a whole chapter to the problems of mergers and acquisitions (see chapter 4, pp. 77–107). The KPMG study is discussed on page 77.

37 **Nutt study of 168 strategic decisions.** Paul C. Nutt (1993), "The Identification of Solution Ideas During Organizational Decision Making," *Management Science* 39: 1071–85. The comparison of failure rates of "whether or not," single-alternative decisions to failure rates of multiple-alternative decisions is in table 4 on page 1079. Nutt explains the perils of "whether or not" decisions on page 78 of Paul C. Nutt (1999), "Surprising but True: Half the Decisions in Organizations Fail," *Academy of Management Executive* 13: 75–90.

40 **Heidi Price helps students.** The Heidi Price story is based on two conversations between Dan Heath and Heidi Price in July 2011 and April 2012 and a conversation with Caufield Schnug in July 2012.

40 **Smart enough to get into Yale.** Economists studied students who had been admitted to two schools of higher and lower prestige but decided to attend the school with lower prestige. Estimated sacrifice in lifetime earnings from attending the less prestigious school: none. See this excellent summary of two studies by Princeton economists Stacy Dale and Alan Krueger: David Leonhardt, "Revisiting the Value of Elite Colleges," *New York Times*, February 21, 2011, http://economix.blogs.nytimes.com/2011/02/21/revisiting-the-value-of-elite-colleges/. The paper that initially established this result is Stacy Berg Dale and Alan B. Krueger (2002), "Estimating the Payoff of Attending a More Selective College: An Application of Selection on Observables and Unobservables," *Quarterly Journal of Economics* 107: 1491–1527. Leonhardt quotes Krueger: "My advice to students: Don't believe that the only school worth attending is one that would not admit you. . . . Your own motivation, ambition and talents will determine your success more than the college name on your diploma."

41 **Father J. Brian Bransfield.** Conversation between Dan Heath and J. Brian Bransfield in June 2011 and a subsequent e-mail exchange.

43 **Keep the $14.99 for other purchases.** The opportunity-cost study is discussed in Shane Frederick, et al. (2009), "Opportunity Cost Neglect," *Journal of Consumer Research* 36: 553–61. The "consider how much hamburger" and Eisenhower quotes are from this same journal article. The stereo story is told in the article without attribution; the additional story background is from a conversation between Chip Heath and Shane Frederick in March 2012.

47 **Should Sanders fire Anna?** Story from an interview between "Margaret Sanders" and Dan Heath in October 2011; both "Margaret Sanders" and "Anna" are disguised names.

Chapter 3: Multitrack

50 **Lexicon.** The Lexicon story is from a conversation between Dan Heath and David Placek in September 2010 and an older case study on Lexicon that was developed by Chip Heath and Victoria Chang (2002), "Lexicon (A)," Stanford GSB M300A. A version of this story first appeared in a *Fast Company* column we wrote: Dan Heath and Chip Heath, "How to Pick the Perfect Brand Name," *Fast Company*, December/January 2011.

53 **Web banner design study.** The study manipulating whether teams designed ads simultaneously or one at a time is Steven P. Dow, et al. (2010), "Parallel Prototyping Leads to Better Design Results, More Divergence, and Increased Self-Efficacy," *Transactions on Computer-Human Interaction* 17 (4). The facts about how participants reacted to the design procedures are on page 16. The Klemmer quotes are from an interview of Scott Klemmer by Chip Heath in September 2010.

55 **Eisenhardt Silicon Valley study.** The Eisenhardt research is in Kathleen M. Eisenhardt (1989), "Making Fast Strategic Decisions in High-Velocity Environments," *Academy of Management Journal* 32: 543–76.

56 **24 different kinds of jam.** Sheena S. Iyengar and Mark R. Lepper (2000), "When Choice Is Demotivating: Can One Desire Too Much of a Good Thing?" *Journal of Personality and Social Psychology* 79: 995–1006.

57 **Triggering decision paralysis.** The best evidence in the research literature is that decision paralysis is not likely to occur until the number of options moves past six, and some recent reviews have questioned whether it exists at all. The typical study in the literature has contrasted a small assortment of 4 to 6 items with a large assortment of 20 to 30 items and, like the jam study discussed here, the initial studies found that people were more likely to delay or resist choosing with the larger, 20- to 30-item assortment. The state of the literature as of the early 2000s was summarized by Barry Schwartz, who argued strongly for choice overload in his 2004 book *The Paradox of Choice: Why More Is Less* (New York: HarperCollins). We wrote about the choice-overload research in our books *Switch* and *Made to Stick*, citing research by Eldar Shafir and others who have found evidence of decision paralysis with as few as two options. But the typical study has implicitly assumed that paralysis kicks in somewhere between 6 options and 20.

Recently some researchers have argued that choice paralysis is not a serious problem even with the larger assortments. The initial demonstrations of choice paralysis attracted a lot of interest, so by 2010 a group of researchers was able to conduct a meta-analysis of over 50 published papers with more than 5,000 participants. They found that in the studies they reviewed, increasing the number of options did not reliably reduce satisfaction or motivation to choose. Indeed, in situations where people had expertise or well-developed preferences (e.g., common food categories like coffee), more choices tended to increase satisfaction. Benjamin Scheibehenne, Rainer Greifeneder, and Peter M. Todd (2010), "Can There Ever Be Too Many Options? A Meta-analytic Review of Choice Overload," *Journal of Consumer Research* 37: 409–25.

The debate is still ongoing, so if we ever rewrite *Made to Stick* or *Switch*, we'll revisit it to decide whether or not to continue highlighting the research studies of overload that we discussed in those books. But in terms of our advice to multitrack, we simply note that even if choice paralysis kicks in for the twentieth option, the research literature suggests that this is unlikely to be a serious problem for someone adding a second or third option, which is our recommendation here. And even if choice overload turns out to be a problem at small numbers, we suspect, based on Paul Nutt's work and the German technology-firm study below, that it would be worth trading off a little pain from choice overload for a lot of benefits of being able to choose from a set of two or three.

57 **Medium-sized German technology firm.** Hans Georg Gemünden and Jürgen Hauschildt (1985), "Number of Alternatives and Efficiency in Different Types of Top-Management Decisions," *European Journal of Operational Research* 22: 178–90. The procedure used to evaluate the decisions retrospectively was rigorous, unfolding in four different sessions of four hours (when was the last time you spent four hours reviewing your previous decisions?), and the distribution suggests the graders were tough on themselves; they rated only 26% of their decisions as very good, with 34% judged as poor and 40% as satisfactory. Of course this evidence is correlational rather than causal, but the researchers eliminated one major possible confound by showing that the superiority of multiple-alternative decisions held for both complex and simple decisions; so it didn't seem to be the case that the only decisions where multiple alternatives were available were the easy ones.

59 **Kissinger on options.** The "only one real option" quote is on page 418 of Henry Kissinger (1979), *White House Years* (New York: Little, Brown).

60 **Prevention and promotion.** In general, the "prevention" mindset is activated when we think about what we "ought" to do, our duties and obligations (as in the conversation with your son about his club presidency) or when we think about losses (your home price) or dangers (the new technology on the radio). The "promotion" mindset is activated when we think about our

goals, aspirations (as in your son's big goals for his club), or ideals (as in your home-improvement ideas) and when we think about gains or opportunities (as with the new technology). Our culture provides aphorisms that are designed to tickle each mindset. The prevention mindset is represented in "Better safe than sorry" and "A bird in the hand . . ." and "Look before you leap." The promotion mindset is represented in "Seize the day" and "Nothing ventured, nothing gained" and "He who hesitates is lost."

The psychologist who discovered these mindsets is Tory Higgins of Columbia University. He has a forthcoming book on this topic: Heidi Grant Halvorson and E. Tory Higgins (2013), *Focus: Use Different Ways of Seeing the World to Power Success and Influence* (New York: Hudson Street Press).

61 **How companies navigated three global recessions.** Ranjay Gulati, Nitin Nohria, and Franz Wohlgezogen (2010), "Roaring Out of Recession," *Harvard Business Review*, March 2010, pp. 4–10.

63 **Doreen.** The Doreen story is on pages 89–91 of Susan Nolen-Hoeksema (2003), *Women Who Think Too Much: How to Break Free of Overthinking and Reclaim Your Life* (New York: Holt).

Chapter 4: Find Someone Who's Solved Your Problem

68 **The massive scale of Walmart.** The 2012 revenue figure is from Michael T. Duke, "To Our Shareholders, Associates and Customers," http://www.walmart stores.com/sites/annual-report/2012/CEOletter.aspx. Other fun facts: Walmart is the world's third-largest employer, behind the U.S. Department of Defense and the People's Liberation Army of China. Ruth Alexander, "Which Is the World's Biggest Employer?" *BBC News Magazine*, March 19, 2012, http://www.bbc.co.uk/news/magazine-17429786. If it were a country, it would have the nineteenth-largest economy in the world. "Scary (but True) Facts About Wal-Mart," *Business Pundit*, July 1, 2012, http://www.businesspundit.com/stats-on-walmart/. Did you know there are no Walmarts in Australia, continental Europe, or New York City? Walmart, "Our Locations"; http://corporate.walmart.com/our-story /locations; Matt Chaban, "Walmart in New York City: Just How Desperate Is the Retail Giant to Open in the Big Apple?" *Huffington Post*, August 6, 2012, http://www.huffingtonpost.com/2012/08/06/wal-mart-in-new -york-city-losing-fight-to-open-store_n_1748039.html.

68 **Sam Walton.** The centralized-checkout story and the "copied" quote are from pages 336–39 of Richard S. Tedlow (2003), *Giants of Enterprise: Seven Business Innovators in the Empires They Built* (New York: Collins). The other examples of borrowing are from Walton's autobiography: Sam Walton and

John Huey (1992), *Sam Walton: Made in America* (New York: Doubleday). The Kmart quote is on page 104, discussion of other discounters on page 54, and distribution-center ideas on page 102. He says that during the early period Walmart was "too small and insignificant for any of the big boys to notice," so he would show up to the headquarters of a discounter in another part of the country and say, "Hi, I'm Sam Walton from Bentonville, Arkansas. We've got a few stores out there." He reports that most people would bring him in to chat, "perhaps out of curiosity," and he says, "I would ask lots of questions about pricing and distribution, whatever. I learned a lot that way" (page 105). This is the discount-store equivalent of the pet owners who raise the cute baby alligator until one day it's big enough to swallow the family dog.

70 **Kaiser Permanente.** This story is based on conversations between Chip Heath and Doctors Robert Pearl, Alan Whippy, and Diane Craig in August 2012. Background for the statistical comparison to prostate and breast cancer: Nationwide, it is estimated that between 210,000 and 350,000 patients a year die from sepsis. National Institutes of Health, "Sepsis Fact Sheet," October 2009, http://www.nigms.nih.gov/education /factsheet_sepsis.htm. Taking the midpoint of that range, if hospitals could match Kaiser Permanente's 28% reduction, it would be the yearly equivalent of saving 78,000 lives. According to the National Vital Statistics Report for 2009, breast cancer kills about 41,000 and prostate cancer kills 28,000. Kenneth D. Kochanek, et al., "Deaths: Final Data for 2009," *National Vital Statistics Reports* 60, no. 3 (December 29, 2011): 105 (http://www.cdc.gov/nchs/data /nvsr/nvsr60/nvsr60_03.pdf). Full disclosure: Chip has consulted with Kaiser Permanente on several of their change efforts, which is where he heard of this story, though he had not talked with Whippy or Craig before the conversations for this case study.

74 **Dion Hughes and Mark Johnson.** This story is from conversations between Chip Heath and Dion Hughes in September 2010 and March 2012. We asked Scott Goodson, the CEO of StrawberryFrog, who has worked with the two, to talk about his experience with them. Goodson's agency was founded on a network model, maintaining relationships with a couple of hundred freelancers around the world and picking a relevant subset to pitch each project for clients such as Frito-Lay, Heineken, Google, and Smart Car. Exposed to creative talent around the world, he has high praise for the ideas he gets from Hughes and Johnson: "When I work with them, I'll give them a couple of days to think about stuff, then I'll get on the phone and every idea will be like, 'Oh f*#@, that's amazing. That's such a perceptive way of thinking.' Dion and Mark have

a unique ability to be super, super strategic, to think about the brand and its promise and what's going on in the world and to tie all that together."

79 **Kevin Dunbar's scientific analogies.** The "search for other problems that have been solved" quote and the idea that scientists are often unaware of the critical role analogies play are in Kevin Dunbar (2000), "How Scientists Think in the Real World: Implications for Science Education," *Journal of Applied Developmental Psychology* 21: 49–58. The other quotes and observations are from Kevin Dunbar (1996), "How Scientists Really Reason," in *The Nature of Insight*, ed. Robert J. Sternberg and Janet E. Davidson (Boston: MIT Press).

82 **Medical plastics designer analogies.** Bo T. Christensen and Christian D. Schunn (2007), "The Relationship of Analogical Distance to Analogical Function and Preinventive Structure: The Case of Engineering Design," *Memory & Cognition* 35: 29–38.

83 **Laddering.** Some marketers use the term "laddering" to talk about processes that get to the core needs of a consumer. A girl may use soap to wash her face, but a marketing "laddering" technique would ask the girl "why" a couple of times to determine that her deeper needs and desires are for "beauty." For the marketers, the movement upward on the ladder is moving upward on an abstract hierarchy of needs. We use the term a little more visually—as you step up the ladder of analogies you will see more, a wider range of analogies and more distant analogies.

84 **Fairhurst swimsuit design.** The bulk of the content of this example and most of the quotes, including the extended scene in the Natural History Museum, come from American Public Media, "The Waldo Canyon Fire," *The Story* (hosted by Dick Gordon), June 29, 2012, available at http://thestory.org /archive/The_Story_62912.mp3/view. The "roughness is the key" quote and "83% of medals" statistic are from a video describing why Fairhurst was a finalist in an award for European Inventor of the Year in 2009, hosted at http:// www.epo.org/news-issues/european-inventor/finalists/2009/fairhurst.html. The "torpedo" quote is from "Inventor Awards to Be Announced," BBC, April 28, 2009, http://news.bbc.co.uk/today/hi/today/newsid_8022000/8022077. stm. An account of the controversy and the ban of Fairhurst-inspired swimsuits is in Deidre Crawford, "London Olympics: Advances in Swimwear for Athletes—and You," *Los Angeles Times*, July 29, 2012, http://articles.latimes .com/2012/jul/29/image/la-ig-olympic-swimwear-20120729.

85 **Reduce drag and increase thrust.** Peter Reuell, "A Swimsuit Like Shark Skin? Not So Fast," *Harvard Gazette*, February 9, 2012, http://news .harvard.edu/gazette/story/2012/02/a-swimsuit-like-shark-skin-not-so

-fast/ (accessed 9/11/2012). What's funny is that the same scientist believes that the Speedo team didn't do a good enough job replicating sharkskin. He thinks, based on some testing, that the performance improvement is largely due to the "torpedo" aspect.

Chapter 5: Consider the Opposite

92 **Hayward and Hambrick, CEO hubris.** The material in this section, including the average 41% premium and the punchline of the Buffett quote, is in Mathew L. A. Hayward and Donald C. Hambrick (1997), "Explaining the Premiums Paid for Large Acquisitions: Evidence of CEO Hubris," *Administrative Science Quarterly* 42: 103–27. We use a longer version of the Buffett quote from pages 137–39 in Warren E. Buffett, "The Essays of Warren Buffett: Lessons for Corporate America," ed. Lawrence A. Cunningham, http://bit.ly/fAQgBX. Hayward and Hambrick also showed that when the CEOs paid a premium, they overpaid: Subsequent performance was measurably worse in situations where CEOs paid bigger premiums.

95 **Alfred Sloan story.** Peter F. Drucker (2006), *The Effective Executive* (New York: HarperBusiness), p. 148.

95 **Meta-analysis of confirmation bias.** William Hart, et al. (2009), "Feeling Validated Versus Being Correct: A Meta-analysis of Selected Exposure to Information," *Psychological Bulletin* 135: 555–58.

96 **Devil's advocate.** Discussion of the devil's advocate and its role in the Catholic Church is from Paul B. Carroll and Chunka Mui (2008), *Billion Dollar Lessons: What You Can Learn from the Most Inexcusable Business Failures of the Last Twenty-Five Years* (New York: Portfolio Books). The value of seeking out existing (authentic) dissent is consistent with research at the University of California at Berkeley: Charlan Nemeth, Keith Brown, and John Rogers (2001), "Devil's Advocate Versus Authentic Dissent: Stimulating Quantity and Quality," *European Journal of Social Psychology* 31: 707–20.

97 **Murder board, *Gong Show*.** Chip Heath, Richard P. Larrick, and Joshua Klayman (1998), "Cognitive Repairs: How Organizational Practices Can Compensate for Individual Shortcomings," *Research in Organizational Behavior* 20: 1–37.

98 **Roger Martin and Copper Range mine.** The Copper Range mining story is based on interviews by Chip Heath of Roger Martin (March 2012), Richard Ross (April 2012), and John Sanders (May 2012). It also draws from a blog post by Roger Martin: "My Eureka Moment with Strategy," *Harvard Business Review: HBR Blog Network*, May 30, 2010, http://blogs

.hbr.org/martin/2010/05/the-day-i-discovered-the-most.html. The "If you think an idea is the wrong way to approach a problem" quote is from this blog post.

103 **Judge Schiltz advice to law students.** U.S. District Court Judge Patrick J. Schiltz (1999), "On Being a Happy, Healthy, and Ethical Member of an Unhappy, Unhealthy, and Unethical Profession," *Vanderbilt Law Review* 52: 945–48. We found a PDF available online, but the link did not seem permanent enough to cite here; our advice is to search for "Schiltz unhappy unethical" and, with any luck, you will find a source too.

103 **iPod study.** Julie A. Minson, Nicole E. Ruedy, and Maurice E. Schweitzer (2012), "There *Is* Such a Thing as a Stupid Question: Question Disclosure in Strategic Communication," Working paper, Wharton School of Business, University of Pennsylvania.

104 **Joseph H. case study.** Allen Barbour (1995), *Caring for Patients* (Stanford, CA: Stanford University Press), pp. 10–12.

107 **18 seconds.** This study by Dr. Howard Beckman at the University of Rochester and his coauthors caused consternation when it was published in 1984. In 1999, after 15 years of efforts by medical schools to train doctors to be more patient focused, Beckman and his colleagues published a follow-up study that found that doctors had improved . . . to 23 seconds. At that rate of improvement, patients in the year 2110 will be able to talk for over a minute without interruption. Meredith Levine, "Tell the Doctor All Your Problems, but Keep It to Less Than a Minute," *New York Times*, June 1, 2004, http://www.nytimes.com/2004/06/01/health/tell-the-doctor-all-your-problems-but-keep-it-to-less-than-a-minute.html.

108 **Beck's marriage diaries.** See Aaron T. Beck (1989), *Love Is Never Enough* (New York: HarperPerennial). The Goldstein study is described on page 248, and the marriage-diary exercise for Ted and Karen is on pages 245–46.

109 **Assume positive intent.** The Indra Nooyi quote is in "The Best Advice I Ever Got," *CNNMoney*, April 30, 2008, http://money.cnn.com/galleries/2008/fortune/0804/gallery.bestadvice.fortune/7.html. The quote from Rochelle Arnold-Simmons is from Rochelle Arnold-Simmons, "Day 158 Honoring My Husband Beyond Affection," *I Will Honor My Husband*, July 22, 2011, http://iwillhonormyhusband.blogspot.com/2011/07/day-158-honoring-my-husband.html. The Industrial Scientific example is from Malia Spencer, "Conversational Nuances Come with Working in Asia," *Pittsburgh Business Times*, June 15, 2012, http://www.bizjournals.com/pittsburgh/print-edition/2012/06/15/conversational-nuances-asia.html.

110 **See endnotes for more.** The value of "consider the opposite" is re-

viewed in Katherine L. Milkman, Dolly Chugh, and Max H. Bazerman (2009), "How Can Decision Making Be Improved?" *Perspectives on Psychological Science* 4: 379–85. Considering the opposite has been shown to reduce several biases that have been regarded as especially thorny: the overconfident conclusions that we highlight in chapter 10 (and that were demonstrated by CEOs in the hubris study in this chapter) and other, quite different, biases ranging from a hindsight bias that leads us to see anything that happens as inevitable to a tendency to anchor too strongly on a specific numerical value (e.g., basing this year's budget allocation heavily on last year's, even if the situation has changed dramatically).

110 **Schoemaker's deliberate mistake.** The RFP deliberate mistake story is told in Paul J. H. Schoemaker (2011), *Brilliant Mistakes: Finding Success on the Far Side of Failure* (Philadelphia: Wharton Press). The "why leave mistakes to serendipity?" quote is from a conversation between Chip Heath and Schoemaker in August 2012. The other quotes are from Schoemaker's account in *Brilliant Mistakes*.

112 **Deliberate mistakes in dating.** See John T. Molloy (2003), *Why Men Marry Some Women and Not Others* (New York: Warner Books), p. 73.

Chapter 6: Zoom Out, Zoom In

115 **Polynesian Resort.** The beautiful pictures are at http://polynesian-resort .com/Amenities.html (accessed on July 8, 2011), the dirty hotel awards are described at http://www.tripadvisor.com/PressCenter-i4557-c1-Press _Releases.html (accessed on September 27, 2012), and all the reviews are from TripAdvisor, http://www.tripadvisor.com/ShowUserReviews-g54359-d259744 -r115031196-Polynesian_Beach_Golf_Resort-Myrtle_Beach_South_Carolina .html#CHECK_RATES_CONT (accessed on July 8, 2011). The "debaucherous spring break" review came from dangle2011, posted on October 27, 2009 (and accessed on September 27, 2012).

118 **On computing base rates.** One of the challenges of using base rates is knowing which base rates to trust. Do we examine the set of all entrepreneurs who have started a business or just those who have started a restaurant? Or those who've started restaurants in Texas? Or in Austin? Or do we hold out for an exact hit—the set of people who've started Thai restaurants in downtown Austin? One decision-making expert, Josh Klayman, a professor at the University of Chicago's business school, suggests a rule of thumb: Pick the narrowest possible set that still provides 10 to 20 examples. So if there are 15 Thai res-

taurants in Austin, that's your set; if there are only 6, you could broaden your sample, perhaps to all Asian restaurants in Austin.

118 **Kahneman curriculum development story.** The "unnatural exercise" quote and the curriculum-team story are from a class Kahneman taught to a very distinguished group of scientists and entrepreneurs (including the founders of Google and Amazon). Daniel Kahneman, "A Short Course on Thinking About Thinking" (Edge Master Class 07, Rutherford, CA, July 20–22, 2007). An online transcript, located at edge.org/3rd_culture/kahneman07 /kahneman07_index.html, shows what he covered with this group.

119 **Expert doesn't have to be credentialed authority.** Studies of dyadic interaction find that people are almost always more accurate when they incorporate the opinions of others, even if the other doesn't have specialized expertise. In these studies, where people tend to have similar expertise, they tend to weight their own opinion at 70% and the other person's at 30%, whereas they would typically perform better if they weighted the other person equal to themselves. (In one study where people were paired with a partner from another country, people still rated their own views more strongly than their partner's about 65% of the time, even on questions about their partner's country!) If you're consulting someone who knows a little more than you, you should probably err on the side of weighting your own views less than you are tempted to. Jack B. Soll and Richard P. Larrick (2009), "Strategies for Revising Judgment: How (and How Well) People Use Others' Opinions," *Journal of Experimental Psychology: Learning, Memory, and Cognition* 35: 780–805.

123 **Brian Zikmund-Fisher.** Details of Brian Zikmund-Fisher's story are from conversations between Chip Heath and Brian in March and July 2012.

127 **The right kind of emotion.** Notice that Zikmund-Fisher makes his final decision by stepping out of his own perspective and seeing things through the eyes of another (his future daughter). This is something we saw before in Andy Grove's revolving-door test in chapter 1 and we will see again in the chapter on overcoming short-term emotions through simulating social distance (the "what would you advise a friend to do?" question). Priorities often become clarified when we step out of the short-term fog of our emotions by adding some distance.

128 **FDR.** We found many of the examples in this section in a great paper by Lorraine Riley, a student fellow at the Center for the Study of the Presidency and Congress. See Lorraine Ashley Riley, "A Finger in Every Pie: FDR's Mastery of Alternative Channels of Information Gathering," in *A Dialogue on Presidential*

Challenges and Leadership: Papers of the 2006–2007 Center Fellows (Washington: Center for the Study of the Presidency and Congress, 2007), pp. 22–32. The document can be accessed here: http://www.thepresidency.org/storage/ documents/Vater/Section1.pdf. Roosevelt's use of the mail was particularly important in an era in which the science of polling had not yet developed. The staffer quote on presenting a "juicy morsel" only to find out FDR already knew it is from Richard E. Neustadt (1960), *Presidential Power: The Politics of Leadership* (New York: Wiley), p. 132. From Schlesinger's book on the New Deal are the "wind in your nose" and Eleanor Roosevelt quotes (p. 498), the Ickes complaint (p. 524), and the "finger in every pie" quote (p. 528). Arthur M. Schlesinger (1958), *The Coming of the New Deal* (New York: Houghton Mifflin). Interestingly, FDR understood that experts didn't have to be credentialed authorities; he would often ask visitors questions "outside their jurisdiction," and he would drag smart people from a meeting during one hour into his next scheduled meeting regardless of topic. Schlesinger comments, "All this, irritating as it was to tidy minds, enlarged the variety of reactions to him in areas where no one was infallible" (p. 498). These were great techniques for Widening Options and for Reality-Testing by getting people in the room who were more likely to consider different options and to ask disconfirming questions.

130 **Anne Mulcahy, Xerox.** The Customer Officer of the Day and Focus 500 programs are described in Bertrand Marotte, "The New Xerox Battle Cry," *Globe and Mail*, October 15, 2005, p. B3. The background financial information is in Kevin Maney, "Mulcahy Traces Steps of Xerox's Comeback," *USA Today*, September 21, 2006, p. B4.

131 **Genba.** *Genba* background comes from Wikipedia: http://en.wikipedia.org /wiki/Gemba.

131 **Paul Smith, P&G.** The Paul Smith story is from conversations between Chip Heath and Paul Smith in February and July 2012.

Chapter 7: Ooch

136 **"Ooch before we leap."** The material in this case study is from a conversation between Chip Heath and John Hanks in December 2010 and a follow-up between Dan Heath and Hanks in April 2011.

138 **Physical therapy requirement.** See http://www.hunter.cuny.edu/pt /admissions/clinical-experience-requirement.

138 **Peggy, legal secretary.** The story of Peggy is in Matthew McKay, Martha Davis, and Patrick Fanning (2011), *Thoughts and Feelings: Taking Control of*

Your Moods and Your Life, 4th ed. (Oakland, CA: New Harbinger Publications). Kindle location 1669/5148.

140 **Small experiments, prototypes, etc.** "Fire bullets then cannonballs"—in their studies of which companies survive market dislocations, Collins and Hansen find that the survivors don't make big bets on innovations before they run simple, low-cost tests; the failed companies are just as likely to do something "innovative," but they bet all in before testing and sometimes fail big. Jim Collins and Morten T. Hansen (2011), *Great by Choice: Uncertainty, Chaos, and Luck—Why Some Thrive* (New York: HarperBusiness); Peter Sims (2011), *Little Bets: How Breakthrough Ideas Emerge from Small Discoveries* (New York: Free Press).

142 **Tetlock study of experts.** Philip E. Tetlock (2005), *Expert Political Judgment: How Good Is It? How Can We Know?* (Princeton, NJ: Princeton University Press). The sample prediction questions for the experts are from pages 246–47. The opening "sky was not falling" anecdote is in Tetlock's introduction at page xiv. The academic paper with the clever subtitle is Colin F. Camerer and Eric J. Johnson (1991), "The Process-Performance Paradox in Expert Judgment: How Can the Experts Know So Much and Predict So Badly?" in *Toward a General Theory of Expertise: Prospects and Limits,* ed. K. A. Ericsson and J. Smith (Cambridge, England: Cambridge University Press), pp. 195–217.

145 **CarsDirect.com.** Interview: "Andy Zimmerman on How Fresh Ideas Turn into Real, Live Internet-Related Companies at idealab!" *Business News New Jersey* 13 (September 26, 2000), p. 15.

145 **Sarasvathy entrepreneurs vs. executives.** See Saras D. Sarasvathy (2002), "What Makes Entrepreneurs Entrepreneurial?" Working paper, Darden Graduate School of Business Administration. The quote is from page 6 of the PDF version at http://papers.ssrn.com/sol3/papers.cfm?abstract_id= 909038. See also the popular account by Leigh Buchanan: "How Great Entrepreneurs Think," *Inc.,* February 1, 2001, http://www.inc.com/magazine/20110201 /how-great-entrepreneurs-think_pagen_2.html.

146 **Scott Cook, Intuit India example.** This example is from a conversation between Chip Heath and Scott Cook in August 2011. The "politics, persuasion, and PowerPoint" line is from a speech by Cook: "Leadership in an Agile Age" (lecture at Innovation 2011: Entrepreneurship for a Disruptive World conference, March 2011), transcribed at http://network.intuit.com/2011/04/20 /leadership-in-the-agile-age/.

149 **Interviews are less predictive.** See discussion on page 189 of David

G. Myers (2002), *Intuition: Its Power and Perils*. New Haven, CT: Yale University Press. The Richard Nisbett comments about the "interview illusion" are on pages 190–91. Note that this section draws from one of our columns: "Why It Might Be Wiser to Hire People Without Meeting Them," *Fast Company*, June 2009.

150 **Accept 50 more students.** The experience of the University of Texas Medical School is described on pages 87–88 of Robyn M. Dawes (1994), *House of Cards: Psychology and Psychotherapy Built on Myth* (New York: Free Press).

151 **Steve Cole, HopeLab hiring.** Cole quotes are from an interview of Cole by Chip Heath in May 2011.

Chapter 8: Overcome Short-Term Emotion

156 **Car sales tactics.** Chandler Phillips, "Confessions of a Car Salesman," Edmunds.com, January 18, 2001, http://www.edmunds.com/car-buying /confessions-of-a-car-salesman.html.

158 **Millionaire teacher buys car.** This story is from a great book: Andrew Hallam (2011), *Millionaire Teacher: The Nine Rules of Wealth You Should Have Learned in School* (New York: Wiley). He discusses his car-buying technique and his frugal hints for saving in the first chapter. Rule 1: Spend like you want to grow rich.

160 **10/10/10.** Suzy Welch (2009), *10/10/10* (New York: Scribner). Welch has created one of the world's most clever and compact pieces of decision advice. The Annie and Karl story (names disguised) is from a conversation between "Annie" and Dan Heath in May 2012; the e-mail follow-up is from August 2012.

164 **Mere exposure.** The blackboard study is Rick Crandall (1972), "Field Extension of the Frequency-Affect Findings," *Psychological Reports* 31: 371–74. Robert Zajonc's classic paper on mere exposure, one of the most highly cited in the social psychology literature, is Robert Zajonc (1968), "Attitudinal Effects of Mere Exposure," *Journal of Personality and Social Psychology* 9: 1–27. The face-flipping study is Theodore H. Mita, Marshall Dermer, and Jeffrey Knight (1977), "Reversed Facial Images and the Mere Exposure Hypothesis," *Journal of Personality and Social Psychology* 35: 597–601. Repetition sparked trust: Alice Dechêne, et al. (2010), "The Truth About the Truth: A Meta-analytic Review of the Truth Effect," *Personality and Social Psychology Review* 14: 238–57.

165 **Loss aversion.** The classic first discussion of loss aversion is Daniel Kahneman and Amos Tversky (1979), "Prospect Theory: An Analysis of Decision

Under Risk," *Econometrica* 47: 263–92. This paper by two psychologists appeared in the journal that is the high temple of technical economics and became the most cited paper ever to appear in the journal. It was one of the pieces of research discussed in Kahneman's Nobel Prize citation (sadly, Amos Tversky had died a few years earlier). The coin-flip example is from that paper. Purchase protection: David M. Cutler and Richard Zeckhauser (2004), "Extending the Theory to Meet the Practice of Insurance," Working paper, Harvard University. Coffee-mug study: Daniel Kahneman, Jack L. Knetsch, and Richard Thaler (1990), "Experimental Tests of the Endowment Effect and the Coase Theorem," *Journal of Political Economy* 98: 1325–48.

166 **Max Levchin cofounded PayPal.** PayPal was actually first called Confinity, and it produced a product called PayPal, but it was later renamed PayPal after a merger. To keep it simple, we just call it PayPal. This case study is from a fun book by Jessica Livingston where she interviews the founders of almost three dozen start-ups, including Craigslist, Adobe, Hotmail, and others. Jessica Livingston (2008), *Founders at Work: Stories of Startup's Early Days* (New York: Apress), pp. 1–17.

170 **Construal-level theory.** This is a recent area of research, and there are few accounts of it written for nonresearchers. A good review of the research is Yaacove Trope and Nira Liberman (2010), "Construal Level Theory of Psychological Distance," *Psychological Review* 117: 440–63.

170 **Job A or Job B study.** This is study 1 in Laura Kray and Richard Gonzalez (1999), "Weighting in Choice Versus Advice: I'll Do This, You Do That," *Journal of Behavioral Decision Making* 12: 207–17.

171 **Girl from your psychology class study.** See Amy H. Beisswanger, et al. (2003), "Risk Taking in Relationships: Differences in Deciding for Oneself Versus for a Friend," *Basic and Applied Social Psychology* 25: 121–35.

Chapter 9: Honor Your Core Priorities

175 **Kim Ramirez.** This story is from a conversation between Dan Heath and "Kim Ramirez" in February 2012. "Kim Ramirez" and "Josh" are disguised names; all other details are accurate.

183 **Interplast.** The Interplast discussion is from a Stanford GSB case and video by Jim Phills (2006), "Interplast's Dilemma," Stanford Graduate School of Business, Case SI-14. The "it changed everything" quote and other background details are from an interview of Susan Hayes by Chip Heath in March 2012.

186 **Wayne's Rules at Dell Computer.** This story is taken from interviews of Wayne Roberts by Chip Heath in November 2011 and July 2012.

187 **"No manager reported any activity."** The Pounds quote is from page 40 of Morgan W. McCall and Robert E. Kaplan (1990), *Whatever It Takes: The Realities of Managerial Decision-Making.* Upper Saddle River, NJ: Prentice-Hall.

187 **Jim Collins's "stop-doing" list.** Jim Collins, "Best New Year's Resolution? A 'Stop Doing' List," *USA Today,* December 30, 2003.

188 **Captain Abrashoff, USS *Benfold*.** The list A/list B story is on pages 46–48, and the "mini-Olympics" testing procedure is on pages 102–3 of Captain D. Michael Abrashoff (2002), *It's Your Ship: Management Techniques from the Best Damn Ship in the Navy* (New York: Business Plus).

190 **"To be doing right now."** See Daniel H. Pink, "The Power of an Hourly Beep," October 24, 2011, http://www.danpink.com/archives/2011/10/the-power-of-an-hourly-beep. Bregman's book on how to remove distractions and focus on priorities is filled with good advice: Peter Bregman (2011), *Eighteen Minutes* (New York: Business Plus).

Chapter 10: Bookend the Future

194 **Byron Penstock, Coinstar investment.** The Penstock/Coinstar story comes from interviews of Byron Penstock by Dan Heath in September 2011, March 2012, and August 2012. Revenue (p. 63) and kiosk count (p. 35) are from CSTR 2009 10K. In the aftermath of the sale, the Coinstar stock promptly shot through the roof, reaching a peak of $66.98 on November 24 before receding again in the months that followed. Penstock wishes he had sold in November rather than October, of course, but he is untroubled about missing the second spike. If he'd maintained the investment, it would have meant betting that the stock would hit its upper bookend, which was not a bet he was comfortable with.

199 **Invest in index funds.** For our full-fledged soapbox treatment of this topic, see our article "The Horror of Mutual Funds" in our collection *The Myth of the Garage*, which is available for free at http://www.heathbrothers.com/the-myth-of-the-garage/. For a clear and understandable account of the research on the advantages of index funds, see the book by the millionaire teacher Andrew Hallam, from the short-term emotion chapter, who figured out how to buy a car without falling victim to sleazy car sales tactics. Andrew Hallam (2011), *Millionaire Teacher: The Nine Rules of Wealth You Should Have Learned in School* (New York: Wiley). On investments, see his brilliant chapter on rule 3, which quotes four Nobel Prize winners in economics recommending the index-funds strategy, then unpacks the hidden costs and expenses in the typical mutual fund. He quotes one study from the *Journal of Portfolio Man-*

agement that found that over a 15-year period *96%* of actively managed mutual funds underperformed an index fund. And individual investors frequently do worse, particularly when they trade more because of overconfidence. See Brad M. Barber and Terrance Odean (2001), "Boys Will Be Boys: Gender, Overconfidence, and Common Stock Investment," *Quarterly Journal of Economics* 116: 261–92.

200 **Jack Soll and Joshua Klayman.** The 80% confidence interval study is Jack B. Soll and Joshua Klayman (2004), "Overconfidence in Interval Estimates," *Journal of Experimental Psychology: Learning, Memory, and Cognition* 30, 299–314. The box-office statistics for Angelina Jolie are from http://boxofficemojo.com/people/chart/?view=Actor&id=angelinajolie.htm.

202 **First Asian American president.** Our future-president scenario was inspired by an example given by Jay E. Russo and Paul J. H. Schoemaker (2002), *Winning Decisions* (New York: Currency/Doubleday), pp. 111–12. The employee scenario is from the original study of the phenomenon: Deborah J. Mitchell, J. Edward Russo, and Nancy Pennington (1989), "Back to the Future: Temporal Perspective in the Explanation of Events," *Journal of Behavioral Decision Making* 2: 25–38.

203 **Premortem.** Gary Klein (2009), *Streetlights and Shadows: Searching for the Keys to Adaptive Decision Making* (Cambridge, MA: MIT Press), pp. 63, 235–236.

203 **100,000 Homes.** The FMEA and Myron stories are from interviews by Dan Heath of Christina Gunther-Murphy in September 2011, Beth Sandor and Jessica Venegas (of the Community Solutions team) in September 2011, and Mattie Lord in July 2012, as well as periodic communications with Becky Kanis. The launch date for the campaign can be found at 100,000 Homes, "100,000 Homes Campaign Launch Video," http://100khomes.org/blog/watch-100000-homes-campaign-launch-video. Gunther-Murphy works for the Institute for Healthcare Improvement (IHI), which launched the 100,000 Lives Campaign. The campaign succeeded—it's an incredible story, and many people have written about it. (See the first chapter of *Switch* for our take on it.)

207 **Minnetonka Softsoap.** The pump lockup is described on pages 60–61 of Hugh Courtney (2001), *20/20 Foresight: Crafting Strategy in an Uncertain World* (Boston: Harvard Business School Press). The background details of the story are told in a Harvard Business School case study by Adam Brandenburger and Vijay Krishna (1995), "Minnetonka Corporation: From Softsoap to Eternity" (HBS case 9-795-163).

208 **An emergency landing.** Readers in the United States will remember the

remarkable story of US Airways Flight 1549, which experienced this event in 2009. See http://en.wikipedia.org/wiki/US_Airways_Flight_1549.

209 **Safety factor.** The safety factors given here come from Wayne Hale, "Factors of Safety," *Wayne Hale's Blog*, http://blogs.nasa.gov/cm/blog/waynehalesblog/posts/post_1229459081779.html.

209 **Schedule buffers at Microsoft.** See Michael A. Cusumano and Richard Selby (1995), *Microsoft Secrets* (New York: Free Press), p. 94.

210 **Call center case study, Evolv.** Max Simkoff (CEO of Evolv), interviews with Chip Heath and Dan Heath in August and September 2011.

212 **40 studies of realistic job previews.** Jean M. Phillips (1998), "Effects of Realistic Job Previews on Multiple Organizational Outcomes: a Meta-analysis," *Academy of Management Journal* 41: 673–90.

Chapter 11: Set a Tripwire

218 **Zappos.** The forgotten-shoes story has been widely reported, e.g., here: Jim Ryan, "Outstanding Customer Service Beyond Zappos," *Interactive Depot*, May 15, 2012, http://talk2rep-call-centers-idea-depot.com/tag/zappos/. The white-lilies-and-roses story is from Meg Marco, "Zappos Sends You Flowers," *The Consumerist*, October 16, 2007, http://con.st/311369. Chip Heath interviewed Jon Wolske in August 2011.

221 **Peel a banana.** See video at http://www.youtube.com/watch?v=nBJV56WUDng. (The video claims this is how monkeys eat a banana, but even a few minutes of YouTube research shows that monkeys dive in directly in the middle.) Kirschner responded via e-mail to a request we put out on our newsletter for autopilot stories in August 2012. He says his other "aha" video was one of Martha Stewart folding a T-shirt. "The hardest part of doing laundry for me was folding it. And any technique I could find to decrease the time would be helpful." See how Martha Stewart saves time here: http://www.youtube.com/watch?v=Jvcuy4k17DI. On better conversations at dinner, Chip and his family borrowed a "sad, mad, glad" technique from a parenting advice board—the family goes around the table and each person talks about one thing in their day that made them sad, mad, and glad. So far, it has worked to produce great conversations with kids ages 2 to 10, but we offer no warranties for kids past puberty.

223 **Kodak.** The Kodak story is from pages 88–100 of Paul B. Carroll and Chunka Mui (2008), *Billion Dollar Lessons: What You Can Learn from the Most Inexcusable Business Failures of the Last Twenty-five Years* (New York: Portfolio). The market-cap history is from Wolfram Alpha http://www.wolframalpha.com

/input/?i=market+cap+eastman+kodak+history&dataset= (accessed on July 20, 2012).

227 **Amos Tversky and Eldar Shafir.** Amos Tversky and Eldar Shafir (1992), "Choice Under Conflict: The Dynamics of Deferred Decision," *Psychological Science* 3: 358–61.

227 **Decided to eliminate submission deadlines.** The Economic and Social Research Council example is from Colin Camerer, et al. (2003), "Regulation for Conservatives: Behavioral Economics and the Case for 'Asymmetric Paternalism,' " *University of Pennsylvania Law Review* 151: 1211–54.

229 **Partitioning study.** The cookie study is from Dilip Soman and Amar Cheema, "The Effects of Partitioning on Consumption," *Rotman*, Spring 2008, pp. 20–24. The day-laborer study is from Dilip Soman, "Earmarking Money," *Rotman*, Fall 2009, pp. 96–98.

230 **Mental budgets and escalation.** See Chip Heath (1995), "Escalation and De-escalation of Commitment in Response to Sunk Costs: The Role of Budgeting in Mental Accounting," *Organizational Behavior and Human Decision Processes* 62: 38–54.

232 **Lucile Packard, rapid-response teams.** The quotes in this article are from interviews of Kit Leong and Karla Earnest by Chip Heath in March 2012. The paper reporting their work is Paul J. Sharek, et al. (2007), "Mortality and Code Rates Outside the ICU in a Children's Hospital," *Journal of the American Medical Association* 298: 2267–74.

234 **Unexpected success.** The Drucker quote is in Drucker Institute, "We'll Accept It if You Like This Post for Reasons We Didn't Anticipate," *Drucker Exchange*, November 14, 2011, http://thedx.druckerinstitute.com /2011/11/well-accept-it-if-you-like-this-post-for-reasons-we-didnt -anticipate/. The Rogaine story is told in Wikipedia at http://en.wikipedia.org /wiki/Minoxidil. The Viagra story is from "Viagra: A Chronology," *Viagra.md*, http://www.about-ed.com/viagra-history. The journalist's quote is from Simon Davies, "The Discovery of Viagra," *Biotech/Pharmaceuticals@Suite101*, August 1, 2007, http://suite101.com/article/the-discovery-of-viagra-a27733.

236 **Awesome Thing #523.** "When You Learn a New Word and Then Suddenly Start Seeing It Everywhere," *1000 Awesome Things*, April 20, 2010, http://1000awesomethings.com/2010/04/20/523-when-you-learn-a-new -word-and-then-suddenly-start-seeing-it-everywhere/.

Chapter 12: Trusting the Process

240 **Bargaining study by Nutt.** Paul C. Nutt (2005), "Search During Decision Making," *European Journal of Operational Research* 160: 851–76. On the quality of decisions: Decisions using bargaining were more often rated by independent raters as "good" or "outstanding." On the time advantages of bargaining: Compare two of the decision patterns that Nutt studied, championed ideas and bargains. Championed ideas happened when an idea champion spotted a good thing to do and set off to convince the organization to pursue it. (*We should adopt the order processing system used by Lands' End; it's more efficient!*) This is the pattern of innovation often celebrated in the popular press: *Find an idea champion! Support your innovators!* Not surprisingly, since the idea champion already has a prepackaged idea, these decisions are made quickly—in six months on average, compared with nine months for the typical decision in Nutt's database. Bargains were slower at 7.5 months (though, interestingly, still faster than the average).

But the championed ideas, though fast in the decision stage, suffered in the implementation phase. Once the decision was "made," championed ideas were initially implemented only 56% of the time, compared with 79% of the bargains. And a couple of years later, only 40% of the championed ideas had been completely implemented, compared with 75% of the bargains. This pattern suggests that what idea champions gain in speed from the initial decision stage they more than sacrifice on speed and success during the implementation period. (Note that Nutt calls championed ideas "emergent opportunities"—we feel that the "championed ideas" terminology is more accurate.)

243 **Procedural justice.** The conclusions about the relative happiness of Mike, Carlos, and Jen are based on a robust statistical interaction effect described in Joel Brockner and Batia M. Wisenfeld (1996), "An Integrative Framework for Explaining Reactions to Decisions: Interactive Effects of Outcomes and Procedures," *Psychological Bulletin* 120: 189–208.

244 **"State back the other side's position better than they could."** Chip remembers Mnookin making this comment in a decision-making/negotiation workshop around 1989. It was striking enough that he has remembered it ever since.

244 **Dave Hitz, the founder of NetApp.** This strategy for handling opposition is found in Dave Hitz (2009), *How to Castrate a Bull: Unexpected Lessons on Risk, Growth, and Success in Business* (San Francisco: Jossey-Bass), p. 152. This book is insightful and very funny, and it should be on the reading list of any entrepreneur who is trying to grow a business.

246 **Matt D'Arrigo.** This case is based on conversations between Chip Heath or Dan Heath and Matt D'Arrigo in June 2010, August 2010, February 2012, March 2012, and July 2012.

252 **Regrets of the elderly.** See Nina Hattiangadi, Victoria Husted Medvec, and Thomas Gilovich (1995), "Failing to Act: Regrets of Terman's Geniuses," *International Journal of Aging and Human Development* 40: 175–85. This paper uses the responses of "Terman's geniuses," a set of children with genius-level IQs who were initially enrolled in the study by Stanford psychologist Lewis Terman in the 1920s and were followed actively by researchers until their deaths around the turn of the century. Even for this group of very successful and accomplished people, regrets of not acting outnumbered regrets from action more than four to one. In general, Gilovich and Medvec's research has found that our short-run regrets focus on things we did do that we shouldn't have, but in the long run we regret those things we might have done. In this paper, they quote poet John Greenleaf Whittier: "Of all sad words of tongue or pen, the saddest are these: 'it might have been' " (p. 176).

Clinics

257 **Clinic 1: Should a Small Company Sue?** The *Inc.* magazine case study is Jennifer Alsever (January 24, 2012). "Case Study: To Sue or Not to Sue." *Inc.,* http://www.inc.com/magazine/201202/case-study-the-rival-mixed-chicks-sally-beauty.html.

ACKNOWLEDGMENTS

Anyone who writes about decision making owes a deep debt to Daniel Kahneman and Amos Tversky. Chip is grateful to Amos for introducing him to decision making and teaching him to admire elegant results. Some readers—you know who you are—gave us critical feedback on an early draft of the book. Your comments made such a difference; we hope you can see it in the final draft. It's a lot better, thanks to you. (Good-bye to the lemon-juice burglar . . .)

Thanks to Lars Flatmo for his clever archaeology skills in locating obscure references.

Thanks to those of you who attended workshops to help us pilot-test the ideas in this book: Bill Tobin, Phil Wickham, and the Kauffman fellows; Janine Mason and the group at the Fieldstone Foundation (where we first talked to Matt D'Arrigo about his decision); Cary Matsuoka and the California Superintendents retreat; Carla O'Dell and the APQC team; Gay Hoagland and the Bay Area principals; Rosella Derickson and the GSB Insider attendees; Andrew Ellner, Somava Stout, and the innovation fellows at Harvard Medical School; Michael Norton and participants at Harvard Business School; Eric Johnson, Elke Weber, Michael Morris, and participants at the Columbia decision colloquium; Dean Mike Smith and the participants at the UNC School of Government workshop; and Kevin Trapani, Curt Hazelbaker, and the participants at the YMCA Metro South Conference.

A sincere thanks to the people who participated in one-on-one coaching calls to discuss important decisions in their lives. Your candor and feedback were critical to the development of the ideas in this book.

Thank you to the following people for conversations about decisions and decision making: Jeff Belkora, Hilary Briggs, Rachael Brown, Chip Conley, Rob Delamater, Karen Douglas, James Durbin, Andy Epstein, Chris Flink, Jay Freedman, Brian Gibbs, Ric Grefe, Christina Gunther-Murphy, Marcela Gutierrez, Steve Heller, Sarah Hernholm, Karl Kempf, Clint Korver, Sharon Lawrence, Dan Leemon, Jean Martin, Paige Nesis, Don Norman, Dr. Robert Pearl, Martha Piper, David Reinke, Ginger Rona, Kevin Skelly, Carl Spetzler, Devlyn Torres, Beth Viner, Shelley Volz, Donna Wiktorowski, John Willard, and Soon Yu.

Special thanks to those who read the whole manuscript and provided in-depth feedback: Jonah Berger, Rob Gertner, Barbara Kiviat, Rick Larrick, Michael Morris, Carla O'Dell, and Hersh Shefrin. And for many long conversations about the book and decision making, we are grateful to George Wu and Josh Klayman.

We are lucky to have such great partners: Justin Gammon, Christy Darnell, Christy Fletcher and her team at Fletcher & Co; Les Tuerk and Tom Neilssen and everyone at BrightSight; and of course the team at Crown Business, especially Tara Gilbride and Roger Scholl. You have all done so much to help us and to give a life to our ideas. Thank you.

And we could not be more thankful for the family that we have: Mom and Dad (over 50 years of marriage and counting!), Susan, Emory, Aubrey, Amanda, Susan, Oksana, Hunter, and Darby. Thanks for putting up with us.

INDEX

CHIP HEATH is a professor at the Graduate School of Business at Stanford University. He lives in Los Gatos, California.

DAN HEATH is a senior fellow at Duke University's Center for the Advancement of Social Entrepreneurship (CASE). He lives in Raleigh, North Carolina.

The Heath brothers are the authors of the national bestsellers *Switch* and *Made to Stick*.